# THE ALDINE EDITION
# OF THE BRITISH
# POETS

THE POEMS OF MARK AKENSIDE

Akenside

# THE POETICAL WORKS OF
# MARK AKENSIDE

AMS PRESS
NEW YORK

Reprinted from the edition of 1845, London
First AMS EDITION published 1969
Manufactured in the United States of America


Library of Congress Catalogue Card Number: 71-94924

AMS PRESS, INC.
NEW YORK, N. Y. 10003

# PREFACE.

FOUR early Letters from Akenside to Mr. Dyson are for the first time printed in the following Memoir. They are very characteristic of the writer, and valuable as correcting some erroneous statements of his biographers.

For transcripts of these interesting papers, and for several other less important communications, I am indebted to the kindness of J. Dyson, Esq., of Newgrove, Petworth, the son of Akenside's excellent friend and patron.

Every poem which could be traced to the author's pen has been inserted in the present volume.

ALEXANDER DYCE.

London, Dec. 1834.

# CONTENTS.

# LIFE OF AKENSIDE,[1]

### BY THE REV. ALEXANDER DYCE.

MARK AKENSIDE[2] was born at Newcastle upon Tyne, November 9th, 1721, and was baptized on the 30th of the same month by the minister of a meeting-house, which his parents used to frequent.[3] His father, Mark, was a respectable butcher. His mother's maiden name was Mary Lumsden. He was their second son. It is said that in after life he was ashamed of the lowness of his birth, which was constantly brought to his recollection by a lameness, originating in a cut on his foot from the fall of his father's cleaver, when he was about seven years old.[4]

After receiving some instruction at the free-school of

---

[1] During the earlier years of his life, the poet spelt his name, both on the title pages of his publications and in his letters, *Akinside;* but at a later period he adopted the form *Akenside.*

[2] "Mark Akenside, born the 9th November, 1721 : baptized y^e 30th of the same month by the Rev. Mr. Benjamin Bennet."—*History of Newcastle,* ii. 513, by Brand, who adds: "The above was communicated by Mr. Addison, glazier at Newcastle upon Tyne, who married Dr. Akenside's sister, and is in possession of some drawings, which were the works of that ingenious poet in an early period of his life. Mr. Bennet was a dissenting minister at the new meeting-house in Hanover Square, Newcastle upon Tyne."

[3] According to the *Biogr. Brit.,* Akenside's "parents and relations were in general of the Presbyterian persuasion."

[4] Brand's *Obs. on Pop. Antiq.* 114, ed. 1777.

Newcastle, he was sent to a private academy in the same town, kept by a Mr. Wilson, a dissenting minister.

His genius, and his love of poetry, were manifested, while he was yet a school-boy. *The Gentleman's Magazine* for April, 1737, contains one of his earliest attempts at versification, entitled *The Virtuoso, in imitation of Spenser's style and stanza*:[1] it is far superior to the sing-song inanities, which in those days generally adorned the pages of that miscellany, and is prefaced thus by a letter to the editor :

" Newcastle upon Tyne, April, 23.

" I HOPE, Sir, you'll excuse the following Poem, (being the Performance of one in his sixteenth year), and insert it in your next Magazine, which will oblige. Yours &c.
" MARCUS."

To the same popular work he contributed, in the next month, an ingenious fable called *Ambition and Content ;*[2] and, in July following, *The Poet, a Rhapsody*.[3]

When about the age of seventeen, Akenside used to visit some relations at Morpeth, where it has been rather hastily supposed that he wrote his *Pleasures of Imagination*.[4] Passages of it were, probably, composed there : at various times and places, during several years before its publication, that great work had, no doubt, occupied his mind. In a fragment of the fourth book of the remodelled copy, he pleasingly describes his early sensibility to the beauties of nature, and his lonely wanderings in the vicinity both of Newcastle and of Morpeth :

" O ye dales
Of Tyne, and ye most ancient woodlands, where
Oft as the giant flood obliquely strides,
And his banks open and his lawns extend,
Stops short the pleased traveller to view
Presiding o'er the scene some rustic tower

---

[1] *Gent. Mag.* vii. 244.—Mr. Bucke thinks it was suggested by a passage in Shaftesbury's *Characteristics,* iii. 156. ed. 1737. *Life of Akenside,* 5.
[2] *Gent. Mag.* vii. 309.  [3] *Ibid.* vii. 441.
[4] *Biog. Brit.*

Founded by Norman or by Saxon hands ;
O ye Northumbrian shades, which overlook
The rocky pavement and the mossy falls
Of solitary Wensbeck's limpid stream,
How gladly I recall your well-known seats
Belov'd of old, and that delightful time
When all alone, for many a summer's day,
I wander'd through your calm recesses, led
In silence by some powerful hand unseen."

To the *Gentleman's Magazine* for August, 1738,[1] he communicated *A British Philippic, occasioned by the insults of the Spaniards, and the present preparations for war.* That its flaming patriotism was quite to the taste of Mr. Urban, appears from the following advertisement: " N. B. It often turning to our Inconvenience to sell a greater Number of one Magazine than of another, and believing the above noble-spirited Poem will be acceptable to many, not our constant Readers, we have printed it in Folio, Price Six Pence, together with the Motto at large, for which, receiving the Manuscript late, we could not make room. And if the ingenious Author will inform us how we may direct a Packet to his Hands, we will send him our Acknowledgments for so great a Favour, with a Parcel of the Folio Edition."

His *Hymn to Science* was printed in the *Gentleman's Magazine* for October, 1739.[2] It is doubtless a production of considerable merit; but Mr. Bucke is probably the only reader whom it ever moved to rapturous admiration.

Our poet was about eighteen years of age when he was sent to Edinburgh, with some pecuniary assistance from the Dissenter's Society, that he might qualify himself for the office of one of their ministers ; but, after pursuing the requisite studies for one winter, he changed his mind with respect to a profession, entered himself a medical

---

[1] viii. 427, where it is signed " *Britannicus.*"
[2] ix. 544, where it is dated " Newcastle upon Tyne." Mr. Bucke, not aware of this, supposes that it was written at Edinburgh. He pronounces it to be " worthy the lyre of Collins," to whose imaginative odes it bears no resemblance, and after quoting the two following stanzas, ex-

student,[1] and repaid the contribution which he had received from the Dissenters. " Whether," says Johnson,
" when he resolved not to be a dissenting minister, he
ceased to be a dissenter, I know not. He certainly re-
tained an unnecessary and outrageous zeal for what he
called and thought liberty ; a zeal which sometimes dis-
guises from the world, and not rarely from the mind
which it possesses, an envious desire of plundering
wealth or degrading greatness ; and of which the immediate tendency is innovation and anarchy, an impetuous
eagerness to subvert and confound, with very little care
what shall be established." [2]

---

claims, " Has Horace or Gray any thing superior to this ?"
I confidently answer,—many things infinitely superior :

> " That last best effort of thy skill,
> To form the life and rule the will,
>     Propitious Power ! impart :
> Teach me to cool my passion's fires,
> Make me the judge of my desires,
>     The master of my heart.

> " Raise me above the vulgar breath,
> Pursuit of fortune, fear of death,
>     And all in life that's mean :
> Still true to reason be my plan,
> Still let my actions speak the man,
>     Through every various scene."
>                         *Life of Akenside*, 19.

In the same vol. of the *Gent. Mag.* p. 153, is *an imitation
of Horace*, Ode I. B. iii., signed " *M. A.*" and p. 599, an
Ode, with a Greek motto instead of a title, which begins,
" Hail, Melancholy, gloomy Power :" Qy. Are they by
Akenside ?

When the *Pleasures of Imagination* appeared, the editor
of the *Gent. Mag.* gave an extract from that poem, headed
by an announcement that it was written by the author of the
*British Philippic* and the *Hymn to Science*, xiv. 219. Both
pieces were reprinted in the third vol. of Pearch's *Coll. of
Poems.*

[1] In a letter written from Newcastle in 1742 (which will
be afterwards given) he calls himself " Surgeon."

[2] *Life of Akenside.*

At Edinburgh he was elected a member of the Medical Society, December 30th, 1740,[1] and became acquainted with several persons of his own age, who afterwards rose to eminence; but though, during his residence there, he prosecuted the study of medicine,[2] we learn from the following authentic statement that he was by no means satisfied with his new profession, and thirsted for a celebrity very different from that which its most successful practice could confer. "Akenside," says the late Dugald Stewart, "when a student at Edinburgh, was a member of the Medical Society, then recently formed, and was eminently distinguished by the eloquence which he displayed in the course of the debates. Dr. Robertson (who was at that time a student of divinity in the same university) told me that he was frequently led to attend their meetings, chiefly to hear the speeches of Akenside; the great object of whose ambition then was a seat in Parliament; a situation which, he was sanguine enough to flatter himself, he had some prospect of obtaining; and for which he conceived his talents to be much better adapted than for the profession he had chosen. In this opinion he was probably in the right, as he was generally considered by his fellow-students as far inferior in medical science to several of his companions."[3] To the ardour of youth, and the consciousness of high endowments, we ought probably to attribute such ambitious dreams; and we may suppose, that as

---

[1] Anderson's *Life of Akenside.—Brit. Poets*, ix. 725.

[2] Mr. Bucke says that Akenside " seems to have made *great progress*" in his medical studies at Edinburgh (*Life of Akenside*, 16), and in quoting from Stewart the passage which I have given above, he *omits the concluding sentence*.

[3] *Elem. of the Phil. of the Human Mind (Notes)*, iii. 501. 4to. The author is led to give the above anecdote by having quoted in his text (p. 299) the following lines in Akenside's *Ode to Sleep*, where, he observes, the poet " has very beautifully touched upon the history of his own mind :"

" The figur'd brass, the choral song,
The rescued people's glad applause,
The listening Senate, and the laws
Fix'd by the counsels of Timoleon's tongue,

judgment ripened with maturer years, they faded gradually away.

At Edinburgh he composed his ode *On the Winter Solstice*, dated 1740, which he soon after re-wrote and amplified. He is said [1] to have originally printed it with another juvenile production, *Love, an Elegy*, for distribution among his friends. His lines *To Cordelia* [2] bear the same date.

We are told by Akenside's biographers, that after staying three years at Edinburgh, he removed to Leyden for the advancement of his medical studies :—that he remained there two (according to others, three) years, till he had taken his degree of Doctor of Physic in 1744 : —that he there formed an intimacy with his future patron, Mr. Jeremiah Dyson, [3] then a student of law at the same university, and returned with him to England— (they " embarked," according to Mr. Bucke's [4] particular account, " in the same vessel at Rotterdam, and arrived safely in London, after an agreeable but protracted voyage!") :—and that the *Pleasures of Imagination* was published soon after the poet's arrival in England. I shall presently show that Akenside's first and only visit to Leyden was in 1744, and subsequent to the appear-

---

Are scenes too grand for fortune's private ways;
And though they shine in youth's ingenuous view,
The sober gainful arts of modern days
To such romantic thoughts have bid a long adieu."

[1] *Biog. Brit.*—In the Ad. and Cor. to the first vol. we are told that *Love* " afterwards appeared in the first edition of Dodsley's *Collection*, but was omitted in succeeding editions by Akenside's desire." It certainly is not in the first ed. of that work, 3 vols. 1748, but may have been inserted in some early edition of those, or the subsequently-published volumes, which I have not seen : it was printed in the third volume of Pearch's *Coll. of Poems*.

[2] I find them in an excellent American ed. of his *Works*, 2 vols. New Brunswick, New Jersey, 1808.

[3] On the authority, I suppose, of Sir John Hawkins.— *Life of Johnson*, 233, 243, ed. 1787.

[4] *Life of Akenside*, 24.

ance of his great work ; and that he and **Mr. Dyson** were never in Holland at the same time.

Having completed his studies in the Scottish capital, Akenside appears to have returned to his native town in 1741. Next year, he addressed the following remarkable letter[1] to Mr. Dyson, a young gentleman of fortune, with whom, perhaps, he had become acquainted during his residence in Edinburgh :

" Newcastle upon Tyne, y<sup>e</sup> 18th of Aug<sup>st</sup>, 1742.

" DEAR SIR,

" I HAVE been long expecting to hear from you since I had the pleasure of seeing you on the road ; but your letter has either miscarry'd or has been prevented perhaps by some unexpected affairs ingaging you after your arrival at London longer than you suppos'd. Upon either of these cases I should not have delay'd to begin a correspondence sooner, but that I knew not how to direct for you. Our acquaintance, Mr. Anderson, has just now inform'd me ; and I take the opportunity of his journey to London to send you this. For where there is a real esteem and affection, it is certainly extremely absurd to act according to those precisenesses of form and punctuality, which in some matters may prevent inconvenience, but can never regulate the mind, and have no connection with the free inclinations of one who would be a friend. The very opportunity of knowing a person of a desirable character, is the means of no slight enjoyment ; but the prospect of contracting a friendship in such a case brings the pleasure much nearer home, and promises a kind of property in those things which all men look upon with honour and good wishes. If you will excuse me for being thus selfish, I sincerely and heartily offer you my friendship ; and tho' in such a compact, where there are no articles of obligation, nothing stipulated, nothing impos'd, it be not very becoming to promise too much, yet I think one may venture to ingage for himself, that he is capable of being a friend : for tho' in our voluntary affairs this be indeed the main article, yet it luckily happens that this pretension, like all those

---

[1] Now first published.

that regard the heart and will, is neither difficult to be made good, nor liable to the censure of vanity : quite differently from all pretensions to what is valuable in the understanding, or in any other respect of nature or fortune.

"Mr. Anderson says he was told you had been somewhat indispos'd since you got home; I hope you are by this time perfectly strong and healthy, so as to continue without fear in your resolution of spending next winter at Leyden. I heartily wish I could spend it with you, but am as yet undetermin'd. Mr. Archer, besides next winter at Edinburgh, intends, I hear, to pass another with Mr. Hucheson; in my opinion he putts off his settling in business too late, if he spend as many years as he talks of in an academical way. It was always my desire to be fix'd in life, as they say, as soon as I could, consistently with the attainments necessary to what I should profess.

"A letter from you, whenever you are at leisure, will be extremely welcome: you will direct it to be left at Mr. Akinside's, Surgeon, in Newcastle upon Tyne.

"I desire you to excuse this blotted scrawl; it is past midnight, and Mr. Anderson goes away early to-morrow. I am, Sir, with the greatest esteem and sincerity, your very affectionate and obedient servant,

"MARK AKINSIDE."

This letter was the prelude to a friendship memorable for the fervour and the constancy with which it was maintained on both sides, as well as for its beneficial results to the poet. At the time it was written, I apprehend that Akenside was busily occupied in the composition of the great didactic poem, over which his genius seems to have brooded even from his boyish days; and that, though he styles himself "Surgeon," he had not commenced any regular practice in that capacity.

Mr. Dyson's "resolution of spending next winter at Leyden," in order to prosecute the study of civil law, was carried into effect. On his return to England, in 1743,[1] he entered himself at one of the Inns of Court

---

[1] As appears from a letter of Professor Alberti to him, dated December 1st, 1743, in the possession of his son, J. Dyson, Esq.

(I believe, Lincoln's Inn), and, in due time, was called to the bar.

*The Pleasures of Imagination*, being now ready for the press, we may suppose that Akenside brought the precious manuscript to London, about the middle, or towards the close, of 1743. " I have heard," says Johnson, " Dodsley relate, that when the copy was offered him, the price demanded for it, which was a hundred and twenty pounds, being such as he was not inclined to give precipitately, he carried the work to Pope, who, having looked into it, advised him not to make a niggardly offer; for ' this was no every-day writer.' "[1] In consequence of this *imprimatur* from Twickenham, the work was published by Dodsley in January, 1744.[2]

---

[1] Johnson's *Life of Akenside.*

[2] Quarto, pr. 4s.: see *The Daily Post* for January 16th, 1744—Mr. Bucke says it was printed by Richardson, the celebrated novelist: a letter addressed to him by Akenside will be afterwards given, and is, I suspect, Mr. Bucke's sole authority for such an assertion! The motto on the title-page is Ἀσεβὲς μὲν ἐςιν ἀνθρώπɞ τὰς παρὰ τɞ̃ Θεɞ̃ χάριτας ἀτιμαζεῖν. *Epict. apud Arrian*, ii. 23. A second edition, 8vo. pr. 2s. is announced in the *Gent. Mag.* for May next. In a copy of the first edition (now in the British Museum), presented by Akenside to Dyson, is the following MS. dedication, which probably the modesty of the latter would not allow to appear in print:

" Viro conjunctissimo
Jeremiæ Dyson,
Vitæ, morumque suorum duci,
Rerum bonarum socio,
Studiorum judici,
Cujus amicitia
Neque sanctius habet quicquam,
Neque optat carius,
Hocce opusculum
(Vos, O tyrannorum impuræ laudes
Et servilium blandimenta poetarum,
Abeste procul)
Dat, dicat, consecratque
Marcus Akinside,
xvii. Calendas Jan. A. Æ. C. MDCCXLIV."

This dedication was not first printed by Mr. Bucke, as that

Notwithstanding its metaphysical subject, so little adapted to the taste of common readers, this splendid production was received with an applause[1] which at once raised the author, who had only completed his twenty-third year, to a distinguished station among the poets of the day. When it first appeared, Pope was sinking under the malady which, a few months after, removed him from the poetic throne; Swift was still alive, but in the stupor of idiotcy; Thomson had won by *The Seasons* an unfading laurel, to which he was destined to add another wreath by *The Castle of Indolence;* Young was in the fulness of fame, though the four concluding portions of the *Night Thoughts* were yet unpublished; Glover enjoyed a very high reputation from *Leonidas;* Johnson was known only as the author of an admired satire, *London;* Dyer had put forth *Grongar Hill,* and *The Ruins of Rome,* with little success,—his *Fleece* was yet to come; Collins had vainly endeavoured to attract

---

gentleman supposes: it had previously appeared in Beloe's *Anecdotes,* vol. i.

*The Pleasures of Imagination* was published anonymously. Johnson told Boswell that when it originally came out, Rolt (a now forgotten author) went over to Dublin, and published an edition of it in his own name; upon the fame of which he lived for several months, being entertained at the best tables as "the ingenious Mr. Rolt;" and that Akenside having been informed of this imposition vindicated his right by publishing the poem with its real author's name. Boswell adds in a note: " I have had enquiry made in Ireland as to this story, but do not find it recollected there. I give it on the authority of Dr. Johnson, to which may be added that of the Biographical Dictionary and Biographia Dramatica, in both of which it has stood many years. Mr. Malone observes, that the truth probably is, not that an edition was published with Rolt's name in the title-page, but that the poem, being then anonymous, Rolt acquiesced in its being attributed to him in conversation." *Life of Johnson,* i. 342, ed. 1816.

[1] Gray, however, who was not yet known to the world as a poet, passed a depreciating criticism on it in a letter to Dr. Wharton, from Cambridge, April 26th, 1744: " You desire to know, it seems, what character the poem of your young friend bears here. I wonder that you ask the opinion

notice by his *Eclogues* and *Epistle to Hanmer,*—his *Odes* being of a later date; Shenstone had produced little, but among that little was *The School-mistress;* Blair had published *The Grave*; and Armstrong, who had only a disgraceful notoriety from a licentious poem,[1] was soon to rival Akenside as a didactic writer.

The applause which hailed the first appearance of *The Pleasures of Imagination* had scarcely subsided, when Akenside found that he had roused an adversary of formidable powers. Having adopted the opinion of Lord Shaftesbury, that ridicule is the test of truth, he had annexed to a passage in the third book of his poem a long note on the subject, in which Warburton chose to discover an offensive allusion to himself. When, therefore, that mighty dogmatist, about two months after, put forth his *Remarks on Several Occasional Reflections, in answer to Dr. Middleton, &c.*[2] he devoted to Akenside the whole of a sneering and caustic Preface,[3] which opens thus :

---

of a nation, where those, who pretend to judge do not judge at all; and the rest (the wiser part) wait to catch the judgment of the world immediately above them; that is, Dick's and the Rainbow Coffee Houses. Your readier way would be to ask the ladies that keep the bars in those two theatres of criticism. However, to show you that I am a Judge, as well as my countrymen, I will tell you, though I have rather turned it over than read it (but no matter; no more have they) that it seems to me above the middling; and now and then, for a little while, rises even to the best, particularly in description. It is often obscure, and even unintelligible; and too much infected with the Hutchinson jargon. In short, its great fault is, that it was published at least nine years too early. And so methinks in a few words 'à la mode du Temple,' I have pertly dispatched what perhaps may for several years have employed a very ingenious man worth fifty of myself." Mason's *Memoirs of Gray*, 178, ed. 1775. His still more unfavourable opinion of some of Akenside's minor poems will be afterwards cited.

[1] The *Economy of Love.* His *Art of Preserving Health* was published in April, 1744: see *The Daily Post* for the 12th of that month.

[2] Published in March, 1744: see *The Daily Post* for the 16th of that month.

[3] This Preface was afterwards reprinted, with some slight

"In the Prefatory Discourse to the first volume of the
D.[ivine] L.[egation] I spoke pretty largely of the *Use
of Ridicule* in religious subjects; as the *Abuse* of it is
amongst the fashionable arts of Free-thinking : for which
I have been just now call'd to account, without any ce-
remony, by the nameless author of a poem entitled *The
Pleasures of Imagination.* For 'tis my fortune to be
still concern'd with those who either *do* go masked, or
those who *should.* I am a plain man, and on my first
appearance in this way, I told my name and who I belonged to. After this, if men will *rudely* come upon me
in disguise, they can have no reason to complain, that
(in my ignorance of their characters) I treat them all
alike upon the same free footing they have put themselves. This gentleman, a follower of Ld. S.[haftes-
bury], and, as it should seem, one of those to whom that
Preface was addressed ; certainly, one of those to whom
I applied the words of Tully, *non decet, non datum est ;*
who affect wit and raillery on subjects not meet, and
with talents unequal; this gentleman, I say, in the 105th
and 106th pages of his Poem, animadverts upon me in
the following manner : *Since it is* (says he) *beyond all
contradiction evident that we have a* natural *sense or
feeling of the ridiculous, and since so good a reason may
be assigned to justify the supreme Being for bestowing
it ; one cannot without* astonishment *reflect on the conduct of those men who imagine it for the service of true
religion to vilify and blacken it without distinction, and
endeavour to persuade us that it is never applied but in a
bad cause.*" Warburton then proceeds to a very minute
examination of the obnoxious note ;[1] he insinuates that
Akenside is a deist, even a favourer of atheism ; and,
though he attacks his philosophy, and not his poetry,
he repeatedly terms him " *our poet,*" in a manner truly
provoking. In conclusion, he asserts that a passage in

---

alterations, as a *Postscript to the Dedication to the Free-
thinkers* in a new edition of the *Divine Legation of Moses.*—
Both Mr. D'Israeli (*Quarrels of Authors,* i. 97), and Mr.
Bucke (*Life of Akenside,* 37) seem not to know where Warburton's attack on the poet originally appeared.

[1] See the note on ver. 259 of the third book of *The
Pleasures of Imagination.*

the third book of the poem is an insult to the whole body
of the clergy.[1]

*An Epistle to the Rev. Mr. Warburton, occasioned by
his treatment of the author of the Pleasures of Imagination,* appeared about six weeks after the publication
which had called it forth.[2] Though this angry letter,
which displays considerable ingenuity of argument without much grace of style, is generally attributed to the
friendly pen of Mr. Dyson, I am inclined to believe that
the greater part of it was composed by Akenside.[3] The
following quotation forms its commencement :—

"SIR,

"NOTWITHSTANDING the pains you have taken to dis-
courage all men from entering into any controversy with
you ; and notwithstanding the severe example you have
just been making of one, who, as you fancied, had pre-
sumed *to call you to account :* you must still be content
to be accountable for your writings, and must once more
bear the mortification of being actually called to account
for them.

"'Tis the Preface to your late Remarks that you are
now called upon to justify: in which you have thought
fit to treat upon a mighty *free footing* (as you stile it,
but in the apprehension of most people, upon a very in-
jurious one), the ingenious and worthy author of the
poem entitled, *The Pleasures of Imagination.* The favourable reception and applause that performance has
met with, render it unnecessary, and indeed impertinent,
for me to enlarge in its praise, especially as you, Sir,
have not condescended to enter into a particular censure

---

"Others of graver mien, behold, adorn'd
With holy ensigns," &c.

[2] Octavo, pr. 6*d.* Published May 1st, 1744 : see *The
Daily Post* of that date. The motto on the title is "*Neque
solum quid istum audire, verum etiam quid me deceat dicere,
considerabo.*" *Cic. in Verr.* It consists of thirty pages.

[3] In a letter to Mr. Dyson (see p. 25 of this Memoir)
Akenside desires "a copy of *that answer to Warburton,*" to
be sent to Holland. If it had been entirely the work of his
loved (or rather, adored) friend, would he have mentioned
it in such terms?

of the poem; however, by some general hints scatter'd
up and down, as well as by the affectation of perpetually
stiling the author *our poet*, you may have let us see how
you stand affected towards it. Whether it be indeed that
dull, trivial, useless thing you seem to represent it, I
shall not dispute with you; but am content to leave, as
to this point, Mr. W's judgment staked against the general reputation of the poem. The point I am immediately concern'd with, is your unbecoming treatment of
the author, which, as it is so interwoven thro' the whole
course of your Preface, as to be sufficiently evident,
without the allegation of particular passages; so we shall
find there are not wanting repeated instances of direct
and notorious ill usage; such usage, as tho' the provocation had been ever so just, and the imagined attack
upon you ever so real, would yet have been unwarrant-
able, and which, therefore, can't admit of the least shadow of an excuse, when it shall appear that you had
really no provocation at all. For the very fact with
which you set out, and which is the foundation, I suppose, of all your indignation, is an entire mistake. You
tell us, *you have been just now called to account, &c.*
This, I say, is an absolute mistake. And, as for my own
part, I never suspected that the note you refer to had
any thing personal in it, so I am authorized to affirm,
that it was not at all intended personally." To this
Letter Warburton returned no answer. In the remodelled copy of his poem, Akenside reduced into a comparatively short passage the lines which treat of Ridicule,
and which were certainly the least pleasing portion of
the work. He, doubtless, writhed under Warburton's
vigorous attack, for which, as will be shown in the
course of this memoir, he, long after, made a sort of re-
quital.

Though the *Epistle to Warburton* appears not to have
been published, it was certainly printed, before Akenside went to Leyden for the purpose of obtaining the
degree of Doctor of Physic. This is proved by an allusion to it in the first of the following very interesting
letters[1] to his beloved friend, Mr. Dyson. The errone-

---

[1] Now first published.

ous statement of his biographers, that he visited Holland at an earlier period than 1744, has been already noticed.

"Leyden, April 7th, N. S. 1744.

" DEAR DYSON,

" AT last I am in a condition to recollect myself sufficiently to write to you. Ever since I left you, I have been from hour to hour ingag'd by a succession of most trivial circumstances, and yet importunate enough to force my attention from those objects, to which it most naturally and habitually inclines. I now begin to respire, and can fancy myself at Lincoln's Inn, meeting you after a very tedious absence of eight days; and telling the little occurrences I have met with; a story in other respects too inconsiderable to be repeated; but which, in repeating it to my friend, acquires an importance superior to the annals of a king's posterity.

" I went on board from Harwich on Thursday morning, and got ashore at Helvoetsluys just about the same time on Saturday. I was not in the least sick. I am now settled in Roebuck's chamber, the same house with Mr. Drew and Brocklesby. This last was the only one of my acquaintance I found here, and I dare say if you were now to return to Leyden, you would think the acquaintance of those who have come hither since you went away, very, very far from compensating the loss of those whose conversation you had the happiness to injoy. There are not above ten or twelve English, Scotch, and Irish now at Leyden.

" As I was in the street yesterday, Mr. Schwartz, who had been told by somebody or other that I was a friend of Mr. Dyson's, came up to me and inquir'd very affectionately after you. I am just come from sitting the afternoon with him; he could hardly talk of any thing but you; yet complains that you neglect to write to him. He is uncertain whether he shall be in London this summer or not; but says he is very well acquainted with all the streets there, he has so carefully studied them in the map. I love the good nature and simplicity of his manners, and love his company more than any body's in Leyden, for I see that whenever we are together we shall fall a talking about you immediately.

" I have been with Mr. Gronovius[1] and the Doctor,
who make an excellent contrast, both as to their manners and studies; about the latter of these they are constantly rallying and joking on each other.    Mr. Gronovius shew'd me his Nicander, about which he has taken
vast pains.    He has above six hundred emendations of
the text, and scholia, but wants an unpublish'd paraphrase of the author, which, it seems, is in a library at
Vienna.    He talks of making this little book as large as
his last Ælian.    I wish you could get the Pindar, which
I hear is probably by this time finish'd at Glasgow, in
one volume, the same size and type with the Theophras-
tus.    Mr. Brocklesby tells me of an edition of Shaftesbury in the press at Dublin, with new copperplates: to
which a fourth volume will be added, consisting of the
two epistolary pamphlets and unpublish'd letters of Ld.
Molesworth to my[2] master.

" I will not spend time in giving you my sentiments
of Holland or Leyden, they are so intirely the same with
what you express'd to me.    One thing struck me very
strongly, the absurd inconsistence between their ceremo-
nious foppishness (miscalled politeness) and their gross
insensibility to the true decorum in numberless instances,
especially among the women.    Such is their architecture, their painting, their music; such their dress, the
furniture of their houses, the air of their chariots, and the
countenance of their polity, that when I think of England, I cannot now help paying it the same veneration
and applause which at London I thought due only to
Athens, to Corinth, or to Syracuse.    You, who know
Holland, will excuse me for talking in this way, after so
short a view of it as I have had ;[3] because you know
how obvious these appearances are, and how great an
uniformity runs through the whole constitution of the
country, natural and moral.

---

[1] i. e. Abraham Gronovius.    The *Nicander*, here mentioned, was never published.

[2] An allusion to the *Preface* to *Remarks on Occasional Reflections*, &c., in which Warburton more than once calls
Shaftesbury Akenside's " Master."

[3] This passage decidedly proves that Akenside had not
previously visited Holland.

" Mr. Ready is well, and sends his service; as do all your other acquaintances. You will soon see Mr. Drew, for he is a printing his Thesis, and takes London in his way home.

" Be so good as to present my compliments to Mrs. Dyson, Miss Dyson, and all the rest of your friends and mine. You will know whom I mean without a list of them; only, lest you should not think on them, allow me to mention Mr. Ward and Mr. Ramsay. And pray forget not to make my apology to Mr. Pickering, for I utterly forgot to call upon him at my leaving London, which has since vex'd me not a little.

" Be sure you write to me immediately. Let me know how you manage about the Basilica, and what information Mr. Ramsay has given you. If you call at Dodsley's, he will give you a copy of that answer to Warburton; I should be glad if you could send it inclos'd in your first letter, and if you could give me your opinion about Dr. Armstrong's poem.[1] Write me a very long letter, and direct it to Mc-Carthy's. I think I am rather freer than I should have been if boarding; tho', heaven knows, my pleasure at noon is meerly in dining, properly so call'd. Farewell, my friend, my good genius, and above all things, believe me for ever most affectionately, most intirely, only yours,

" M. AKINSIDE."

" Leyden, April 17th, N. S. 1744.

" DEAR MR. DYSON,
" I HAD not been above four days at Leyden before two of my Edinburgh acquaintances, Mr. Austin and Mr. Hume, came hither from their winter quarters at Ghent, to make the tour of Holland. I was glad of the opportunity to go along with them, as I had no prospect of any company so desirable. At my return, I found your letter, by which I see we had been writing to each other precisely at the same time. I always was afraid you would be uneasy in waiting so long for a letter; and indeed I should have wrote directly from Helvoetsluys, but for a mistaken supposition that the post went from

---

[1] *The Art of Preserving Health.*

Leyden on Saturday night, and that consequently I should save no time by writing before I got to my journey's end. Would to God this may find you perfectly recover'd and in free spirits: I dare not, I cannot suffer my imagination to conceive otherwise. The whole day after we parted, I was dreading the consequence of your being abroad in so damp a morning, and lodging in that vile inn, at a time when your health was far from being confirm'd. In every other circumstance, I need not tell you what happiness your letter gave me. Believe me, my dear, my honour'd friend, I look upon my connection with you as the most fortunate circumstance of my life. I never think of it without being happier and better for the reflection. I injoy, by means of it a more animated, a more perfect relish of every social, of every natural pleasure. My own character, by means of it, is become an object of veneration and applause to myself. My sense of the perfection and goodness of the Supreme Being is nobler and more affecting. It is that good, that beauty with which my mind is fill'd, and which serves as a sacred antidote against the influence of that moral evil which is in the world, when it would perplex and distress me. It has the force of an additional conscience, of a new principle of religion: nor do I remember one instance of moral good or evil offer'd to my choice of late, in which the idea of your mind and manners did not come in along with the essential beauty of virtue and the sanction of the divine laws to guide and determine me. It has inlarg'd my knowledge of human nature, and ascertain'd my ideas of the œconomy of the universe. In whatever light I consider, with whatever principle or sensation I compare it, it still continues to receive strength from the best and highest, and in return confirm and inlarge them,

> like the sweet south
> That breathes upon a bank of violets,
> Giving and stealing odours.

I have sometimes, when in a cold or more sceptical turn of thought than is natural to my temper, hesitated whether this affection might not and did not too much engross my mind. But in a moment I saw, and you, my friend, know and feel with what satisfaction not to

be described, that it was impossible to indulge it too
much, in any other sense than as it is possible to carry
too far our regard for the Supreme Being; that is, to
lose sight of its natural tendency and run counter to the
very spirit with which it was instituted : in other words,
while we continue to cultivate our friendship, intire and
extensive as its foundations now are, it cannot ingross
our minds too much, or exert too general an influence
on our conduct.

"Perhaps you expect some account of my travels.
Indeed I cannot say more than that they confirm'd all
my former ideas of the Dutch genius and taste. Minute
and careful in execution, but flat and inelegant and narrow in design. Their buildings, their gardens, their
civil forms, every thing, give the same information. At
Amsterdam I saw a Dutch tragedy, which, tho' intended
to be really distressful, was yet farcical beyond any thing
in Aristophanes, or the Rehearsal. And these farcical
parts were the only things that mov'd the audience in
the very least degree. And in the middle of the distress, in those boxes where people of the best figure use
to sit, the glass and brandy bottle was going about
among both men and women.

"As for my acquaintance here, it lies chiefly, almost
wholly, among the gentlemen that lodge with Mr. Van-
derlas : the others, at the ordinary, have given me no
reason to alter the account you had in my last. Mr.
Ready, as far as I am able to judge, is a very amiable
man, and much a gentleman; and young Mr. Canowan
I hope, will turn out very well in the world, especially
as I see he is much less attach'd to the bigotry and narrow spirit of the Roman Catholic religion. Mr. Schwartz
spent this afternoon with me, and all salute you. I need
not desire you to express for me the warmest sentiments
of friendship and respect to Mrs. Dyson and Miss Dy-
sons, nor to remember me to all our other friends. I
am within five minutes of the post, and very sorry to
part so soon. Farewell, my dearest Dyson. Ever yours,

"M. AKINSIDE."

"Friday Evening.
"To MR. DYSON, at Serle's Coffee-house,
"Lincoln's Inn, London."

"Leyden, April 21st, N. S. 1744.

" MY DEAREST DYSON,

" I HAVE just received and read your letter, by which I find we have been a second time imploy'd in writing to each other at the same instant : from what sympathetic influence of our minds one upon the other, or what invisible agency of superior genii favourable to friendship, I cannot tell. But that your writing was a sort of present and immediate security for your being tolerably well, I should have been much alarm'd at the account you give of the return of your disorder. But now I hope 'tis fairly over, and that you have laid in a stock of health and good spirits for a very long time. For my own part, since I left you, I have indeed been *well,* in the vulgar sense of the phrase, that is to say, my appetite, my sleeps, my pulse, and the rest of that kind have been regular and sound : but the other more desirable sort of good health, that which consists in the perfect, the harmonious possession of one's own mind, in the exercise of its best facultys upon those objects which are most adapted to it by nature and habit, and above all things, in that conscious, that inexplicable *feeling* that *we are happy ;* this kind of health, I confess, I have not injoy'd so intire for these three weeks ; nor do I expect to injoy it, till I return to that situation which taught me first to conceive it. The more I see of Holland (and I imagine the case would be the same were I to travel thro' the world), the more I love and honour my native country. The manners of the people, the political forms, the genius of the constitution, the temper of the laws, the accidental objects of dress and behaviour one meets with in the streets, the very face of their buildings, and outward appearance of the country in general, only serve to put me in mind of England, with a greater desire of returning. In the same manner as all that variety of mix'd company I have pass'd thro' this last year or two, only gave me a stronger sense of my happiness when I got home to you.

" I am [at] present buried among medical books ; collecting facts, and comparing opinions among the dullest of mortal men, and that too, in their dullest capacity, that of authors. However, I hope this necessary task will grow more agreeable, when I shall be at leisure to attend to the justness of argument and the decency of expression. As I spend no time so agreeably as in reading your letters, or (next to that) in conversing with you even after this imperfect manner, I could not forbear sitting down immediately to write, especially as I was so much straitened for time last post. I am very glad that people shew so much unanimity about the war against France; and for my own part, I have not the least doubt of the superiority of our national spirit, and consequently of our success in general: only I am afraid that we shall want generals, and that the war will be too much carried on, on our part, by land. I can't say I was much pleased with the declaration of war (I mean the formula, not the thing), the style seem'd to me rather that of a private man clearing himself from some unbecoming imputations, than that of the chief magistrate of a mighty and free people proclaiming war against the most formidable people in the world, in defence of justice, and drawn to it by the disinterested succour of an oppress'd and insulted ally. The speech to the parliament I could not indeed but approve: there was an expression either in it, or in the declaration against France, quite equal to the occasion; ' I appeal to the whole world for the equity and rectitude of my conduct.' It is certainly very great, and has but one impropriety (indeed, a very essential one), that the honour due to the people of Britain for the generosity and fearless love of justice they have, under such vast pressures, manifested upon this occasion, is by this way of speaking, unavoidable in our government, attributed to *one man*, who has no other merit in the affair, than meerly in not imbezzling the vast sums which have been advanc'd in support of the common cause.

" You would see by my last that I cannot finish my affairs here so soon as you suppos'd. But what time I lost in the beginning by going to Amsterdam, &c., I shall gain towards the end of my stay here: so that I hope to be in London, at least in England, within a month at latest. I have long indulg'd myself in an agreeable prospect of settling at S., chiefly because of my opportunity of seeing you frequently, and next to that (if indeed it be not a consideration more important), in making such acquaintances during the summer seasons,

as might put it sooner in my power to spend the remain-
der of my life without interruption beside you. But
since the expectation was ill founded, we must make
ourselves easy, and look out in Northampton, or any
other place tolerably near home. For of this one thing
I am certain : never to be far from you. I would have
you write as soon as you can, if it be but to tell me how
long your journey to Shropshire will take you; because,
if you determine to go thither, I shall take shipping from
Rotterdam to Newcastle, as you will probably be gone
before I can reach London even by the pacquet. At
this moment, while I write this, I feel something of the
pain of a second parting.

" As the auctions were almost intirely over before I
got hither, I have not bought many books, nor expect to
buy many. I have however, got a few classics, and such
medical books as are most useful at present. Those that
are rather for curiosity and medical erudition, I shall
leave commissions for with some acquaintance or other.
I find what you told me to be very true, that the old and
best editions of the Greek authors are dearer here than
in London. Mr. Gronovius tells me, what perhaps you
do not know, that Mr. Freeman is to return to Leyden :
by which I judge he has intirely dedicated himself to
Greek (properly so call'd) and to editorial criticism (excuse the phrase). I think Gronovius one of the strangest
men I ever met with.

" Farewell, my dear friend. I know you oft think of
me, and need not be told how oft and how affectionately
I remember you.

" Ever and intirely yours,<br>
" MARK AKINSIDE."

" Tuesday Afternoon."

" P.S. I wish you would leave off writing upon gilt
paper, unless you can get sheets of it as large as this. I
forgot to tell you, that Wetstein at Amsterdam shew'd
me the unfinish'd Diodorus Siculus; it is printed exactly
like the last Thucydides, but how accurately I cannot
tell. Forget not my compliments at Charter-house
Square, nor to Mr. Harrison, Mr. Dyson, and the rest
of our friends. Mr. Gronovius, Mr. Schwartz, Mr.
Ready, and all your's here salute you.

" I have just been at Langeratu's to inquire about the Basilica, but not finding him, must refer it to another opportunity."

On the 16th May, 1744,[1] Akenside took his degree of Doctor of Physic, at Leyden, the subject of his *Dissertatio Medica Inauguralis* being *De ortu et incremento fœtus humani;*[2] and, doubtless, as soon as he had obtained his diploma, he hastened back to England. In the collection of odes, which he published in the following year, is an ode *On leaving Holland.*

He was now desirous to commence the practice of his profession; and having heard that he had a prospect of succeeding at Northampton, and having made some necessary enquiries on the spot in June, 1744,[3] he soon after fixed himself there as a physician. It was not long, however, before he found that the chief medical business of the place was in the hands of Dr. Stonehouse, from whom it was not to be wrested by a stranger;[4] and

---

[1] The correctness of this date is ascertained by an entry in the annals of the College of Physicians, London, which states that Akenside, on the 20th June, 1751, produced his Diploma from the University of Leyden, &c.—See p. 46 of this Memoir.

[2] It appears to have been printed. " In this dissertation the author is said to have displayed his medical sagacity by attacking some opinions of Leeuwenhoek and other writers, at that time very generally received, but which have been since discarded by the best physicians and philosophers; and by proposing an hypothesis, which is now considered as founded in truth." *Biog. Brit.*

[3] From the information of Mr. Dyson, (October 25th 1834) who thus describes the contents of one of the poet's letters to his father: " On the 14th June [1744] he writes from Northampton to report the result of his enquiries in relation to the expediency of his settling there, which was such as induced him to do so."

[4] A correspondent (who signs himself Indagator) in the *Gent. Mag.* for October, 1793 (lxiii. 885), writes thus: " The fact, Mr. Urban, is, that this contest for the physical business at Northampton, though unsuccessful on the part of Akenside, had for some time been supported by him with extraordinary violence. I am warranted, by manuscripts in

having maintained a fruitless contest with that gentleman, and perhaps, disliking Northampton on account of
its distance from the capital, he quitted it after a stay of
about eighteen months, and removed to Hampstead.
" The writer of this article," says Kippis, in a note on
our author's *Life*,[1] " who then resided at Northampton
for education, well remembers that Dr. Doddridge and
Dr. Akenside carried on an amicable debate concerning
the opinions of the ancient philosophers with regard to a
future state of rewards and punishments ; in which Dr.
Akenside supported the firm belief of Cicero in particular, in this great article of natural religion."    According
to Johnson, who heartily disliked his political creed, and
never loses an opportunity of stigmatising it, Akenside
" deafened the place with clamours for liberty." [2]

   During his stay at Northampton (in 1744), he produced

---

my possession, when I say, that not only a fair and open
struggle of medical hostilities, but every art and every exertion, personal abuse and private insinuation, had been used
to usurp Dr. Stonehouse's professional emoluments, and
oust him from his established settlement.   Yet, on Akenside's removal from that place to Hampstead, the recommen-
datory letter, a copy of which I send you, was generously
written in his favour by his worthy rival, as an introduction
for him to a gentleman of consequence in the neighbourhood
of his new abode."

   " DEAR SIR,
" The gentleman who presents you with this is Dr. Akenside, a brother physician, whose merit, as a man of refined
sense and elegance of taste, is too well known by his writings (The Pleasures of the Imagination, &c.) to need any
other testimonial ; and, I dare say, from what you already
know of them, you will naturally conclude, without any
praise of mine, that such a man must be proportionably distinguished in his own peculiar profession.
   " I take this opportunity of introducing him to the honour
of your acquaintance ; and make no doubt you will receive
him as a gentleman, whom for his character and abilities I
much esteem, and whose near neighbourhood, in any place
where there had been room for us both, I should have regarded as an addition to my happiness.   I am," &c.

   See, too, *Gent. Mag.* for January, 1794, (lxiv. 12.)
   [1] *Biog. Brit.*                    [2] *Life of Akenside.*

his very powerful satire, *An Epistle to Curio,*[1]—i. e. to
Pulteney, who having been long the strenuous supporter
of the people's cause in opposition to the measures of
government, had suddenly deserted his party, and become
an object of popular execration, for the sake of an empty
title, the Earldom of Bath. This justly-admired piece
he afterwards injudiciously altered into an ode.

The following letter, undoubtedly genuine, and never
before printed in England, is given from a fac-simile of
the original in an American edition of our author's works :[2]

" Northampton, May 21st, 1745.

" DEAR SIR,

" WHEN I look on the date of your letter, I am very glad
that I have any excuse, however disagreeable, for not
answering it long ere this. About a month ago, when I
was thinking every post to write to you, I was thrown
from my horse with a very great hazard of my life, and
confined a good while afterwards from either writing or
reading. But, thank heaven, for these ten days, I have
been perfectly well. You are very good-natured about
the verses. If they gave you any pleasure, I shall conclude my principal end in publishing them to be fairly
answer'd. And that you look upon your reading them
in manuscript, and this way of seeing them in print, as
an instance of real friendship, gives me great satisfaction.
As for public influence, if they have any, I hope it will
be a good one. But my expectations of that kind are
not near so sanguine as they once were. Indeed human
nature in its genuine habit and constitution is adapted
to very powerful impressions from this sort of entertainment ; but in the present state of manners and opinions,
it is almost solely on the retir'd and studious of nature,
that this effect can be looked for ; for hardly any besides

---

[1] Quarto, pr. 1s. : See List of Books for November, 1744,
in the *Gent. Mag.*—On the title page is this motto : " *Neque
tam ulciscendi causa dixi, quam ut et in præsens sceleratos cives
timore ab impugnanda patria detinerem ; et in posterum docu-
mentum statuerem, nequis talem amentiam vellet imitari.*"—
TULL.

[2] Printed at New-Brunswick, New-Jersey, 1808, 2 vols.
8vo.

these have been able to preserve the genuine habit of the mind in any tolerable degree. I am, dear Sir, your most obedient and most humble servant,

"M. AKINSIDE."

"To M. WILKES JUN.
St. John's-street, London."

Here probably he alludes to his *Odes on Several Subjects,* which had been published more than two[1] months before the date of this letter, and which require particular notice, though they have not obtained the slightest mention from Mr. Bucke. They are prefaced by an *Advertisement* worthy of preservation :—" The following Odes were written at very distant intervals, and, with a view to very different manners of expression and versification. The author pretends chiefly to the merit of endeavouring to be correct, and of carefully attending to the best models. From what the ancients have left of this kind, perhaps the Ode may be allowed the most amiable species of poetry ; but certainly there is none which in modern languages has been generally attempted with so little success. For the perfection of lyric poetry depends, beyond that of any other, on the beauty of words and the gracefulness of numbers; in both which

---

[1] Quarto, pr. 1s. 6d. See List of Books for March, 1745, in the *Gent. Mag.* This tract consists of fifty-four pages, and has the following motto from Pindar :

χρυσὸν εὔχονται, πεδίον δ᾽ἕτεροι
ἀπέραντον· ἐγὼ δ᾽ἀστοῖς ἀδὼν, καὶ
χθονὶ·γῦια καλύψαι-
μ᾽, αἰνέων αἰνητὰ, μομ-
φὰν δ᾽ἐπισπείρων ἀλιτροῖς.

Another edition of these *Odes* in small octavo was printed in the same year.—Horace Walpole writes to Sir H. Mann, March 29th, 1745 : " There is another of these tame geniuses, a Mr. Akenside, who writes odes ; in one he has lately published, he says, ' Light the tapers, urge the fire.' Had you not rather make gods jostle in the dark, than light the candles, for fear they should break their heads ?" *Letters, &c.* ii. 32. Walpole's editor, in a kindred spirit, calls the *Pleasures of Imagination* " a poem of *some merit.*"

respects the ancients had infinite advantages above us.
A consideration which will alleviate the author's disap-
pointment, if he too should be found to have miscarried."
The contents of this tract are:—I. *Allusion to Horace*
[now entitled *Preface* to Odes, Book I.]. II. *On the*
*Winter-solstice.* III. *Against Suspicion.* IV. *To a*
*Gentleman, whose Mistress had Married an Old Man*
[now entitled *To a Friend Unsuccessful in Love*].
V. *Hymn to Cheerfulness.* VI. *On the Absence of the*
*Poetic Inclination* [now entitled *To the Muse*]. VII. *To*
*a Friend on the Hazard of Falling in Love* [now entitled
*On Love, to a Friend*]. VIII. *On Leaving Holland.*
IX. *To Sleep.* X. *On Lyric Poetry.* A new edition
of these *Odes*, materially altered and improved, was published in 1760; and after the author's death, they were
again reprinted with still farther alterations, in that collection of his various Odes which he had left behind him
for the press. How the text, as finally arranged, differs
from that of the first edition, the following quotations
will evince. A celebrated stanza in the Ode *On the*
*Winter-solstice* is now read thus:

> " Hence the loud city's busy throngs
> Urge the warm bowl and splendid fire;
> Harmonious dances, festive songs
> Against the spiteful heaven conspire.
> Meantime perhaps with tender fears
> Some village-dame the curfew hears,
> While round the hearth her children play:
> At morn their father went abroad;
> The moon is sunk, and deep the road;
> She sighs, and wonders at his stay."

It stood in the edition of 1745:

> " Now through the town promiscuous throngs
> Urge the warm bowl and ruddy fire;
> Harmonious dances, festive songs
> To charm the midnight hours conspire.
> ·While mute and shrinking with her fears,
> Each blast the cottage-matron hears,
> As o'er the hearth she sits alone:
> At morn her bride-groom went abroad,
> The night is dark and deep the road;
> She sighs, and wishes him at home."

The Ode *To a Friend Unsuccessful in Love* now ends thus:

> " O just escap'd the faithless main,
> Though driven unwilling on the land,
> To guide your favour'd steps again,
> Behold your better Genius stand !
> Where Truth revolves her page divine,
> Where Virtue leads to Honour's shrine,
> Behold he lifts his awful hand !
>
> " Fix but on these your ruling aim,
> And Time, the sire of manly care,
> Will Fancy's dazzling colours tame,
> A soberer dress will Beauty wear ;
> Then shall Esteem, by Knowledge led,
> Enthrone within your heart and head
> Some happier love, some truer fair."

It formerly concluded:

> " O just escap'd the faithless main,
> Though driven unwilling on the land,
> To guide your favour'd steps again,
> Behold your better Genius stand !
> Where Plato's olive courts your eye,
> Where Hamden's laurel blooms on high,
> He lifts his heaven-directed hand.
>
> " When these are blended on your brow,
> The willow will be nam'd no more ;
> Or if that love-deserted bough
> The pitying, laughing girls deplore,
> Yet still shall I most freely swear
> Your dress has much a better air
> Than all that ever bride-groom wore."

In the Ode *On Lyric Poetry* we now find:

> " Yet then did Pleasure's lawless throng,
> Oft rushing forth in loose attire,
> Thy virgin dance, thy graceful song
> Pollute with impious revels dire.
> O fair, O chaste ! thy echoing shade
> May no foul discord here invade ;
> Nor let thy strings one accent move,
> Except what Earth's untroubled ear
> 'Mid all her social tribes may hear,
> And Heaven's unerring throne approve."

The lines were originally :

> " But oft amid the Grecian throng,
> The loose-rob'd forms of wild Desire
> With lawless notes intun'd thy song,
> To shameful steps dissolv'd thy quire.
> O fair, O chaste, be still with me
> From such profaner discord free :
> While I frequent thy tuneful shade,
> No frantic shouts of Thracian dames,
> No Satyrs fierce with savage flames
> Thy pleasing accents shall invade."

When this collection first appeared, the *Odes* of Collins and Gray had not been published ; and it therefore formed (with all its imperfections) the most valuable accession which the lyric poetry of England had received since Dryden's time, if we except the single *Ode* of Pope.[1]

Concerning the Ode *Against Suspicion*, we are told by Mr. Bucke that it was addressed to a self-tormenting friend who had been seized with groundless jealousy, because his wife used to indulge in certain, "innocent freedoms" with her male acquaintances, and who, in his distress, had applied to Akenside for advice.[2]

That our author, after quitting Northampton, proceeded to try his fortune as a physician at Hampstead,

---

[1] Of the mass of nonsense which, under the title of *Pindarick Odes*, was poured out towards the close of the seventeenth, and during the early part of the eighteenth century, the reader who has not examined it, can have no conception. The *very* worst piece of the kind I ever met with, is a long Ode by Theobald *On the Union*, printed in 1707, which begins :

> " Haste, Polyhymnia, haste ; thy shell prepare ;
> I have a message thou must bear,
> *But to the car a salamander tie ;*
> Thou canst not on a sunbeam play," &c.

Yet in an intimate acquaintance with Grecian and early English poetry, Theobald excelled most of his contemporaries !

[2] *Life of Akenside*, 49.   Mr. Bucke does not give his authority for the anecdote.

has been already noticed. In February, 1747, Mr. Hardinge [1] resigned his office of Clerk to the House of Commons in favour of Mr. Dyson, for six thousand pounds; and the latter, bidding adieu to the bar, purchased a villa at North End, Hampstead, for the purpose of introducing Akenside to the chief persons in the neighbourhood. "There," says Sir John Hawkins, "they dwelt together during the summer season, frequenting the long room, and all clubs, and assemblies of the inhabitants." [2] But, if we may believe the statements of this writer who knew him well, Akenside, by a want of " discretion," frustrated the kind endeavours of Mr. Dyson to forward his views. At the meetings just mentioned, which were attended by wealthy persons of ordinary endowments, who could only talk of the occurrences of the day, he made an ostentatious display of that talent for conversation which had distinguished him in more enlightened society,—became involved in disputes that betrayed him into a contempt of those who differed from his opinions,—was tauntingly reminded of his low birth and dependance on Mr. Dyson,—and was reduced to the necessity of asserting in plain terms that he was a gentleman. By a residence of about two years and a half at Hampstead, he gained nothing but the conviction that he had chosen a situation which did not suit him. Mr. Dyson therefore parted with his villa at North End, settled his friend in a small but handsome house in Bloomsbury Square, London, and, with a generosity almost unexampled, allowed him annually such a sum of money (stated to have been three hundred pounds),[3] as enabled him to keep a chariot, and to command the comforts and elegancies of life.

Mr. Bucke has suppressed the observations of Hawkins on Akenside's want of success at Hampstead; and

---

[1] See an account of this gentleman, Mr. Nicholas Hardinge, in Nichols's *Illust. of Lit. Hist.* iii. 5.

[2] *Life of Johnson,* 243. ed. 1787.

[3] The sum was probably greater. Sir John Hawkins says that Mr. Dyson "assigned for his support *such a part of his income* as enabled him to keep a chariot," *Id.* 244; and Mr. Justice Hardinge, in some anecdotes which will be afterwards given in this Memoir, asserts that Akenside " lived incomparably well."

attributes it entirely to the insolence of the purse-proud inhabitants, whom the high-minded poet would not stoop to court. They were, perhaps, not a little supercilious and overbearing; but the tone assumed by Mr. Bucke in treating the subject, could only be warranted by his having resided among them at the period in question, and having frequently witnessed their behaviour towards Akenside.[1]

To return to the notice of his works. In 1746, he wrote his truly classical *Hymn to the Naiads*,[2] and (according to Mr. Bucke) his Ode *To the Evening Star*:[3] he also contributed to Dodsley's excellent periodical publication, *The Museum, or, Literary and Historical Register*, several prose-papers, which deserve to be re-printed, and from which I regret that the necessary short-ness of this Memoir will not allow me to offer some extracts; viz. *On Correctness*,[4] *The Table of Modern Fame, a vision*,[5] *Letter from a Swiss Gentleman on English Liberty*,[6] and *The Balance of Poets*.[7] In 1747 he com-

---

[1] " They required to be sought ; their wives and daughters expected to be escorted and flattered ; and their sons to be treated with an air of obligation," &c. *Life of Akenside*, 70.

[2] First printed in Dodsley's *Coll. of Poems*, vol. vi. 1758.

[3] *Life of Akenside*, 52.—Printed without a date, in Mr. Dyson's ed. of his *Poems*, 1772.

[4] *Museum*, i. 84.—Two passages of this Essay are cited by J. Warton (Pope's *Works*, i. 264. iv. 190), and Mr. Bucke, not knowing from what piece they were derived, supposes that Warton quoted from the conversation of Akenside!" *Life of Akenside*, 105.

[5] *Museum*, i. 481.—It is an imitation of the eighty-first number of *The Tatler*—J. Warton (Pope's *Works*, ii. 83), attributing it to Akenside, says, " the guests are introduced and ranged with that taste and judgment which is peculiar to the author." It is strange that Akenside should have omitted to introduce (though he quotes) Shakespeare in this Vision.

[6] *Museum*, ii. 161.—On the authority of Mr. A. Chalmers, (*Biog. Dict.*, art. *Akenside*) who possesses J. Warton's copy of *The Museum :* see *Brit. Poets*, xviii. 76.

[7] *Museum*, ii. 165. (mispaged).—On the authority of Isaac Reed.

posed a couple of stanzas *On a Sermon against Glory;*[1]
and an *Ode to the Earl of Huntingdon,* which was published in the following[2] year, and is, perhaps, the most
perfect of his efforts in lyric poetry. About the same
time he composed his *Ode to Caleb Hardinge, M. D.,*[3]
a talented and eccentric character, of whom, in connection with our poet, some anecdotes will be afterwards related. Mr. Dyson, we have already seen, had succeeded
this gentleman's brother, Mr. Hardinge, as Clerk to the
House of Commons; and Akenside had consequently
become acquainted with various members of the Hardinge family. The Ode *To Sir Francis Henry Drake,*[4]
was produced, I apprehend, at nearly the same period.
In 1749 he wrote *The Remonstrance of Shakespeare,*
*supposed to have been spoken at the Theatre Royal, while*
*the French Comedians were acting by subscription,*[5] a
piece only remarkable for its illiberality.

Akenside was about the age of twenty-seven, when,
rendered easy in his circumstances by the annual gratuity
of Mr. Dyson, he finally took up his abode in the metro-
polis. Thenceforth his exertions to advance himself in
his profession appear to have been unremitting. Though
he occasionally amused his leisure by composing poetry,
he gave little of it to the press; and published from time
to time various medical essays. His reputation and practice continued to increase till his death; but it is certain
that he never attained the highest rank in his profession,
and that his services were never in much request.[6] " A
physician in a great city," observes Johnson, " seems to
be the mere play-thing of fortune; his degree of reputation is, for the most part, totally casual: they that

---

[1] Printed in Mr. Dyson's ed. of his *Poems,* 1772.
[2] Quarto, pr. 1s. See List of Books for January, 1748,
in *The Gent. Mag.*
[3] Printed in Mr. Dyson's ed. of his Poems, 1772.
[4] Printed *ibid.*        [5] Printed *ibid.*
[6] The newspapers, which announce his decease, describe
him as "a physician of very extensive practice," and Kippis,
in the *Biog. Brit.,* says, " in a course of time, Dr. Akenside
came into very considerable reputation and practice:" on
the contrary, besides the statements of Dr. Johnson and Sir
John Hawkins, it is positively asserted by his friend Mr.

employ him know not his excellence ; they that reject him know not his deficience. By any acute observer, who had looked on the transactions of the medical world for half a century, a very curious book might be written on the ' Fortune of Physicians.' "[1] According to Sir John Hawkins, Akenside's endeavours to become popular were defeated by the high opinion which he every where manifested of himself—his want of condescension to those of inferior talents—and his love of political controversy. At Tom's Coffee-house in Devereux Court, which he frequented in the winter-evenings, and which was then the resort of various eminent men, he would engage in disputes, chiefly on literature and politics, that fixed on his character the stamp of haughtiness and self-conceit.

Among the company who used to assemble there, was a little deformed personage, named Ballow ; a lawyer without practice, holding a place in the exchequer ; vulgar and ill-tempered, but of deep and extensive learning. He envied the eloquence which Akenside displayed in conversation, hated what he thought his republican principles, and affected to treat him as a pretender to literature. A violent dispute having arisen between them, Akenside, in consequence of some expressions uttered by Ballow, demanded an apology ; which not being able to obtain, he sent his adversary a written challenge. Though Ballow wore a sword of remarkable length, he had no inclination to use it : he declined an answer ; and, in spite of Akenside's repeated attempts to see him, kept close in his lodgings, till the interposition of friends had adjusted their difference. Akenside, however, gained little reputation for courage by this affair : it was settled not by the concessions of his adversary, but by their mutual obstinacy,—the one refusing to fight in the morning, the other in the afternoon.[2] " Yet," adds Sir John

---

Justice Hardinge, that " he certainly had no business or fame" as a medical man: see some anecdotes afterwards cited in this Memoir.

[1] *Life of Akenside.*

[2] There is truth in the remark of Mr. Bucke, that " to challenge a man like Ballow, must have been a punishment

D

Hawkins, who writes with no unfriendly feeling towards our poet, " where there was no competition for applause or literary reputation, he was an easy companion, and would bear with such rudeness as would have angered almost any one.  Saxby, of the Custom-house, who was every evening at Tom's, and by the bluntness of his behaviour, and the many shrewd sayings he was used to utter, had acquired the privilege of Thersites, of saying whatever he would, was once in my hearing inveighing against the profession of physic, which Akenside took upon him to defend.  This railer, after labouring to prove that it was all imposture, concluded his discourse with this sentiment: ' Doctor,' said he, ' after all you have said, my opinion of the profession of physic is this, the ancients endeavoured to make it a science and failed, and the moderns to make it a trade and have succeeded.' Akenside took his sarcasm in good part, and joined in the laugh which it occasioned............Akenside was a man of religion and strict virtue, a philosopher, a scholar, and a fine poet.  His conversation was of the most delightful kind, learned, instructive, and without any affectation of wit, cheerful and entertaining.  One of the pleasantest days of my life I passed with him, Mr. Dyson, and another friend, at Putney bowling-green house, where a neat and elegant dinner, the enlivening sunshine of a summer's day, and the view of an unclouded sky, were the least of our gratifications.  In perfect good-humour with himself and all around him, he seemed to feel a joy that he lived, and poured out his gratulations to the great dispenser of all felicity in expressions that Plato himself might have uttered on such an occasion.  In conversations with select friends, and those whose course of study had been nearly the same with his own, it was an usual thing with him in libations to the memory of eminent men among the ancients, to bring their characters into view, and thereby give occasion to expatiate on those particulars of their lives that

---

to the sensitive mind of Akenside, in itself sufficient, for having given way to a weakness so unworthy of a poet of high rank, and more especially a philosopher of no mean order."  *Life of Akenside,* 179.

had rendered them famous: his method was to arrange them into three classes, philosophers, poets, and legislators.

"That a character thus formed should fail of recommending itself to general esteem, and of procuring to the possessor of it those benefits which it is in the power of mankind to bestow, may seem a wonder, but it is often seen that negative qualities are more conducive to this end than positive ; and that, with no higher a character than is attainable by any one who with a studious taciturnity will keep his opinions to himself, conform to the practice of others, and entertain neither friendship for nor enmity against any one, a competitor for the good opinion of the world, nay for emoluments and even dignities, stands a better chance of success, than one of the most established reputation for learning and ingenuity. The truth of this observation Akenside himself lived to experience, who, in a competition for the place of physician to the Charter-house, was unable to prevail against an obscure man, devoid of every quality that might serve to recommend him, and whose sole merit was that of being distantly related to the late Lord Holland." [1]

Akenside's practice, Mr. Bucke informs us, was obstructed by his dislike of being all things to all men, and in a still greater degree, by his fame as a poet.[2] I believe that it was greatly impeded by his forbidding manners to strangers: he was excessively stiff and formal ; and if any one ventured to smile in the apartments of the sick, he checked them with a frown.[3] Some anecdotes, which charge him with cruelty to hospital-patients, will be afterwards cited. That he was a scientific and acute physician,[4] is testified by his works, which I have heard more than one member of the profession mention in terms of praise.

Among his friends, and, it should seem, his patients,

---

[1] *Life of Johnson*, pp. 244—248, ed. 1787.
[2] *Life of Akenside*, 86.
[3] So a Mr. Meyrick told Mr. Bucke. *Id.* 29.
[4] Mr. Justice Hardinge thought otherwise (see some anecdotes afterwards quoted in this Memoir); but his opinion on the subject carries no weight.

he now included the Honourable Charles Townshend, who, for his parliamentary eloquence, has been termed by Burke " a prodigy," and who, at a later period, became Chancellor of the Exchequer. To this distinguished statesman Akenside addressed two *Odes*, the longer of which is dated 1750 :[1] but, from some unknown cause, their friendship subsequently ceased. "Sir," said Johnson to Boswell, " a man is very apt to complain of the ingratitude of those who have risen far above him. A man when he gets into a higher sphere, into other habits of life, cannot keep up all his former connections. Then sir, those who knew him formerly upon a level with themselves, may think that they ought still to be treated as on a level, which cannot be; and an acquaintance in a former situation may bring out things which it would be very disagreeable to have mentioned before higher company, though, perhaps, every body knows of them." Boswell presently adds : "Dr. Johnson's remark as to the jealousy entertained of our friends who rise far above us, is certainly very just. By this was withered the early friendship between Charles Townshend and Akenside." The recent editor of Boswell's work justly observes that " this is no appropriate instance. Charles Townshend, —the nephew of the prime minister,—the son of a peer, who was secretary of state, and leader of the House of Lords—was as much above Akenside in their earliest days, as at any subsequent period ; nor was Akenside in rank inferior to Dr. Brocklesby, with whom Charles Townshend continued in intimate friendship to the end of his life."[2]

In 1750 (according to Mr. Bucke) he also addressed an Ode *To William Hall, Esq., with the Works of Chaulieu.*[3] Mr. Hall belonged to the Middle Temple, and moved in the best society ; composed verses of con-

---

[1] Both printed in Mr. Dyson's ed. of his *Poems,* 1772.

[2] Boswell's *Life of Johnson,* ed. Croker, iii. 367-8.—Mr. Bucke carelessly attributes to Johnson the remark of Boswell, on the friendship of Townshend and our poet. *Life of Akenside,* 117.

[3] Printed in Mr. Dyson's ed. of his *Poems,* 1772, where it has no date.

siderable elegance, and was the intimate friend of Markland ;[1] but in licentiousness of life he seems to have exceeded the French Abbé whose poems were presented to him.

In 1751, on the appearance of a work from the pen of Frederic, King of Prussia, entitled *Memoires pour servir à l'Histoire de la Maison de Brandebourg*, Akenside wrote a short Ode *To the Author*,[2] &c., exposing the dangerous tendency of certain passages ; also, an *Ode to Thomas Edwards*, on Warburton's edition of Pope's *Works*, which will be more particularly mentioned when we arrive at the period of its publication.

During the same year, he was held up to ridicule in the *Peregrine Pickle* of Smollett, who, though his propensity to personal satire scarcely needed such incitement, is said to have been piqued at some reflections [3] which the poet had cast on Scotland, soon after his return from Edinburgh. That the ode-writing " Doctor," who raves about liberty, and treats his friends to an entertainment in the manner of the ancients, was intended for a caricature of Akenside would have been evident enough, even if the pedant had not been made to quote, as his own composition, two lines from the *Ode to the Earl of Huntingdon*.[4]

---

[1] To Mr. Hall, at whose expense it was originally printed, Markland dedicated his treatise *De Græcorum Quinta Declinatione Imparisyllabica, &c.*—Hall frequented Tom's Coffeehouse in Devereux Court (Nichols's *Lit. An.* iv. 327.) where, perhaps, Akenside became acquainted with him. He fell into a wretched state of idiotcy, and died a maniac at Bath in 1766.—For pleasing specimens of his poetical powers, see two copies of verses to Miss Lawrence in Dodsley's *Coll. of Poems*, v. 219, 329,—*Vacation, To a Lady very handsome but too fond of dress*, and *Anacreon, Ode* iii. *Id.* vi. 163 —172, ed. 1782,—also a *Sonnet on Lauder's Forgeries, to Nicholas Hardinge*, in Nichols's *Lit. An.* viii. 520.

[2] Printed in Mr. Dyson's ed. of his *Poems*, 1772.

[3] Moore's *Life of Smollett*, cxxiii.

[4] " *O fool! to think the man, whose ample mind must grasp whatever yonder stars survey*—Pray, Mr. Pallet, what is your opinion of that image of the mind grasping the whole universe? For my own part, 1 can't help thinking it the most happy conception that ever entered my imagination."

In 1753, Akenside was admitted by mandamus to a
Doctor's Degree at Cambridge, and elected Fellow of
the Royal Society : in 1754 he became Fellow of the
College of Physicians.[1]

That he was unwilling to cross the paths of his old an-
tagonist, appears from the following note to Dr. Birch :[2]

" DEAR SIR,

" I RETURN you thanks for the pleasure which I have
had in reading these two books.

---

*Per. Pickle.* ii. 110, ed. 1751,—and Smollett's *Works* (by
Moore), iii. 330.—Desirous, it should seem, of repairing the
injustice he had done to our author, Smollett, in the *Con-
tinuation of the Complete Hist. of England,* says " *Akenside*
and Armstrong excelled in didactic poetry," iv. 126.

[1] See *Cantab. Grad.*—Mr. Bucke erroneously states that
he took his Cambridge degree soon after returning from
Holland. *Life of Akenside,* 173.—The date of his election
by the Royal Society I owe to J. Hudson, Esq.—For the
following extracts from the annals of the College of Physicians, I have to thank Dr. Francis Hawkins, their Registrar :—

" 1751, May 3d, Dr. Akenside was summoned to attend the
    Censor's Board, at the Royal College of Physicians.
    June 6th, examined first time by that Board.
    June 20th, examined second time, when he produced a
      Diploma from the University of Leyden, dated May
      16th, 1744.
    June 25th, admitted Licentiate of the College of Phy-
      sicians.
1752. The College of Physicians wrote to the Vice Chan-
    cellor of the University of Cambridge to signify that
    the College had no objection to the Degree of M. D.
    being conferred on Dr. Akenside by Mandamus.
1753, Feb. 2nd, he was examined a first time as a candidate
    for the Fellowship of the College.
    Feb. 9th, examined a second time, when he produced a
      Diploma from Cambridge, dated Jan. 4th, 1753.
    March 8th, examined third time.
    April 16, admitted a Candidate of the College.
1754, April 8th, admitted Fellow.
1755, Sep. 30th, chosen Fourth Censor of the College, with
    Drs. Heberden, Coxe, and William Pitcairn, Dr. Reeve
    being President."

[2] *Letters to Dr. Birch,* 4300, in the Brit. Mus.

" I see this instant, in the Public Advertiser, that Dr. Warburton is made King's Chaplain, and enters into waiting immediately. Can you tell me whether this be true? If there be any hazard of finding him at Kensington, I shall not chuse to go thither to-day. I am your affectionate humble servant,

" M. AKENSIDE."

" Bloomsb. Square,
" Saturday Morn. [Sept. 28, 1754.]"

His encomiastic *Ode to the Bishop of Winchester* [1] bears date the same year. This prelate was the celebrated controversialist, Dr. Hoadley, whose political opinions accorded with the poet's.

In June,[2] 1755, Akenside read the Gulstonian Lectures before the College of Physicians; a portion of which, on the origin and use of the lymphatic vessels in animals, was again read at a meeting of the Royal Society, and printed in the *Philosophical Transactions* for 1757.[3]

---

[1] Printed in the sixth vol. of Dodsley's *Coll. of Poems*, 1758.

[2] See the two following notes :—but Dr. Francis Hawkins, Registrar to the College, informs me, that, according to the entries in their annals, Akenside read the Gulstonian Lectures on May 28, 29, and 30.

[3] Vol. L. Part I. p 322 :—*Observations on the Origin and Use of the Lymphatic Vessels of Animals : being an extract from the Gulstonian Lectures, read in the Theatre of the College of Physicians of London, in June,* 1755 : consisting of six pages. In consequence of a misprint in this essay, Akenside wrote the following letter to the author of *Clarissa,* who, it may be necessary to inform some readers, was a printer :—

" To MR. RICHARDSON, in Salisbury Court, Fleet Street.

" SIR,

" I RETURN you many thanks for sending me the sheet about which I wrote to you. I find in it an *erratum* of that unlucky sort, which does not make absolute nonsense, but only conveys a false and absurd idea. The sheet is mark'd T t; and in page 328, and line 9th from the bottom, *stream* is printed instead of *steam.* If you can without much trouble either print this as an *erratum,* or rather let somebody with a stroke of a pen blot out the *r,* as the sheets are dried, I should be

Next year he published a short pamphlet,[1] in reply to certain animadversions on this essay by Dr. Alexander Monro of Edinburgh, among which was an insinuation that Akenside's theory was derived from *his* treatise *De Glandulis lymphaticis.*

Here may be introduced another short note[2] to Dr. Birch:—

" DEAR SIR,

" HAVE you got the letters concerning Hume's History?

---

greatly oblig'd. I am, Sir, with true respect, your most humble servant,

" M. AKENSIDE."

" Bloomsb. Square, Jan. 25."

*Letters to Dr. Birch, &c.,* 4300, in the Brit. Mus.

[1] *Notes on the Postscript to a Pamphlet entitled ' Observations Anatomical and Physiological &c., by Alexander Monro, Junior, M.D. Professor of Anatomy, &c., Edinburgh, August,* MDCCLVIII.' 1758, 8vo. p. p. 24. pr. 6d.—Our author writes in the third person, and commences the tract with this clear statement of facts: " Dr. Akenside did, it seems, so long ago as June 1755, in certain annual lectures which he read in his turn at the College of Physicians, advance a new theory concerning these [lymphatic] vessels; a theory which he had at first drawn out for himself, and of which, before that time, no mention had been made to the public. He did not then print any part of what he had read; thinking perhaps, that his notion was already sufficiently made known, by being stated at a public lecture before a numerous audience of physicians and other persons qualified to judge of what he advanc'd, and with an explicit account of the evidence on which he founded it. Some time afterwards when a dispute about this very point had arisen between two other gentlemen, each of them for himself laying claim to the discovery, Dr. A. was prevailed upon to give in at a meeting of the Royal Society so much of his lectures as related to the subject in question. Accordingly this was read as a passage taken from those lectures; the same title being then prefixed to it which it now bears in print; and several gentlemen being then present, who had formerly heard the lectures themselves. The paper was published by the council of the society." Monro's treatise on the Lymphatics, from which he insinuated that Akenside borrowed his ideas, did not arrive in England till 1756.

[2] *Letters to Dr. Birch,* 4300, in the Brit. Mus.

I grudge to buy them.   If you have them, and can spare them so long, I should be much oblig'd if you would let me have them a few hours.   I am a sort of invalid, just enough to confine me.   Your affectionate humble servant,

"M. AKENSIDE."

"Bloomsb. Square,
"Wednesday Morn." [March 3d, 1756.]

On the 7th, 8th, and 9th of September,[1] 1756, he read the Croonian Lectures before the College of Physicians. According to Kippis,[2] their subject was the History of the Revival of Learning, to which some of the members objected as "foreign to the institution," and Akenside, after three lectures, gave up the task in disgust.

The first book of his re-modelled *Pleasures of Imagination* is dated 1757.   The poem, says Mr. Dyson appeared originally " at a very early part of the author's life : that it wanted revision and correction he was sufficiently sensible ;  but so quick was the demand for several successive republications, that in any of the intervals to have completed the whole of his corrections was utterly impossible ; and yet to have gone on from time to time in making farther improvements in every new edition, would, he thought, have had the appearance at least of abusing the favour of the public : he chose, therefore, to continue for some time reprinting it without alteration, and to forbear publishing any corrections or improvements until he should be able at once to give them to the public complete : and with this view he went on for several years to review and correct the poem at his leisure, till at length he found the task grow so much upon his hands, that, despairing of ever being able to execute it sufficiently to his own satisfaction, he abandoned the purpose of correcting, and resolved to write the poem over anew, upon a somewhat different and an enlarged plan."[3]

---

[1] From the information of Dr. Francis Hawkins, Registrar to the C. of Ph.

[2] *Biog. Brit.*

[3] Advertisement to Mr. Dyson's ed. of Akenside's *Poems*, 1772.

In 1758 [1] he endeavoured to excite the martial spirit
of the nation by an *Ode to the Country Gentlemen of
England.* " Mr. Elliott, father of Lord Minto," says
the late Mr. Justice Hardinge,[2] " made an admirable
speech in support of the Scotch Militia, which I had the
good fortune to hear when I was a boy : and it was re-
ported, that, when commended as he was on every side
for that performance, ' If I was above myself,' he answered, ' I can account for it ; for I had been animated
by the sublime Ode of Dr. Akenside.' "

He, soon after,[3] suffered a severe attack of sickness ;
on the abatement of which, he removed, for change of
air, to Goulder's Hill, the seat of Mr. Dyson; and during
a short stay under that friendly roof, he composed his
*Ode on Recovering, &c.,* which contains an elegant allusion to the recent marriage of his patron.

Few miscellanies had been so favourably received by
the public as Dodsley's *Collection of Poems;* and in
consequence of its undiminished popularity, it was enlarged by two additional volumes in 1758.[4]  To the sixth

---

[1] Quarto, pr. 6d.: see List of Books for March, 1758, in
*Gent. Mag.*  Its motto is,

> ——" rusticorum mascula militum
> Proles, Sabellis docta ligonibus
> Versare glebas."    HOR.

Whitehead, the laureat, published at the same time *Verses
to the People of England.*  On these two effusions Byrom
wrote some rhyming *Remarks,* in which he says :

> " Really these fighting poets want a tutor,
> To teach them *ultra crepidam ne sutor ;*
> To teach the doctor, and to teach the laureat,
> *Ex Helicone sanguinem ne hauriat:*
> Tho' blood and wounds infect its limpid stream,
> It should run clear before they sing a theme."

[2] In a long letter concerning Akenside (the rest of which
will be afterwards quoted).   Nichols's *Ill. of Lit. Hist.* viii.
524.

[3] " My harp, which *late* resounded o'er the land
The voice of glory," &c.

*Ode on Recovering from a fit of Sickness, in the Country,*
1758,—printed in Mr. Dyson's ed. of his *Poems,* 1772.

[4] Dodsley's *Collection* appeared first, in three volumes,

volume Akenside contributed a *Hymn to the Naiads;
Ode to the Earl of Huntingdon; Ode to the Bishop of
Winchester; Inscription for a Grotto; For a statue of
Chaucer at Woodstock;* one beginning " Whoe'er thou
art," &c.; *For a statue of Shakespeare; On William
the Third; For a column at Runnymede;* and an *Ode,*
" If rightly tuneful bards decide," &c.   None of these
pieces, except the second in the list, had previously
appeared.

A publication of this year, (1758), addressed to our
author, must not pass unnoticed.   It is *The Call of Aristippus,*[1] an Epistle in rhyme, by the ingenious John Gil-
bert Cooper, who, designating Akenside as the "Twofold
Disciple of Apollo," assures him that in Elysium Plato
and Virgil shall weave him a never-fading crown, while
Lucretius, Pindar, and Horace shall willingly yield him
precedence.   The panegyric is rendered worthless by its
extravagance.

In January, 1759, Akenside was appointed assistant

---

in 1748; the fourth volume came out in 1755; the fifth and
sixth volumes were published in 1758.

Gray's remarks on the *Pleasures of Imagination* have
been already cited (see page 18, note, of this Memoir).
In March, 1758, he writes thus to Dr. Wharton :—" Then
here is the Miscellany (Mr. Dodsley has sent me the whole
set gilt and lettered, I thank him).   Why, the two last volumes are worse than the four first; particularly Dr. Akenside is in a deplorable way.   What signifies Learning and
the Ancients (Mason will say triumphantly), why should
people read Greek to lose their imagination, their ear, and
their mother tongue ?"   *Memoirs of Gray,* by Mason, 261,
ed. 1775.—Could such a scholar as Gray be insensible to
the classic beauty of the *Hymn to the Naiads,* and the *Inscriptions* of Akenside?

Mr. Bucke, on the authority of Sir Grey Cooper, states
that the Inscription, " Whoe'er thou art," &c., tells faithfully the melancholy fate of a young gentleman, named
Weybridge, who came early into possession of a small property in the County of Northumberland.   *Life of Akenside,* 83.

[1] It was a sequel to three *Epistles to the Great, from
Aristippus in Retirement,* 4to.—Cooper had previously mentioned Akenside with absurdly exaggerated commendation
in *Letters concerning Taste:* see ed. 1755, p. 101.

Physician to St. Thomas's Hospital, and two months
after, principal Physician. In the same year he became
assistant Physician to Christ's Hospital. Of his behaviour, in his official capacity, at the former institution,
the following anecdotes are preserved. As they must
tend to lower him in the estimation of the reader, I
transcribe them with a feeling of reluctance; but I should
not have thought myself justified in suppressing them, as
Mr. Bucke has done, even if they had been derived from
a less respectable source than the *Memoirs of Dr. Lettsom.* I am willing, however, to believe that practice at
an hospital may frequently present occurrences to disturb
the temper of the mildest physician.

Lettsom, when a young man, says Mr. Pettigrew,
" entered [at St. Thomas's Hospital] as a surgeon's
dresser, under Benjamin Cowell, Esq. The other Sur-
geons were Mr. Baker, and Mr. Smith, men of no great
eminence. The Physicians were Akenside, Russell, and
Grieve. Lettsom was early fond of poetry, and had
read the ' Pleasures of Imagination' with admiration.
He anticipated great pleasure in coming under the Author's notice; for, by a small premium, a Surgeon's
pupil is admitted to the practice of the Physicians of the
Hospital. Great, however, was his disappointment in
finding Dr. Akenside the most supercilious and unfeeling physician that he had hitherto known. If the
poor affrighted patients did not return a direct answer to
his queries, he would often instantly discharge them from
the Hospital. He evinced a particular disgust to females,
and generally treated them with harshness. It was
stated that this moroseness was occasioned by disappointment in love; but hapless must have been that
female who should have been placed under his tyranny.
Lettsom was inexpressibly shocked at an instance of Dr.
Akenside's inhumanity, exercised towards a patient in
Abraham's Ward, to whom he had ordered bark in bo-
luses; who, in consequence of not being able to swallow
them, so irritated Akenside, as to order the sister of the
Ward to discharge him from the hospital; adding, ' he
shall not die under my care.' As the sister was removing
him, in obedience to the Doctor, the patient expired.
One leg of Dr. Akenside was considerably shorter than the
other, which was in some measure remedied by the aid of

a false heel. He had a pale strumous countenance, but was always very neat and elegant in his dress. He wore a large white wig, and carried a long sword. Lettsom never knew him to spit, nor would he suffer any pupil to spit in his presence. One of them once accidentally did so, yet standing at some distance behind him. The Doctor instantly spun round on his artificial heel, and hastily demanded, who was the person that spit in his face? Sometimes he would order some of the patients, on his visiting days, to precede him with brooms to clear the way, and prevent the patients from too nearly approaching him. On one of these occasions, Richard Chester, one of the Governors, upbraided him for his cruel behaviour: 'Know,' said he, 'thou art a servant of this Charity.' On one occasion his anger was excited to a very high pitch, by the answer which Mr. Baker, the Surgeon, gave to a question the Doctor put to him, respecting one of his sons, who was subject to epilepsy, which had somewhat impaired his understanding,—'To what study do you purpose to place him?' said Akenside to Baker. 'I find,' replied Baker, 'he is not capable of making a Surgeon, so I have sent him to Edinburgh to make a Physician of him.' Akenside turned round from Baker with impetuosity, and would not speak to him for a considerable time afterwards. Dr. Russell was as condescending as Akenside was petulant. Akenside, however, would sometimes condescend to explain a case of disease to the pupils, which always appeared sagacious; and, notwithstanding his irritable temper, he was more followed than Russell by the pupils." [1]

In October, 1759, Akenside delivered the Harveian Oration before the College of Physicians, by whose order it was next year given to the press. [2]

In June, 1761, Mr. Thomas Hollis (as his biographer informs us) "bought a bed which once belonged to John

---

[1] Pettigrew's *Memoirs of Dr. Lettsom.* i. 21.

[2] *Oratio Anniversaria, quam ex Harveii instituto in theatro Collegii Regalis Medicorum Londinensis Die Octobris xviii A. MDCCLIX habuit Marcus Akenside, M. D. Coll. Med. et Reg. Societ. Socius.* 1760, 4to. pp. 24.—It is dedicated to Dr. Reeve, the President, and to the Fellows of the College of Physicians.

Milton, and on which he died. This bed he sent as a present to Dr. Akenside, with the following card : ' An English gentleman is desirous of having the honour to present a bed, which once belonged to John Milton, and on which he died, to Dr. Akenside ; and if the Doctor's genius, believing himself obliged, and having slept in that bed, should prompt him to write an ode to the memory of John Milton, and the assertors of British liberty, that gentleman would think himself abundantly recompensed.' The Doctor seemed wonderfully de-lighted with this bed, and had it put up in his house. But more we do not know of the *delight* the Doctor took in his present; nor the least memorandum of an acknow-ledgment to Mr. Hollis, through Mr. Payne or other-wise, for it appearing. And as to the ode, the Doctor might learn from his friend Dyson, that an encomium of Milton, as an assertor of British liberty, at that time of the day, was not the thing."[1] The sneering allusion in the latter part of this passage will be explained by the circumstances which I have now to relate, and which, perhaps, made the democrat Hollis think Akenside no longer fit to occupy the bed of Milton.

Hitherto both Mr. Dyson and our poet had espoused the cause of liberty with such an ardour, as to induce suspicions, certainly unjust, that they were the advocates of republicanism. On the accession, however, of George the Third, the former suddenly became a Tory, and the supporter of Lord Bute ; and though the general excel-lence of his character forbids us to believe for one mo-ment, that his conversion was purchased, it would be difficult to clear him from the charge of inconsistency. By Mr. Dyson's influence, Akenside was appointed one of the Physicians to the Queen, on the settlement of her Majesty's household in 1761 ;[2] and, from that period, his Whig acquaintances, in whose eyes the acceptance of such a situation was a dereliction of principle, regarded

---

[1] *Memoirs of Thomas Hollis,* 111.

[2] In the " List of the establishment made by his Majesty for the household of the future Queen," printed in *The St. James's Chronicle* for September 5th, 1761, we find,—
   " *Physicians,* Dr. Letherland, Dr. Akenside.
   *Physician to the Household,* Dr. Pringle."

his political apostacy as not less flagrant than that of his patron. The subject now in question being several times alluded to in the following curious anecdotes, I have reserved them for this part of the memoir. They are from the pen of Mr. Justice Hardinge,[1] whose father Mr. Dyson succeeded as Clerk to the House of Commons,[2] and to whose uncle, the physician, our poet has addressed an Ode.[3]

" Dr. Akenside was known to my father, as being Mr. Dyson's friend, long before he was known to me. As to Mr. Dyson's knowledge of Mr. Hardinge, it originated in their contract for the succession of Mr. Dyson to the post of Chief Clerk in the House of Commons, when Mr. Hardinge was preparing to resign it; and the intercourse, ripening into mutual esteem, produced a cordial friendship, which lasted as long as Mr. Hardinge lived.

"The first I can recollect of my own personal acquaintance with Dr. Akenside's name and Muse, was my father's recital to me, when I was a boy at Eton School, of the invocation to ancient Greece, in that celebrated Poem which has been so depreciated by Dr. Johnson, that I fear no error of judgment and of taste, manifest in that criticism, can redeem the censure from heavier imputations. This inspired passage, as I think it still, was recommended additionally to me by the charm of recitation, in which not even Garrick himself could be superior to Mr. Nicholas Hardinge; though he wanted either nerves or powers to make a figure in the House of Commons, and though he had no musical ear. But his *reading* and *repeating* ear, if I may use that phrase, was exquisite; and his accent, prompted by his judgment, uniformly just. It is very singular, but it is

---

[1] George Hardinge, senior Justice of the Counties of Brecon, Glamorgan, and Radnor, died at Presteigne, April 26th, 1816, in his seventy-second year. The talents and acquirements of this eccentric man were of a superior order. See his *Essence of Malone, &c.,*—his contributions to Nichols's *Illust. of Lit. History* and *Literary Anecdotes,*—and his *Miscellaneous Works in Prose and Verse,* 3 vols, with *Memoirs of the author.*

[2] See page 38 of this Memoir.          [3] See page 40 *id.*

true, that Akenside was not a good reader of his own verse.

" My father admired him, as a gifted poet, as a man of genius, of learning, and of taste. They were upon friendly terms. I have heard Akenside represent my father as a man of admirable taste and judgment, of perfect honour, and of the kindest affections that ever breathed in a human breast. As I grew up into man, Akenside honoured me with a most affectionate regard ; which I forfeited, as you will have occasion to see, a little before his death, to my infinite regret ; but, I am sorry to add, with no remorse ; for I was more ' *sinn'd against than sinning.'*

" When I was at College, he sent me a letter of advice and of directions for the course of my academical studies, which in style and conception was the most ingenious and masterly work that ever that arduous topic has produced. In general, to do him justice, he wrote English prose with purity, with ease, and with spirit; in verse, he was occasionally a little quaint, laboured, and inflated; but I never discerned any such vice in his prose.

" When I came from College to the Inns of Court, besides the opportunity of seeing him often at Mr. Dyson's house, and with my uncle Dr. Hardinge, I was often his dinner-guest, and generally with him alone. In addition to all his powers, arising from his genius and his eloquence, I had the enjoyment of his portfolio, enriched by capital prints from the most eminent painters of Italy and Holland, which he illustrated with admirable taste.

" He had in general society a pomp and stiffness of *manner*, not of *expression*, in which last he was no less chaste than flowing and correct. But the misfortune of this *manner* was in some degree connected with his figure and appearance. He looked as if he never could be undressed; and the hitch in his gait, whatever gave rise to it (a subject of obloquy too despicable to be answered, and which I am sorry to see that you have transcribed), compared with a solemn cast in his features, was, at the best, of a kind that was not companionable, and rather kept strangers at a distance from him. Though his features were good, manly, and expressive, a pale complexion of rather a sickly hue, and the laboured primness

of a powdered wig in stiff curl, made his appearance al-
together unpromising, if not grotesque. But, where he
was intimate, was admired, and was pleased with his
party, he conversed most eloquently and gracefully. He
had the misfortune, however, to have little or no taste for
*humour;* and he took a jest[1] very ill. Except in his
*political morality,* which I could not admire, Dr. Akenside was a man of perfect honour, friendly, and liberal.
His religious opinions were, I believe, a little whimsical
and peculiar ; but in general he kept them very much to
himself. He and Mr. Dyson had both originally been
Dissenters. He was irritable ; had little restraint upon
his temper among strangers, and was either peevish, or
too oracular and sententious. He wanted gaiety of heart
in society, and had no wit in his Muse or in his eloquence.
I don't believe he had much depth of medical science, or
much acuteness of medical sagacity ; he certainly had no
business or fame in that line. His great powers, besides
the talent of poetry, were those of eloquent reasoning,
historical knowledge, and philosophical taste, enlivened
by the happiest and most brilliant allusions. He had
an astonishing memory, and a most luminous application
of it. I recollect that he read *gratis* all the modern books
of any character, and that he had the right conferred upon
him of opening the leaves. His comments were cherished ;
and if the book struck him with a powerful impression,
I believe it was generally given to him by the bookseller.
   " He lived incomparably well; and as I knew of no
other source to his income but his constant friend Mr.
Dyson's munificence to him, I rejoiced in it, for the
honour of them both. I never saw any thing like their
friendship, and their union of sentiments ; yet nothing
was more dissimilar than were the two men. Mr. Dyson
was quite a man of business, of order, and figures—of
parliamentary forms—and of political argument. His
character (bating an amiable partiality in the Eulogist)
is well drawn by Mr. Hatsell. He had neither fancy nor
eloquence ; and though he had strong prejudices, he
veiled them in obliging manners.

---

[1] " Dr. Akenside had no wit," says Mr. Justice Hardinge, in a subsequent communication to Mr. Nichols. *Lit.
Anec.* viii. 525.

E

" The misfortune of their politics (and I was the victim of it in some degree) was, that, upon the accession of this reign, they entirely and radically changed them; for they became bigoted adherents to Lord Bute and the Tories, having at every earlier period been, as it were, the High Priests of the opposite creed.  Mr. Dyson was preferred, and was ultimately pensioned.  His friend, whom he always bore in mind, was made Physician to the Queen—*Ex illo fluere*—from that period both of them were converts, and zealots, of course, for the *New Religion*. My uncle, Dr. Hardinge, whose wit and penetrating judgment had no delicacy in their blow, often told them both when they were young men (and with an oath which I must not repeat) ' that, like a couple of idiots, they did not leave themselves *a loop-hole*—they could not *sidle away* into the opposite creed.'

" As my opinions were naturally upon the same line of politics which Lord Camden[1] uniformly adopted and pursued, I offended my admired friend the Poet by too open a disclosure of my political faith, insignificant, qualified, and perfectly unassuming, as it was.  It made a coolness between us—but I believe that his original friendship to me was never essentially impaired.

" My uncle, Dr. Hardinge, was a comic tyrant over all his friends.  I shall never be able to forget an evening of Civil War, and another of Peace, between these two Physicians.  Dr. Akenside was the guest; and at supper, by a whimsical accident, they fell into a dispute upon the subject of a bilious colic.  They were both of them absurdly eager.  Dr. Hardinge had a contempt for every Physician but himself; and he held the Poet very cheap in that line.  He laughed at him, and said the rudest things to him.  The other, who never'took a jest in good part, flamed into invective; and Mrs. Hardinge, as clever in a different way as either of them, could with difficulty keep the peace between them.  Dr. Akenside ordered his chariot, and swore that he would never come into the house again.  The other, who was the kindest-hearted of men, feeling that he had goaded his friend, called upon him the next morning, and, in a manner

---

[1] Mr. Justice Hardinge was the nephew of this nobleman.

quite his own, made a perfect reconcilement, which terminated in a pacific supper the following night, when,
by a powerful stroke of humour, the Host convulsed the
sides of his Guest with laughter, and they were in delightful unison together the whole evening. 'Do you kn—
kn—know, Doctor,' said he (for he stammered), 'that I
b—bought a curious pamphlet this m—morning upon a
st—stall, and I'll give you the t—title of it; An Acc—
count of a curious dispute between D—Dr. Y. and D—
Dr. Z. concerning a b—b—bilious c—colic, which terminated in a d—duel between the two Ph—Physicians,
which *t—terminated in the d—death of both.*' [1] . . . . .

" As far as I can recollect, his friends, besides Mr.
Dyson, were chiefly Dr. Heberden, Dr. Hardinge, Mr.
Cracherode, Mr. Thomas Townshend, the first Lord
Sydney's father, Mr. Tyrwhitt, the Archbishop of York,
and Mr. Wray. He was a most unprejudiced and candid estimator of contemporary poets, for which I admired
him the more on account of its amiable *singularity.*

" But I must not forget here to mention perhaps the
most curious feature of his life. It is in the partial but
very awkward change which his new *Politics at Court*
made in those of *the Poet.* You will find a memorable
proof to this point. In the first edition of the work these
lines appear :

'Wilt thou, kind Harmony, descend,
And join the festive train; for with thee comes
Majestic TRUTH; and where TRUTH deigns to come,
Her Sister LIBERTY will not be far.'

And in the second edition:

'for with thee comes
Wise ORDER; and where ORDER deigns to come,
Her Sister LIBERTY will not be far.'" [2]

After all, neither in the alterations just pointed out, nor
in others made by the author in his *Odes,*[3] is there any

---

[1] Here I have omitted some critical remarks by Mr. Hardinge on Akenside's poetry, and the anecdote of Mr. Elliott
already quoted, see p. 50 of this Memoir.

[2] Nichols's *Lit. Anec.* viii. 521, 525.

[3] " In the Ode *On leaving Holland,* the three following
lines,

thing indicative of violent Tory zeal; and it should be remembered, that Mr. Hardinge, who asserts in the above Anecdotes that Akenside became as bigoted a partisan of the Tories as he had been of the Whigs, has elsewhere declared, that " his politics were *illegible.*"[1]

We have been told in the preceding page that Akenside " was a most unprejudiced and candid estimator of contemporary poets;" and the remark will be illustrated by the scattered notices which I shall now throw together.

In the course of a conversation on Pope's *Essay on Man*, he assented to the opinion of Joseph Warton, that " the fourth Epistle on Happiness is adscititious, and out of its proper place, and ought to have made part of the second Epistle, where Man is considered with respect to himself." [2]

He was a great admirer of Gothic architecture, and would frequently sit, by moonlight, on the benches in St. James's Park, to gaze on Westminster Abbey; " and

---

' I go where freedom in the streets is known,
And tells a monarch on his throne,
*Tells him he reigns, he lives but by her voice.*'

are thus changed in the last edition :

' I go where liberty to all is known,
And tells a monarch on his throne,
He reigns not but by her preserving voice.'

In the Ode *To the Earl of Huntingdon*, the four subsequent lines which originally were,

' But here where freedom's equal throne
To all her valiant sons is known;
*Where all direct the sword she wears,*
And each the power which rules him shares,'

are corrected as follows, in the third line,

' *Where all are conscious of her cares.*'

Whatever may be thought of these particular alterations, it is certain that a most ardent spirit of liberty breathes through Dr. Akenside's works." *Biogr. Brit.—note by Kippis.*

[1] " His [H. Walpole's] politics were as *illegible*, if I may use that phrase, as those of Dr. Akenside." Nichols's *Ill. of Lit. Hist.* viii. 526.

[2] Warton's ed. of Pope's *Works*, iii. 123.

I remember," adds Mr. Meyrick, " he once told me that he seldom thought of the passage in his own poem,

' The radiant sun, the moon's nocturnal lamp,' &c.

but he thought of a still finer one in Pope's Homer:

' As when the moon, refulgent lamp of night,' " &c.[1]

It has been rashly supposed that in the following passage of *The Pleasures of Imagination*, he alludes to Pope:

" Thee, too, facetious Momion, wandering here;
Thee, dreaded censor! *oft have I beheld*
Bewilder'd unawares," &c. &c.  B. iii. 179.

But there is every reason to believe that Akenside never saw Pope, who died a few months after the appearance of the poem, for which he had advised Dodsley to make a handsome offer.[2]

With Thomson's *Castle of Indolence* he was enraptured : among many stanzas, to which, in his own copy, he had put an emphatic mark of approbation, was that beginning,

" I care not, fortune, what you me deny," &c.[3]

He repeatedly mentioned Fenton's *Ode to Lord Gower* as "the best in our language, next to Alexander's Feast;"[4] and, at his desire, Welsted's Ode, *The Genius, written in* 1717, *on occasion of the Duke of Marlborough's Apoplexy*, was inserted in the fourth volume of Dodsley's *Collection of Poems*.[5]

That he was on Terms of intimacy with the author of *The Fleece*, and lent him some assistance in the composition of that poem, appears from a letter of Dyer to Duncombe, November 24th, 1756 :—" Your humble servant is become a deaf, and dull, and languid creature;

---

[1] Bucke's *Life of Akenside*, 212.
[2] See p. 17 of this Memoir.
[3] Bucke's *Life of Akenside*, 31.
[4] Warton's ed. of Pope's *Works*, ii. 401.
[5] *Id.* v. 198.—With Welsted, who died in 1747, Akenside is said to have been acquainted. His *Works*, published by Nichols in 1787, contain several pieces which show that his talents at least did not deserve the contempt of Pope.

who, however, in his poor change of constitution, being a little recompensed with the critic's phlegm, has made shift, by many blottings and corrections, and some helps from his kind friend, Dr. Akenside, to give a sort of finishing to the ' Fleece,' which is just sent up to Mr. Dodsley."[1]  Johnson informs us that Akenside declared " he would regulate his opinion of the reigning taste by the rule of Dyer's Fleece ; for if that were ill-received, he should not think it any longer reasonable to expect fame from excellence."[2]  The works of Dyer, though neglected by the multitude, will be always esteemed by the reader of taste and feeling for the true poetic fancy and the love of natural objects which they every where display.

A passage in *The Pleasures of Imagination,*

> " To muse at last amid the ghostly gloom
> Of graves, and hoary vaults," &c.   B. i. 396.

and a stanza in the *Preface to the Odes,*

> " Nor where the boding raven chaunts," &c.

are said to have been aimed at Young, though I cannot perceive in them such " a palpable stroke" as Mrs. Barbauld[3] has discovered.  It has not, however, been noticed that in the first edition of the *Hymn to Cheerfulness* Akenside mentions the author of the *Night Thoughts* by name :

> " Let Melancholy's plaintive tongue
> *Instruct the nightly strains of Young :*"

a couplet which he afterwards altered thus :

> " Let Melancholy's plaintive tongue
> *Repeat what later bards have sung."*

The Ode *On Lyric Poetry* closes with a stanza remarkable for its allusion to an epic poem which the author meditated, as well as to a celebrated work of the same kind by a contemporary writer :

---

[1] *Letters by several eminent persons, including the Correspondence of Hughes,* iii. 58.—Yet Mr. Bucke says, it does not appear that Akenside was intimate with Dyer !  *Life of Akenside,* 90.

[2] *Life of Dyer.*

[3] *Essay on The Pleasures of Imagination.*

" But when from envy and from death to claim
A hero bleeding for his native land,
When to throw incense on the vestal flame
Of Liberty my genius gives command,
Nor Theban voice, nor Lesbian lyre
From thee, O Muse, do I require,
While my presaging mind,
Conscious of powers she never knew,
Astonish'd grasps at things beyond her view,
Nor by another's fate submits to be confin'd."

Akenside had selected Timoleon[1] for the hero of his poem, in which, it appears, he had even made some progress. The last line of the stanza (as he told Warton) is pointed at the *Leonidas* of Glover.[2]

From this digression I return to the regular annals of the poet's life. Among Birch's MSS.[3] is the following note, which shews that he accompanied the deputation, sent by the University of Cambridge to congratulate the King and Queen on their nuptials:

" Dr. AKENSIDE presents his compliments to Dr. Birch, and begs the favour that he would lend him a band, in order that he may attend the Cambridge address tomorrow.

" Craven Street,
" Sept. 13." [1761.]

---

[1] Warton's ed. of Pope's *Works*, ii. 73.—A writer, who signs 'himself Indagátor, in the *Gent. Mag.* for October, 1793 (lxiii. 885), says, " I have proof, though it has never been mentioned to the world, that he had made some progress in an Epic Poem, the plan of which I know not; the title of it was *Timoleon.*"—An Epic poem on the same subject was once designed by Pope; and was also proposed by Lord Melcombe to Thomson.

[2] Warton's ed. of Pope's *Works*, ii. 73.—I may add here, that Akenside agreed with Warton, Lowth, and Harris, in thinking that no critical treatise was better calculated to form the taste of young men of genius than Spence's *Essay on Pope's Odyssey, Id. Life*, xxxvi.—and that he considered *The Memoirs of Lord Bolingbroke* as a worthless production. —*Letter from Birch to Wray*, in Nichols's *Ill. of Lit. Hist.* iv. 534.

[3] *Letters to Birch*, 4300, in the Brit. Mus.

About two years before this date, Akenside had quitted his house in Bloomsbury Square for one in Craven Street ; and after having stayed in the latter about twelve months, he removed to Burlington Street, where he continued to reside till his decease.[1]

The MSS. of Birch[2] furnish one more note from our author's pen :

" DR. AKENSIDE presents his compliments to Dr. Birch, and returns many thanks for his kind present. He has left an unpublish'd letter of Ld. Bacon, which he thinks a valuable one, and which he had leave from Mr. Tyrwhitt to communicate to Dr. Birch ; and desires that when he has done with it, he would be so good as to send it to Burlington Street.

"Nov. 29, 1762."

To the very learned Tyrwhitt (who has been previously mentioned among the friends of Akenside) Mr. Dyson resigned, during this yèar, the clerkship of the House of Commons.[3]

In December, 1763, Akenside read before the Royal Society, a paper, which was afterwards published in the *Philosophical Transactions* for the same year,—*An account of a Blow upon the Heart, and of its effects*.[4]

His *De Dysenteria Commentarius*[5] appeared in 1764;

---

[1] According to the *Sheet Catalogues of the Fellows, &c. of the College of Physicians* (in the Brit. Mus.), his residence from 1759 to 1761 inclusive, was in Craven Street,—from 1762 till his decease, in Burlington Street.

[2] *Letters to Birch*, 4300, in the Brit. Mus.

[3] " This gentleman [Tyrwhitt] is well known as the editor of Chaucer, and [for] a part he took in the controversy in regard to Rowley's poems :" so says Mr. Bucke (*Life of Akenside*, 176), who seems not to know that Tyrwhitt has done more for Greek than English literature. Since the time of Bentley to the present day, what classical scholar in this country, with the exception of Porson, has displayed such acuteness and felicity of emendation as Tyrwhitt ? But his edition of the *Canterbury Tales* exhibits a text which by no means satisfies the antiquarian reader.

[4] *Phil. Trans.* liii. 353 : it consists of two pages and a half.

[5] *De Dysenteria Commentarius, auctore Marco Akenside,*

a production still esteemed by the medical student for the valuable information it imparts, and admired by the scholar for its choice and elegant Latinity.

When Warburton, now dignified with the mitre, put forth a new edition of the first and second volumes[1] of the *Divine Legation of Moses*, in 1766, he reprinted, as a *Postscript to the Dedication to the Free-thinkers*, his severe strictures on our poet's theory concerning Ridicule, &c., without condescending to notice the arguments which had been adduced in its defence. Irritated by what he regarded as a renewal of hostilities, Akenside displayed less magnanimity than might have been ex-

---

*Coll. Med. Londin. Socio. Reg. Societ. Sodali, et Magnæ Britanniæ Reginæ Medico*, 1764, $oc^{tvo}$. It consists of eighty-one pages, and is divided thus :

    *Cap*. I. *De Dysenteria historia.*
        II. *De dysentericorum curatione.*
        III. *De causis dysenteriæ.*
        IV. *De actione ipecacounhæ in dysentericos.*

There are two English translations of this work,—by Ryan and Motteux : that of the former is extremely inaccurate (see Monthly Review, xxxv. 373), that of the latter is not free from faults.

[1] These volumes are advertised, as published in the *London Chronicle*, April 3, 1766,—which it is necessary to mention, because a writer in the *Monthly Review* seems to have thought that they appeared subsequently to Akenside's *Ode to Edwards:* "The discerning reader will be at no loss to account for this attack upon Dr. Akenside, when he recollects a late short publication of the Doctor's," xxxv. 227.— Mr. Bucke talks of "the obnoxious postscript he had before appended to his preface" (*Life of Akenside*, 150), not knowing that Warburton's attack on Akenside was originally made in the Preface to *Remarks on Several Occasional Reflections, &c.* (see p. 19 of this Memoir).—The Preface, when altered into a Postscript, opened thus : " A Poet and a Critic [Lord Kaimes] of equal eminence, have concurred, though they did not start together, to censure what was occasionally said in this Dedication (as if it had been addressed to them) of the use and abuse of Ridicule. The Poet was a follower of Lord Shaftesbury's fancies ; the Critic a follower of his own. Both men of TASTE, and equally anxious for the well-doing of Ridicule."

pected in such an admirer of the ancient sages, and had
recourse to an ingenious method of mortifying his an-
tagonist.  He published a lyrical satire, which he had
composed long before this period, on the appearance of
the Bishop's edition of Pope's *Works*, and which probably but for this fresh provocation, would have never
seen the light,—*An Ode to the late Thomas Edwards,
Esq.*, *written in the year* 1751;[1] and a note on the
fifth stanza surprised the reader by the following piece of
information: " During Mr. Pope's war with Theobald,
Concanen, and the rest of their tribe, Mr. Warburton,
the present Lord Bishop of Gloucester, did with great
zeal cultivate their friendship ; having been introduced,
forsooth, at the meetings of that respectable confederacy :
a favour which he afterwards spoke of in very high terms
of complacency and thankfulness.  At the same time in
his intercourse with them he treated Mr. Pope in a most
contemptuous manner, and as a writer without genius.
Of the truth of these assertions his Lordship can have no

---

[1] In folio, pr. 6*d.*, published May, 1766 : see *The St.
James's Chronicle* for the first of that month, into which it is
copied, with the following paragraph prefixed to it : " While
Peace has spread her wing over the greatest Nations of
Europe, War has sounded his trump in the regions of Parnassus.  We have lately been witnesses to a fierce Conflict
between a Right Rev. Prelate, and a Learned and Reverend
Professor ; each of whom have disputed about Job, without
one Drachm or Scruple of his Patience between them.  At
present another son of Apollo, in his two-fold Capacity of
God of Poetry and Physic, enters the lists ; and tilts, we
know not why, with the Episcopal Militant.  In a word, to
drop all Metaphor, we are at a Loss to account why the following Ode, written so long ago, is made Public at this particular Period.  We doubt not, however, but its appearance
here will be agreeable to our Readers."—See also two *Letters to the Printer of the Public Advertiser* (in the *Ap.* to *Memoirs of T. Hollis*, 722).  In the first of them, dated May 6,
1766, the writer, accounting for the publication of the *Ode*,
says : " The secret, I suppose, is no more than this : the
bishop has, just now, given a new édition of the first volume
of his Divine Legation ; and has thought fit to reprint the
Censure he had before made on a certain note of this poet,"
&c.

doubt, if he recollects his own correspondence with Concanen ; a part of which is still in being, and will probably be remembered as long as any of this prelate's writings." A letter from Warburton to Concanen,[1] dated January 2d, 1726, had fallen into the hands of Akenside, who knew that in announcing the existence of such a document, he should cause no slight vexation to his adversary. Though never published [2] by our poet, it has been printed in a note on Shakespeare's *Julius Cæsar*,[3] from a copy which he communicated to George Steevens, and which was thus endorsed : " The foregoing Letter was found about the year 1750 by Dr. Gawin Knight, first librarian to the British Museum, in fitting up a house which he had taken in Crane Court, Fleet Street. The house had, for a long time before, been let in lodgings, and in all probability Concanen had lodged there. The original letter has been many years in my possession, and is here most exactly copied, with its several little peculiarities in Grammar, spelling, and punctuation. April 30, 1766, M. A." In this curious Epistle (too long for insertion here) the object of Warburton is to point out passages from various writers, which Addison had imitated in his *Cato;* and having occasion to quote some lines from *Julius Cæsar*,[4] he illustrates them by an absurd comment, which he afterwards introduced, with little variation, into his edition of *Shakespeare*. It decidedly proves his intimacy with Theobald [5] and Concanen ; but contains no mention of Pope, except an observation that he " borrows for want of genius."

The *Ode* in question was with propriety addressed to Thomas Edwards, whose well-known *Canons of Criticism* had destroyed the reputation of Warburton in one de-

---

[1] Matthew Concanen, celebrated in *The Dunciad*, ii. 299, where vide note.

[2] Misled, perhaps, by Warton (note on Pope's *Works*, v. 164), Mr. Bucke supposes that Akenside *published* the Letter together with the Ode. *Life of Akenside*, 157.

[3] By Malone,—*Supplement to Shakespeare*, i. 223.

[4] " Between the acting of a dreadful thing," &c.

[5] See also Letters between Warburton and Theobald, of a later date, in which they call each other " dearest friend." Nichols's *Illust. of Lit. Hist.* ii. 630, 649.

partment of literature. This amiable and accomplished
man, who died in 1757, had long been intimately acquainted with Akenside; and was, I believe, the " Phædria," who had called forth our author's Odes,—*To a
friend unsuccessful in love*,[1] and *Affected Indifference*.[2]
Nor should it be forgotten that by his *Sonnets*,[3]—some of
them possessing no ordinary beauty,—Edwards revived
among his countrymen a taste for that species of composition, which had been neglected since the days of Milton.

In 1765, Akenside had finished the second book of
the re-modelled *Pleasures of Imagination;* and in September of the following year, Mr. Daniel Wray writes
thus to one of his correspondents :[4]—" I was at Mount
Ararat sooner than usual, to attend Lord and Lady Dacre,
accompanied by Akenside, who passed the evening
there, and communicated the second and part of a third
book in his great work. In the former, and in the same
philosophical way, he is eloquent on the topics of truth,
and virtue, vice, and the passions. In the latter Solon
is introduced giving a Fable, on the Origin of Evil. It
is introduced by an Episode from Herodotus of Arga-
rista's marriage, the daughter of Clisthenes, which is de-
lightfully poetical." Mr. Wray,—a friend both of Akenside and Edwards,—was a contributor to the well-known
work *The Athenian Letters.* He was Fellow of the
Royal Society, and of the Society of Antiquaries; deputy
Teller of the Exchequer; and one of the Trustees of the
British Museum, on its first establishment.

From the annals of the College of Physicians we learn
that, in 1766, " Dr. Akenside was thanked by the College for his trouble in preparing Harvey's Works for the

---

[1] See p. 35 of this Memoir.

[2] Printed in Mr. Dyson's ed. of his *Poems*, 1772.

[3] See forty-five *Sonnets* appended to *The Canons of Criticism*, ed. 1765, several of which had previously appeared in
Dodsley's *Coll. of Poems, &c.* : the five best will be found in
my *Specimens of English Sonnets*, 1833.

[4] Nichols's *Illust. of Lit. Hist.* i. 104.—Mount Ararat
(which Mr. Bucke calls " the seat of Lord and Lady Dacre,"
—*Life of Akenside*, 195) was the name of Mr. Wray's house
at Richmond.

press, and for prefixing a Preface, which was printed with them, together with the Life of Harvey, by Dr. Lawrence." [1]

On the 6th of June, 1767, he read before the College two papers,—*Observations on Cancers*, and *Of the Use of Ipecacoanha in Asthmas;* and on the 6th of July, a third, —*A Method of treating White Swellings of the Joints.* These essays were published, next year, in the first volume of the *Medical Transactions.* [2]

In 1767, appeared a small volume, entitled *Lexi-phanes, a Dialogue, Imitated from Lucian, and suited to the present times*,—a piece of ill-natured drollery, which, though levelled chiefly at the prose of Johnson, contains also an attack on the poetry of Akenside. It was written by an obscure Scotchman, Archibald Campbell, [3] who hoped that its publication would involve him in a controversy with " the two Lexiphaneses," from which he would acquire at least notoriety; but he was disappointed; for neither Johnson nor Akenside deigned to reply.

The following *jeu d'esprit* [4] is from the pen of Mr. Daniel Wray, whose intimacy with Akenside has just been noticed :

" The Arbitrator was out of town, when the applications from Ld. Dacre and Dr. Akenside were left at his house; and, when he found them, he was fully employed in dis-

---

[1] On the information of Dr. Francis Hawkins, Registrar to the Col. of Ph.

[2] See the first vol. of the *Medical Transactions*, third ed. 1785.—The first of Akenside's essays consists of twenty-nine pages, the second of ten and a-half, the third of eight.

[3] He was a purser in the navy, and " as well for the malignancy of his heart, as his terrific countenance, was called horrible Campbell." Hawkins's *Life of Johnson*, 347, ed. 1787. In a note on *Lexiphanes*, Campbell declares, that Akenside's " words, and especially his phrases, are generally so execrable, and his meaning, where any can be picked out, always so trifling; in short, he has imbibed so much of Plato's nonsense," &c. &c. p. 76: sec. ed. 1767.—Campbell published another little volume,—*A Sale of Authors.*

[4] Now first published, from the original in the possession of J. Dyson, Esq.

patching some business, in order to return to Richmond :
Ld. Dacre asked for the Decision only at the leisure of
the Court : and it has been thought proper and decorous
to take some time for judgment.

" Ld. D. has offered no arguments, nor even stated
the point in dispute. Dr. A. has fairly stated it to be
whether Buchanan praised Q. Mary as a woman of
virtue.

"In the second passage of the *Pompæ*, *virtus* has
nothing that confines it to moral virtue, but it may include it : and there occurs a line in the Epithalamium,

Et genus et virtus et forma,

where that idea may also be included in *virtus*. This
verse is not indeed in Ld. D.'s plea, and so perhaps not
strictly admissible.

" Upon the whole, the classical *virtus* is not generally
virtue in English : but Buchanan, however classical he
was, might be willing to leave his idea in these compliments, dim and confused ; or perhaps might put these
*brave words* together without much consideration or pre-
cision, not expecting they would be so nicely canvassed
two centurys after.

" From such imperfect documents, therefore, the court
will not determine so important a cause, so warmly agi-
tated and of such expectation. But hereby declares *the
wager to be drawn;* each party to sit down with the
trouble they have had in debating and searching for materials and precedents ; and that the respective characters
of the Queen and the writer remain in *statu quo,* un-
affected by any arguments drawn from these verses, being
matters of another jurisdiction.

" D. W. Arbitrator.

"M. ARARAT,
" 26 May, 1770.

" Dr. A. will transmit the above sentence to Ld. D.

" To DR. AKENSIDE,
" In Burlington Street, London."

The unfinished third book of the re-modelled *Pleasures of Imagination,* and the fragment of the fourth
book, bear the date of this year ; and Akenside was looking forward to the period when the publication of the

work was to increase his already established fame as a poet. His practice, as a physician,[1] was now considerable, and promised to be more extensive. But a putrid fever, with which he was suddenly seized, put an end to his existence, after a short illness, on the 23d June, 1770, in the forty-ninth year of his age. He died at his residence in Burlington Street,[2] and was buried[3] in St. James's Church.

Some *Observations on the putrid erysipelas, made at St. Thomas's Hospital,* which he had read[4] before the College of Physicians, and intended for the second volume of the *Medical Transactions,* were among his papers at the time of his decease, but were never printed.

Mr. Dyson, who had become possessor of the books, prints, MSS., and other effects of Akenside, gave to the world an edition of his *Poems,* in 1772.[5] The contents of this elegant volume are,—1. *The Pleasures of Imagination,* as originally published. 2. As much of that Poem, on an enlarged plan, as the author had prepared for the press. "What reason there may be," says the Advertisement, "to regret that he did not live to execute the whole of it, will best appear from the perusal of the plan itself, as stated in the General Argument, and of the Parts which he had executed, and which are here published. For the Person, to whom he entrusted the Disposal of his Papers, would have thought himself wanting, as well to the service of the Public, as to the Fame of his Friend, if he had not produced as much of the work as appeared to have been prepared for publication. In this light he considered the intire first and second Books, of which a few Copies had been printed for the

---

[1] See what has been said on this subject,—pp. 40. 41. 43.

[2] Mr. Bucke erroneously states that he died in Bloomsbury Square (*Life of Akenside,* 216): but see p. 64 of this Memoir; also the *General Evening Post, from Saturday, June 23d, to Tuesday, June 26th,* 1770, the *Middlesex Journal,* &c.

[3] On the 28th June.

[4] About the same period that he read the Croonian Lectures, says Mr. Bucke, without any authority. *Life of Akenside,* 197.—See page 49 of this Memoir.

[5] Both in 4to. and 8vo.

use only of the Author and certain Friends : also a very
considerable part of the third Book, which had been
transcribed in order to its being printed in the same
manner: and to these is added the Introduction to a
subsequent Book, which in the Manuscript is called the
Fourth, and which appears to have been composed at
the time when the Author intended to comprize the
whole in Four Books; but which, as he had afterwards
determined to distribute the Poem into more Books,
might perhaps more properly be called the Last Book."[1]
3. *Odes*[2] :—of which nineteen are for the first time

---

[1] The late Mr. Pinkerton, in a volume entitled *Letters of
Literature, by Robert Heron*, 1785, printed, for the first time,
some alterations made by Akenside in *The Pleasures of
Imagination*. " They were inserted," he tells us, " in the
margin of the Doctor's copy, which afterwards passed into
the hands of a gentleman, from a friend of whom, and of my
own, a very ingenious young Templar, I received them.
At what time they were written I cannot pretend to say,
much less to reveal the author's reasons for not giving an
edition according to them. Most of them are evidently
much for the better, one or two, I am afraid, for the worse.
You will observe that a few of them have been adopted by
the author in his proposed alteration of the Poem; as
appears from the two books, and part of the third, of that
alteration, published by Mr. Dyson in his edition of Akenside's Poems, 1772, 4to., but far the greater part is unpublished ; and that the most valuable, as being evidently written ere the author had taken up the strange idea, that
poetry was only perfect oratory. So that I will venture to
say, that an edition of the Pleasures of Imagination, adopt-
ing most of these corrections, would be the most perfect
ever yet known."—*Letter* iv. p. 21. Pinkerton's taste was
not " the most perfect ever known ;" neither, I think, is that
of Mr. Bucke, who seems to have meditated an edition of
the kind, and who (according to his custom of giving garbled
extracts) quotes the above passage from Pinkerton, omitting
the observation that " one or two of the corrections are for
the worse." *Life of Akenside*, 286.
The *Pleasures of Imagination* has been translated into
French prose by Baron d'Holbach, 1759, and into Italian
verse by Abbate Angelo Mazza, 1764.
[2] Those not already mentioned in this Memoir, are *On the
use of Poetry, To the Cuckoo, On the Love of Praise, At Study,
The Complaint*, and *On Domestic Manners*.

printed ; the rest (most of them now greatly altered) had been previously published. 4. The *Hymn to the Naiads*, corrected, with the addition of some notes. 5. *Inscriptions;* of which the three last[1] had not before appeared. The *Epistle to Curio*, in its original state, and several smaller pieces,[2] which the author had produced during his early years, are not reprinted in the volume just described. The only biographical notice of Akenside, which accompanies it, is comprised in a paragraph of the Advertisement : "The frigidity of this account," observed the Monthly Reviewer, " must be disgustful to every reader, who is endued with the least portion of sensibility,"[3] a censure which has been frequently repeated. But there can be no doubt that modesty alone prevented Mr. Dyson from undertaking the office of Akenside's biographer ; for how could he have discharged it faithfully, without being, in some degree, the herald of his own munificence ? He was exemplary in all the relations of private life ; he rose to considerable political eminence ; and, as the friend and patron of the poet, he has left a name which can never cease to be remembered with respect.[4]

Akenside had a pale and rather sickly complexion, but manly and expressive features. The formality of his deportment, the precise elegance of his dress, his ample wig in stiff curl, his long sword, his hobbling gait, and his artificial heel, rendered his appearance far from prepossessing, and somewhat akin to the ludicrous.

His irritability of temper at times betrayed him into

---

[1] Namely, *The Wood Nymph*, " Ye powers unseen," &c., and " Me, tho' in life's sequester'd vale," &c.—Two Latin *Inscriptions* of the poet's " copying," which were in the possession of Mr. Meyrick, are printed by Mr. Bucke (*Life of Akenside*, 81), who calls them " very beautiful."—They are defective in sense, grammar, and metre !

[2] Already enumerated in this Memoir, with the exception of the *Song*, which closes the present volume, and which is attributed to Akenside by Ritson,—*English Songs*, i. 207.

[3] *Monthly Review* for Dec. 1772,—xlvii. 436.

[4] Mr. Dyson died Sep. 16, 1776. " He was at that time M. P. for Horsham, a member of the Privy Council, and Cofferer to his Majesty's Household."—Nichols's *Ill. of Lit. Hist.* viii. 555.

conduct, from which a very unfavourable and unjust idea of his character was conceived by strangers.[1] An early disappointment in love is said to have occasioned this infirmity. In a passage of *The Pleasures of Imagination*, where he touches on the fate of Parthenia,[2] he has been supposed to allude to a young lady, who died when about to become his wife; and in several *Odes*[3] he mentions, as the object of his passion, Olympia, whom, it appears, he also lost by death. " But he celebrates other ladies, and speaks of them *even with affection;* Amoret[4] and Melissa:"[5] such is the remark of Mr. Bucke,[6] who might have added the names of Lucinda,[7] Eudora,[8] Dione,[9] and Cordelia,[10] and so made up a list of mistresses only exceeded by *The Chronicle* of Cowley! Though we cannot read in Akenside's poetry the true history of his loves, we learn from it that there were moments when he felt the dreary solitude of celibacy, and sighed for domestic comforts;

> " Though the day have smoothly gone,
> Or to letter'd leisure known,
> Or in social duty spent,
> Yet at eve my lonely breast
> Seeks in vain for perfect rest,
> Languishes for true content." [11]

In general society his manners were not agreeable: he seemed to want gaiety of heart; and was apt to be dictatorial in conversation. But when surrounded only by

---

[1] See the anecdotes at p. 52 of this Memoir.

[2] B. ii. 193 *( Original Poem ).*

[3] *To the Muse, On Love, To Sir Francis Drake, On Lyric Poetry,* and *To the Evening Star.*

[4] *Ode* (without a title) X. B. ii.

[5] *Pleas. of Imag. ( Sec. Poem )* i. 367.

[6] *Life of Akenside,* 127. In the next page Mr. Bucke observes that " Akenside's respect for women *peeps out every where.*" !

[7] Ode *On the Winter-solstice,* ed. 1745.

[8] *Id. ibid.* as the text now stands.

[9] Ode *On Lyric Poetry,* eds. 1745, and 1760 : afterwards altered to " Olympia."

[10] *Song,*—at the end of this volume.

[11] Ode, *At Study.*

his intimate friends, he would instruct and delight them
by the eloquence of his reasoning, the felicity of his allusions, and the variety of his knowledge. He had no wit
himself, and took ill the jests of others. He was gifted
with a memory of extraordinary power, and perfect readi-
ness in the application of its stores. With the exception
of Ben Johnson, Milton, and Gray, it would be difficult
to name an English poet, whose scholarship was of a
higher order than Akenside's.

In his life-long friendship with Mr. Dyson the warmth
and constancy of his affections are strikingly displayed.
He had a noble independence of spirit; and, notwithstanding his alleged political inconsistency, it should seem
that the love of liberty, for which he was distinguished
during the earlier part of his career, was but little impaired by the atmosphere of a court. His respect for
Christianity he has testified more than once;[1] but his
religious creed, as indicated in his poetry, appears to
have been nearly that of "his Master," Shaftesbury,
pure theism. " ' People would assert,' he was accus-
tomed to say, ' that I imitated Newton, or I should never
allude to the Deity, or hear him alluded to by others,
but I should make an inclination of my body.' And
one day, being in company with Mr. Meyrick's father at
a coffee-house, in the neighbourhood of Charing-cross,
having listened, for some time, with impatience to the
oratory of a Mr. Warnefield, who was making some
severe remarks not only on Warburton's Divine Legation of Moses, but on the Bible itself, he, at length, in-
terrupted him. ' I tell you what, sir,' said he; ' Warburton is no friend of mine;—but I detest hearing a
man of learning abused. As to the Bible—believe or
not, just as you please; but let it contain as many absur-
dities, untruths, and unsound doctrines, as you say it
does, there is one passage, at least, that I am sure, you,

---

[1] See his Odes *To the Author of Memoirs of the House of
Brandenburgh*, and *To the Bishop of Winchester*.—His towns-
man, Sir Gray Cooper, had a paraphrase of the Benedicite,
which he "had good reasons for believing was written by
Akenside;" and he had heard that a Christmas Carol, which
used to be sung in the streets of Newcastle, was also composed by our author. See Bucke's *Life of Akenside*, 183.

with all your ingenuity, and with all the eloquence you possess, have not the power to surpass. It is where the prophet says,—'The children of men are much wiser than the children of light.' "[1] A hasty assertion of Walker, that " the immortality of the soul is scarcely once hinted at throughout *The Pleasures of Imagination*," is cited by Johnson,[2] who yet allows, as an excuse for this "great defect," that Akenside "has omitted what was not properly in his plan." But if either of them had carefully perused the work, could they have overlooked, among other passages of similar tendency,[3] the following lines?

> " Led by that hope sublime, whose cloudless eye,
> Through the fair toils and ornaments of earth,
> Discerns *the nobler life reserv'd for Heaven.*" &c.
> I. 489 *(Sec. Poem)*.

---

[1] Bucke's *Life of Akenside*, 180.

[2] *Life of Akenside.* In 1772, talking of *The Pleasures of Imagination*, Johnson said to Boswell, " Sir, I could not read it through." *Life of Johnson*, ii. 167, ed. 1816.

[3] See the original Poem, B. i. 163, 183, 212, 436 ; B. ii. 359 ; and the re-modelled Poem, B. ii. 145.—Mr. Bucke was assured by " an octogenarian of great learning," that he had every reason to think that the following passage formed part of a letter from Akenside to Dr. Grainger : " Your friend seems to doubt whether he has a soul or not ; and yet surely he will not attempt to place himself on a level with Kepler ; and so far was he from doubting that he had a soul, he gives one even to the earth itself." " In respect to its nature," said he, on another occasion, " it is past my judgment, whether material or immaterial. Perhaps it may partake of both natures. Tertullian not only makes the soul material, but he gives a corporal body even to God himself, and Job says, ' In my flesh I shall see God.' The Christian doctrine, also, implies it ; since it speaks of the resurrection of the body. Certainly, every thing that exists must have shape ; and if shape, form ; and if form, substance. But there may be many substances, and no doubt there are, beyond what we know of at present. Simplicius says, there is in nature an active principle and a passive one : the soul may partake of the same differences ; the former principle, associating with light, the latter with colour. Maximus Tyrius makes even a bolder assertion ;

On a series of papers by Addison, in *The Spectator*,[1] Akenside founded his great didactic poem. To Shaftesbury and Hutcheson [2] also, he is considerably indebted ; and from the writers of Greece and Rome he has derived a few of his ideas, and, perhaps, a portion of his inspiration,—for never had the genius and wisdom of antiquity a more ardent admirer, or a more unwearied student. In this celebrated work, if little invention is exhibited, the taste and skill with which the author has selected and combined his materials, are everywhere conspicuous ; if the thoughts are not always stamped with originality, they have a general loftiness and an occasional sublimity ; if some passages are not lighted up with poetic fire, they glow with rhetorical beauty ; while ingenious illustration and brilliant imagery enliven and adorn the whole. Akenside has chosen no unimportant theme, and he treats it with an earnestness and an enthusiasm which at once command attention. He pours forth a moral and philosophic strain, which elevates the mind ; but he dwells so little on actual existencies and on human interests, that it rarely moves the heart. His diction is rich and curious ; sometimes, however, so redundant, as slightly to obscure the meaning, and sometimes so remote from common phraseology, as to impart an air of stiffness and turgidity to the lines. His versification is sweet and flowing ; and, perhaps, those only, who are familiar with the cadences of Milton, will complain of its monotony.

To *The Pleasures of Imagination*, as published in 1744, the preceding observations are intended to apply.

---

for, he says, that God's oracles and men's understandings are of near alliance. Hence the assertion of Proclus, that all our souls are the children of God. But the fact is, we know little of these things. It is a great satisfaction, however, that we live in a world presenting every moment something to exercise our faculties ; and that the grand mover of the whole will, no doubt, make ample allowances for human infirmity."—*Life of Akenside*, 181.

[1] *No.* 411, *et seq.*

[2] Shaftesbury's *Characteristics.*—Hutcheson's *Inquiry into the Original of our Ideas of Beauty and Virtue.*

The second Poem, which in the estimation of some critics [1] is an improvement on the first, appears to me comparatively flat and prosaic, notwithstanding its superior correctness. Had Akenside devoted the leisure of his later years to an entirely new work, it would have formed a more acceptable bequest to posterity than the remoulded production of his youth.

That he possessed powers for the graver kind of satire, is evinced by his *Epistle to Curio,*—a composition remarkable for keen but not coarse invective, for dignity of reproof, and intensity of scorn.

Throughout the range of English literature there is nothing more deeply imbued with the spirit of the ancient world than our author's *Hymn to the Naiads*. In its solemnity, its pomp of expression, and its mythologic lore, he has shewn himself a most successful imitator of Callimachus; yet is it far from being the mere echo of a Grecian hymn.[2] Nor are his terse and energetic *Inscriptions* less worthy of praise.

In some of Akenside's *Odes,*—especially those *On the Winter-solstice* and *On Lyric Poetry,*—there are stanzas of pleasing picturesqueness; but in the greater number, he appeals chiefly to the understanding of the reader,[3] and is not solicitous to heighten the effect of the sentiments by wreathing them with the flowers of fancy. In those *To the Earl of Huntingdon*, and *To the Country Gentlemen of England*, he rises to a gnomic grandeur, which has seldom been surpassed. His *Odes*, on the whole, are deficient in impetuousness, warmth of colouring, tenderness, and melody.

---

[1] Among whom was Hazlitt,—*Lectures on English Poets*, 236.

[2] In 1594, Chapman, the fine old dramatist, and translator of Homer, published a tract, entitled Σκία νυκτὸς, *The Shadow of Night*, which consists of two *Hymns, To Night*, and *To Cynthia,*—very learned and mystical effusions, with occasional gleams of poetry. To attempt some Hymns in the manner of Callimachus, was among the literary projects of Milton : see *The Reason of Church Government urged against Prelaty*, 1641, p. 39.

[3] Mason had been told that Akenside " entertained, some years before his death, a notion that *poetry was only true eloquence in metre.*"—*Memoirs of Gray*, 261. ed. 1775.

# APPENDIX

## TO THE LIFE OF AKENSIDE.

### P. 12 note.

THE Ode beginning " Hail, melancholy," was written by Mrs. Carter, and may be found in her *Poems*.

P. 45, note 4. " Would to heaven," said he [i. e. the " Doctor"], "my Muse were blessed with an occasion to emulate that glorious testimony on *the trophy in Cyprus, erected by Cimon, for two great victories gained on the same day over the Persians by sea and land; in which it is very remarkable, that the greatness of the occasion has raised the manner of expression above the usual simplicity and modesty of all other ancient inscriptions."—Peregrine Pickle*, ii. 248. ed. 1751. What I have marked in Italics, is from Akenside's note on the *Ode to the Earl of Huntingdon:* which see.

P. 61, " Thee, too facetious Momion," &c. The *Archæologia Æliana*, vol. ii. part ii. Newcastle, 1830, containing *An Account of the Life and Writings of Richard Dawes*, has just fallen into my hands. I learn from it that Akenside had been a pupil of Dawes, when that great scholar was head-master of the Grammar School of Newcastle, to which office he was appointed in 1738; and that in the character of Momion the poet was supposed to have described his old master. In a strange pamphlet (so scarce that I have never been able to procure a sight of it) called *Extracts from a MS. Pamphlet, entitled the Tittle Tattle Mongers*, which Dawes published at Newcastle in 1747, are the following observations on the passage of the *Pleasures of Imagination*, where Momion is mentioned. " A certain illustrious collection of genii have thought proper to apply this character personally. The part of the brotherhood they take to themselves, and are so kind as to confer that of Momion upon Philhomerus [Dawes]. The poet, indeed, has absolutely denied that the character was intended personally, and has professed himself astonished at the application. But his pleading non-intention with respect to another gentleman, after having

declared himself astonished at what was his doctrine, makes
me entertain but a moderate opinion of his veracity. And
in this opinion I am confirmed by the conduct of his friends,
the genii, who, notwithstanding his remonstrance, persist in
the application. Nay, I am apt to believe, that they, being
acquainted with his *blushing diffidence*, instigated, if not
hired, him to undertake so notable a prank." The words
"*blushing diffidence*," allude to a passage in the *Pleasures of
Imagination*, B. iii. 205, first ed.

"forgive my song,
That for the *blushing diffidence* of youth," &c.

P. 61. In an unpublished letter from J. Edwards to
Daniel Wray, dated Turrick, April 28, 1756, is the following
passage: "I am glad to hear that Dr. Akenside has recovered Dyer again; but has Dyer recovered his poetical
vein? Alas, I fear we shall have no *Fleece* at last. I hope
the Doctor will publish the Ode you mention to the Bishop
of Winchester. [see *Life of Akenside*, p. 47.] I could have
wished he had not recalled the liberty he once gave me to
print that he honoured me with." [See *Life of Akenside*,
p. 66.]

P. 73. That "Akenside, when he walked in the streets,
looked for all the world like one of his own Alexandrines
set upright;" was a saying of Henderson, the actor,—for
which I am indebted to a true poet of our own day, Mr.
Rogers, who heard it repeated many years ago.

# ADVERTISEMENT.[1]

THIS volume contains a complete collection of the Poems of the late Dr. Akenside, either reprinted from the original editions, or faithfully published from copies which had been prepared by himself for publication.

That the principal Poem should appear in so disadvantageous a state, may require some explanation. The first publication of it was at a very early part of the author's life. That it wanted revision and correction, he was sufficiently sensible ; but so quick was the demand for several successive republications, that in any of the intervals to have completed the whole of his corrections was utterly impossible ; and yet to have gone on from time to time making farther improvements in every new edition would (he thought) have had the appearance at least of abusing the favour of the public. He chose therefore to continue for some time reprinting it without alteration, and to forbear publishing any corrections or improvements until he should be able at once to give them to the public complete. And with this view, he went on for several years to review and correct the poem at his leisure ; till at length he found the task grow so much upon his hands, that despairing of ever being able to execute it sufficiently to his own satisfaction, he abandoned the purpose of correcting, and resolved to write the poem over anew upon a somewhat different and an enlarged plan. And in the execution of this design he had made a considerable progress. What reason there may be to regret that he did not live to execute the whole of it, will best appear from the perusal of the plan itself, as stated in the General Argument, and of the parts which he had executed, and which are here published. For the person, to whom he intrusted the disposal of his papers, would have thought himself wanting, as well to the service of the public, as to the fame of his friend, if he had not produced as much of the work as appeared to have been prepared for publication. In this light he considered the entire first and second books, of which a few copies had been printed for the use only of the author and

---

[1] To Mr. Dyson's edition of Akenside's Poems, 1772.

certain friends: also a very considerable part of the Third Book, which had been transcribed in order to its being printed in the same manner: and to these is added the Introduction to a subsequent Book, which in the manuscript is called the Fourth, and which appears to have been composed at the time when the author intended to comprize the whole in Four Books; but which, as he had afterwards determined to distribute the Poem into more Books, might perhaps more properly be called the Last Book. And this is all that is executed of the new work, which although it appeared to the editor too valuable, even in its imperfect state, to be witholden from the public, yet, (he conceives) takes in by much too small a part of the original Poem to supply its place, and to supersede the re-publication of it. For which reason both the Poems are inserted in this collection.

Of Odes the author had designed to make up Two Books, consisting of twenty Odes each, including the several Odes which he had before published at different times.

The Hymn to the Naiads is reprinted from the sixth volume of Dodsley's Miscellanies, with a few corrections and the addition of some notes. To the Inscriptions taken from the same volume three new Inscriptions are added; the last of which is the only instance wherein a liberty has been taken of inserting any thing in this Collection which did not appear to have been intended by the author for publication; among whose papers no copy of this was found, but it is printed from a copy which he had many years since given to the editor.

The author of these Poems was born at Newcastle upon Tyne, on the 9th day of November, 1721. He was educated at the Grammar School at Newcastle, and at the Universities of Edinburgh and Leyden, at the latter of which he took his degree of Doctor in Physic. He was afterwards admitted by mandamus to the degree of Doctor in Physic in the University of Cambridge: elected a Fellow of the Royal College of Physicians, and one of the Physicians of St. Thomas's Hospital: and upon the establishment of the Queen's Household, appointed one of the Physicians to Her Majesty. He died of a putrid fever, on the 23d day of June, 1770, and is buried in the parish church of St. James, Westminster.

# THE
# PLEASURES OF IMAGINATION.

## A POEM. IN THREE BOOKS.

Ἀσεβὲς μέν ἐστιν ἀνθρώπω τὰς παρὰ τῶ Θεῶ χάριτας
ἀτιμάζειν.     Epict. apud Arrian. II. 23.

## THE DESIGN.

THERE are certain powers in human nature which seem to hold a middle place between the organs of bodily sense and the faculties of moral perception : they have been called by a very general name, the Powers of Imagination. Like the external senses, they relate to matter and motion ; and, at the same time, give the mind ideas analogous to those of moral approbation and dislike. As they are the inlets of some of the most exquisite pleasures with which we are acquainted, it has naturally happened that men of warm and sensible tempers have sought means to recall the delightful perceptions which they afford, independent of the objects which originally produced them. This gave rise to the imitative or designing arts; some of which, as painting and sculpture, directly copy the external appearances which were admired in nature ; others, as music and poetry, bring them back to remembrance by signs universally established and understood.

But these arts, as they grew more correct and deliberate, were of course led to extend their imitation beyond the peculiar objects of the imaginative powers ; especially poetry, which, making use of language as the instrument by which it imitates, is consequently become an unlimited representative of every species and mode of being. Yet as their intention was only to express the objects of imagination, and as they still abound chiefly in ideas of that class, they of

course retain their original character; and all the different
pleasures which they excite, are termed, in general, Pleasures of Imagination.

The design of the following poem is to give a view of
these in the largest acceptation of the term; so that whatever our imagination feels from the agreeable appearances
of nature, and all the various entertainment we meet with
either in poetry, painting, music, or any of the elegant arts,
might be deducible from one or other of those principles in
the constitution of the human mind which are here established and explained.

In executing this general plan, it was necessary first of
all to distinguish the imagination from our other faculties;
and in the next place to characterize those original forms or
properties of being, about which it is conversant, and which
are by nature adapted to it, as light is to the eyes, or truth
to the understanding. These properties Mr. Addison had
reduced to the three general classes of greatness, novelty,
and beauty; and into these we may analyze every object,
however complex, which, properly speaking, is delightful
to the imagination. But such an object may also include
many other sources of pleasure; and its beauty, or novelty,
or grandeur, will make a stronger impression by reason of
this concurrence. Besides which, the imitative arts, especially poetry, owe much of their effect to a similar exhibi-
tion of properties quite foreign to the imagination, insomuch
that in every line of the most applauded poems, we meet
with either ideas drawn from the external senses, or truths
discovered to the understanding, or illustrations of contrivance and final causes, or, above all the rest, with circumstances proper to awaken and engage the passions. It was
therefore necessary to enumerate and exemplify these different species of pleasure; especially that from the passions,
which, as it is supreme in the noblest work of human genius, so being in some particulars not a little surprising,
gave an opportunity to enliven the didactic turn of the
poem, by introducing an allegory to account for the appearance.

After these parts of the subject which hold chiefly of admiration, or naturally warm and interest the mind, a pleasure of a very different nature, that which arises from ridicule, came next to be considered. As this is the foundation of the comic manner in all the arts, and has been but
very imperfectly treated by moral writers, it was thought
proper to give it a particular illustration, and to distinguish
the general sources from which the ridicule of characters
is derived. Here too a change of style became necessary;

such a one as might yet be consistent, if possible, with the general taste of composition in the serious parts of the subject : nor is it an easy task to give any tolerable force to images of this kind, without running either into the gigantic expressions of the mock heroic, or the familiar and poetical raillery of professed satire ; neither of which would have been proper here.

The materials of all imitation being thus laid open, nothing now remained but to illustrate some particular pleasures which arise either from the relations of different objects one to another, or from the nature of imitation itself. Of the first kind is that various and complicated resemblance existing between several parts of the material and immaterial worlds, which is the foundation of metaphor and wit. As it seems in a great measure to depend on the early association of our ideas, and as this habit of associating is the source of many pleasures and pains in life, and on that account bears a great share in the influence of poetry and the other arts, it is therefore mentioned here and its effects described. Then follows a general account of the production of these elegant arts, and of the secondary pleasure, as it is called, arising from the resemblance of their imitations to the original appearances of nature. After which, the work concludes with some reflections on the general conduct of the powers of imagination, and on their natural and moral usefulness in life.

Concerning the manner or turn of composition which prevails in this piece, little can be said with propriety by the author. He had two models ; that ancient and simple one of the first Grecian poets, as it is refined by Virgil in the Georgics, and the familiar epistolary way of Horace. This latter has several advantages. It admits of a greater variety of style ; it more readily engages the generality of readers, as partaking more of the air of conversation ; and, especially with the assistance of rhyme, leads to a closer and more concise expression. Add to this the example of the most perfect of modern poets, who has so happily applied this manner to the noblest parts of philosophy, that the public taste is in a great measure formed to it alone. Yet, after all, the subject before us, tending almost constantly to admiration and enthusiasm, seemed rather to demand a more open, pathetic, and figured style. This too appeared more natural, as the author's aim was not so much to give formal precepts, or enter into the way of direct argumentation, as, by exhibiting the most engaging prospects of nature, to enlarge and harmonize the imagination, and by that means insensibly dispose the minds of men to a

similar taste and habit of thinking in religion, morals, and
civil life. 'Tis on this account that he is so careful to
point out the benevolent intention of the author of nature
in every principle of the human constitution here insisted
on; and also to unite the moral excellencies of life in the
same point of view with the mere external objects of good
taste; thus recommending them in common to our natural
propensity for admiring what is beautiful and lovely. The
same views have also led him to introduce some sentiments
which may perhaps be looked upon as not quite direct to
the subject; but since they bear an obvious relation to it,
the authority of Virgil, the faultless model of didactic
poetry, will best support him in this particular. For the
sentiments themselves he makes no apology.

## BOOK I.

### ARGUMENT.

THE subject proposed. Difficulty of treating it poetically.
The ideas of the divine mind, the origin of every quality
pleasing to the imagination. The natural variety of constitution in the minds of men; with its final cause. The idea
of a fine imagination, and the state of the mind in the enjoyment of those pleasures which it affords. All the primary
pleasures of the imagination result from the perception of
greatness, or wonderfulness, or beauty in objects. The
pleasure from greatness, with its final cause. Pleasure from
novelty or wonderfulness, with its final cause. Pleasure
from beauty, with its final cause. The connection of beauty
with truth and good, applied to the conduct of life. Invi-
tation to the study of moral philosophy. The different degrees of beauty in different species of objects: colour, shape,
natural concretes, vegetables, animals, the mind. The sublime, the fair, the wonderful of the mind. The connection
of the imagination and the moral faculty. Conclusion.

WITH what attractive charms this goodly
frame
Of nature touches the consenting hearts
Of mortal men; and what the pleasing stores
Which beauteous Imitation thence derives
To deck the poet's, or the painter's toil;
My verse unfolds. Attend, ye gentle powers

Of musical delight! and while I sing
Your gifts, your honours, dance around my strain.
Thou, smiling queen of every tuneful breast,
Indulgent Fancy! from the fruitful banks    10
Of Avon, whence thy rosy fingers cull
Fresh flowers and dews to sprinkle on the turf
Where Shakespeare lies, be present: and with thee
Let Fiction come, upon her vagrant wings
Wafting ten thousand colours through the air,
Which, by the glances of her magic eye,
She blends and shifts at will, thro' countless forms,
Her wild creation. Goddess of the lyre,
Which rules the accents of the moving sphere,
Wilt thou, eternal Harmony, descend    20
And join this festive train? for with thee comes
The guide, the guardian of their lovely sports,
Majestic Truth; and where Truth deigns to come,
Her sister Liberty will not be far.
Be present all ye Genii, who conduct
The wandering footsteps of the youthful bard,
New to your springs and shades: who touch his ear
With finer sounds: who heighten to his eye
The bloom of Nature, and before him turn
The gayest, happiest attitude of things.    30
   Oft have the laws of each poetic strain
The critic-verse employ'd; yet still unsung
Lay this prime subject, though importing most
A poet's name: for fruitless is the attempt,
By dull obedience and by creeping toil
Obscure to conquer the severe ascent
Of high Parnassus. Nature's kindling breath
Must fire the chosen genius; Nature's hand
Must string his nerves, and imp his eagle-wings
Impatient of the painful steep, to soar    40
High as the summit; there to breathe at large
Æthereal air: with bards and sages old,
Immortal sons of praise. These flattering scenes,
To this neglected labour court my song;
Yet not unconscious what a doubtful task

To paint the finest features of the mind,
And to most subtile and mysterious things
Give colour, strength, and motion.  But the love
Of Nature and the Muses bids explore,
Through secret paths erewhile untrod by man,  50
The fair poetic region, to detect
Untasted springs, to drink inspiring draughts,
And shade my temples with unfading flowers
Cull'd from the laureate vale's profound recess,
Where never poet gain'd a wreath before.
      From Heaven my strains begin: from Heaven
            descends
The flame of genius to the human breast,
And love and beauty, and poetic joy
And inspiration.  Ere the radiant sun
Sprang from the east, or 'mid the vault of night
The moon suspended her serener lamp;
Ere mountains, woods, or streams adorn'd the globe,
Or Wisdom taught the sons of men her lore;
Then liv'd the Almighty One: then, deep-retir'd
In his unfathom'd essence, view'd the forms,
The forms eternal of created things;
The radiant sun, the moon's nocturnal lamp,
The mountains, woods and streams, the rolling globe,
And Wisdom's mien celestial.  From the first
Of days, on them his love divine he fix'd,  70
His admiration: till in time complete
What he admir'd and lov'd, his vital smile
Unfolded into being.  Hence the breath
Of life informing each organic frame,
Hence the green earth, and wild resounding waves;
Hence light and shade alternate; warmth and cold;
And clear autumnal skies and vernal showers,
And all the fair variety of things.
    But not alike to every mortal eye
Is this great scene unveil'd.  For since the claims
Of social life, to different labours urge
The active powers of man; with wise intent
The hand of Nature on peculiar minds

Imprints a different bias, and to each
Decrees its province in the common toil.
To some she taught the fabric of the sphere,
The changeful moon, the circuit of the stars,
The golden zones of heaven : to some she gave
To weigh the moment of eternal things,
Of time, and space, and fate's unbroken chain,  90
And will's quick impulse: others by the hand
She led o'er vales and mountains, to explore
What healing virtue swells the tender veins
Of herbs and flowers ; or what the beams of morn
Draw forth, distilling from the clifted rind
In balmy tears.   But some, to higher hopes
Were destin'd ; some within a finer mould
She wrought, and temper'd with a purer flame.
To these the Sire Omnipotent unfolds
The world's harmonious volume, there to read  100
The transcript of Himself.   On every part
They trace the bright impressions of his hand :
In earth or air, the meadow's purple stores,
The moon's mild radiance, or the virgin's form
Blooming with rosy smiles, they see portray'd
That uncreated beauty, which delights
The mind supreme.   They also feel her charms,
Enamour'd ; they partake the eternal joy.
    For as old Memnon's image, long renown'd
By fabling Nilus, to the quivering touch  110
Of Titan's ray, with each repulsive string
Consenting, sounded through the warbling air
Unbidden strains ; even so did Nature's hand
To certain species of external things,
Attune the finer organs of the mind :
So the glad impulse of congenial powers,
Or of sweet sound, or fair proportion'd form,
The grace of motion, or the bloom of light,
Thrills through Imagination's tender frame,
From nerve to nerve : all naked and alive  120
They catch the spreading rays : till now the soul
At length discloses every tuneful spring,

G

To that harmonious movement from without
Responsive.   Then the inexpressive strain
Diffuses its enchantment : Fancy dreams
Of sacred fountains and Elysian groves,
And vales of bliss : the intellectual power
Bends from his awful throne a wondering ear,
And smiles : the passions, gently sooth'd away,
Sink to divine repose, and love and joy        130
Alone are waking; love and joy, serene
As airs that fan the summer.   O ! attend,
Whoe'er thou art, whom these delights can touch,
Whose candid bosom the refining love
Of Nature warms, O ! listen to my song ;
And I will guide thee to her favourite walks,
And teach thy solitude her voice to hear,
And point her loveliest features to thy view.
    Know then, whate'er of Nature's pregnant stores,
Whate'er of mimic Art's reflected forms        140
With love and admiration thus inflame
The powers of Fancy, her delighted sons
To three illustrious orders have referr'd ;
Three sister graces, whom the painter's hand,
The poet's tongue confesses ; the sublime,
The wonderful, the fair.   I see them dawn !
I see the radiant visions, where they rise,
More lovely than when Lucifer displays
His beaming forehead through the gates of morn,
To lead the train of Phœbus and the spring.     150
    Say, why was man so eminently rais'd
Amid the vast Creation ; why ordain'd
Through life and death to dart his piercing eye,
With thoughts beyond the limit of his frame :
But that the Omnipotent might send him forth
In sight of mortal and immortal powers,
As on a boundless theatre, to run
The great career of justice ; to exalt
His generous aim to all diviner deeds ;
To chase each partial purpose from his breast ;   160
And through the mists of passion and of sense,

And through the tossing tide of chance and pain,
To hold his course unfaltering, while the voice
Of truth and virtue, up the steep ascent
Of nature, calls him to his high reward,
The applauding smile of Heaven? Else wherefore
In mortal bosoms this unquenched hope, [burns
That breathes from day to day sublimer things,
And mocks possession? wherefore darts the mind,
With such resistless ardour to embrace     170
Majestic forms; impatient to be free,
Spurning the gross control of wilful might;
Proud of the strong contention of her toils;
Proud to be daring? Who but rather turns
To heaven's broad fire his unconstrained view,
Than to the glimmering of a waxen flame?
Who that, from Alpine heights, his labouring eye
Shoots round the wide horizon, to survey
Nilus or Ganges rolling his bright wave [shade,
Thro' mountains, plains, thro' empires black with
And continents of sand; will turn his gaze
To mark the windings of a scanty rill
That murmurs at his feet? The high-born soul
Disdains to rest her heaven-aspiring wing
Beneath its native quarry. Tir'd of earth
And this diurnal scene, she springs aloft
Through fields of air; pursues the flying storm;
Rides on the vollied lightning through the heavens;
Or, yok'd with whirlwinds and the northern blast,
Sweeps the long tract of day. Then high she soars
The blue profound, and hovering round the sun
Beholds him pouring the redundant stream
Of light; beholds his unrelenting sway
Bend the reluctant planets to absolve
The fated rounds of Time. Thence far effus'd
She darts her swiftness up the long career
Of devious comets; through its burning signs
Exulting measures the perennial wheel
Of Nature, and looks back on all the stars,
Whose blended light, as with a milky zone,     200

Invests the orient.   Now amaz'd she views
The empyreal waste, where happy spirits hold
Beyond this concave heaven, their calm abode ;
And fields of radiance, whose unfading light
Has travell'd the profound six thousand years,
Nor yet arrives in sight of mortal things.
Even on the barriers of the world untir'd
She meditates the eternal depth below;
Till half recoiling, down the headlong steep
She plunges; soon o'erwhelm'd and swallowed up
In that immense of being.   There her hopes
Rest at the fated goal.   For from the birth
Of mortal man, the Sovereign Maker said,
That not in humble nor in brief delight,
Not in the fading echoes of renown,
Power's purple robes, nor pleasure's flowery lap,
The soul should find enjoyment : but from these
Turning disdainful to an equal good,
Through all the ascent of things enlarge her view,
Till every bound at length should disappear,      220
And infinite perfection close the scene.
   Call now to mind what high capacious powers
Lie folded up in man ; how far beyond
The praise of mortals, may the eternal growth
Of Nature to perfection half divine,
Expand the blooming soul?  What pity then
Should sloth's unkindly fogs depress to earth
Her tender blossom ; choke the streams of life,
And blast her spring !  Far otherwise design'd
Almighty Wisdom ; Nature's happy cares      230
The obedient heart far otherwise incline.
Witness the sprightly joy when aught unknown
Strikes the quick sense, and wakes each active power
To brisker measures : witness the neglect
Of all familiar prospects, though beheld
With transport once ; the fond attentive gaze
Of young astonishment ; the sober zeal
Of age, commenting on prodigious things.
For such the bounteous providence of heaven,

In every breast implanting this desire     240
Of objects new and strange, to urge us on
With unremitted labour to pursué
Those sacred stores that wait the ripening soul,
In Truth's exhaustless bosom. What need words
To paint its power? For this the daring youth
Breaks from his weeping mother's anxious arms,
In foreign climes to rove: the pensive sage,
Heedless of sleep, or midnight's harmful damp,
Hangs o'er the sickly taper; and untir'd
The virgin follows, with enchanted step,     250
The mazes of some wild and wondrous tale,
From morn to eve; unmindful of her form,
Unmindful of the happy dress that stole
The wishes of the youth, when every maid
With envy pin'd. Hence, finally, by night
The village-matron, round the blazing hearth,
Suspends the infant audience with her tales,
Breathing astonishment! of witching rhymes,
And evil spirits; of the death-bed call
Of him who robb'd the widow, and devour'd     260
The orphan's portion; of unquiet souls
Risen from the grave to ease the heavy guilt
Of deeds in life conceal'd; of shapes that walk
At dead of night, and clank their chains, and wave
The torch of hell around the murderer's bed.
At every solemn pause the crowd recoil,
Gazing each other speechless, and congeal'd
With shivering sighs: till eager for the event,
Around the beldame all erect they hang,
Each trembling heart with grateful terrors quell'd.
   But lo! disclos'd in all her smiling pomp,
Where Beauty onward moving claims the verse
Her charms inspire: the freely-flowing verse
In thy immortal praise, O form divine,
Smooths her mellifluent stream. Thee, Beauty, thee
The regal dome, and thy enlivening ray
The mossy roofs adore: thou, better sun!
For ever beamest on the enchanted heart

Love, and harmonious wonder, and delight
Poetic.  Brightest progeny of Heaven!        280
How shall I trace thy features? where select
The roseate hues to emulate thy bloom?
Haste then, my song, thro' Nature's wide expanse,
Haste then, and gather all her comeliest wealth,
Whate'er bright spoils the florid earth contains,
Whate'er the waters, or the liquid air,
To deck thy lovely labour.  Wilt thou fly
With laughing Autumn to the Atlantic isles,
And range with him the Hesperian field, and see
Where'er his fingers touch the fruitful grove,   290
The branches shoot with gold; where'er his step
Marks the glad soil, the tender clusters grow
With purple ripeness, and invest each hill
As with the blushes of an evening sky?
Or wilt thou rather stoop thy vagrant plume,
Where gliding thro' his daughter's honour'd shades,
The smooth Penéus from his glassy flood
Reflects purpureal Tempe's pleasant scene?
Fair Tempe! haunt belov'd of sylvan Powers,
Of Nymphs and Fauns; where in the golden age 300
They play'd in secret on the shady brink
With ancient Pan: while round their choral steps
Young Hours and genial Gales with constant hand
Shower'd blossoms, odours, shower'd ambrosial
        dews,
And spring's Elysian bloom.  Her flowery store
To thee nor Tempe shall refuse; nor watch
Of winged Hydra guard Hesperian fruits
From thy free spoil.  O bear then, unreprov'd,
Thy smiling treasures to the green recess
Where young Dione stays.  With sweetest airs 310
Entice her forth to lend her angel form
For Beauty's honour'd image.  Hither turn
Thy graceful footsteps; hither, gentle maid,
Incline thy polish'd forehead: let thy eyes
Effuse the mildness of their azure dawn;
And may the fanning breezes waft aside

Thy radiant locks: disclosing, as it bends
With airy softness from the marble neck,
The cheek fair-blooming, and the rosy lip,
Where winning smiles and pleasures sweet as love,
With sanctity and wisdom, tempering blend
Their soft allurement.  Then the pleasing force
Of Nature, and her kind parental care
Worthier I'd sing: then all the enamour'd youth,
With each admiring virgin, to my lyre
Should throng attentive, while I point on high
Where Beauty's living image, like the Morn
That wakes in Zephyr's arms the blushing May,
Moves onward; or as Venus, when she stood
Effulgent on the pearly car, and smil'd,          330
Fresh from the deep, and conscious of her form,
To see the Tritons tune their vocal shells,
And each cerulean sister of the flood
With loud acclaim attend her o'er the waves,
To seek the Idalian bower.  Ye smiling band
Of youths and virgins, who through all the maze
Of young desire with rival steps pursue
This charm of Beauty; if the pleasing toil
Can yield a moment's respite, hither turn
Your favourable ear, and trust my words.          340
I do not mean to wake the gloomy form
Of Superstition dress'd in Wisdom's garb,
To damp your tender hopes; I do not mean
To bid the jealous thunderer fire the heavens,
Or shapes infernal rend the groaning earth
To fright you from your joys: my cheerful song
With better omens calls you to the field,
Pleas'd with your generous ardour in the chase,
And warm like you.  Then tell me, for ye know,
Does Beauty ever deign to dwell where health 350
And active use are strangers?  Is her charm
Confess'd in aught, whose most peculiar ends
Are lame and fruitless?  Or did Nature mean
This pleasing call the herald of a lie;
To hide the shame of discord and disease,

And catch with fair hypocrisy the heart  
Of idle faith ?   O no ! with better cares  
The indulgent mother, conscious how infirm  
Her offspring tread the paths of good and ill,  
By this illustrious image, in each kind          360  
Still most illustrious where the object holds  
Its native powers most perfect, she by this  
Illumes the headstrong impulse of desire,  
And sanctifies his choice.   The generous glebe  
Whose bosom smiles with verdure, the clear tract  
Of streams delicious to the thirsty soul,  
The bloom of nectar'd fruitage ripe to sense,  
And every charm of animated things,  
Are only pledges of a state sincere,  
The integrity and order of their frame,          370  
When all is well within, and every end  
Accomplish'd.   Thus was Beauty sent from heaven,  
The lovely ministress of Truth and Good  
In this dark world: for Truth and Good are one,  
And Beauty dwells in them, and they in her,  
With like participation.   Wherefore then,  
O sons of earth ! would ye dissolve the tie ?  
O wherefore, with a rash impetuous aim,  
Seek ye those flowery joys with which the hand  
Of lavish Fancy paints each flattering scene     380  
Where Beauty seems to dwell, nor once inquire  
Where is the sanction of eternal Truth,  
Or where the seal of undeceitful good,  
To save your search from folly !   Wanting these,  
Lo ! Beauty withers in your void embrace,  
And with the glittering of an idiot's toy  
Did Fancy mock your vows.   Nor let the gleam  
Of youthful hope that shines upon your hearts,  
Be chill'd or clouded at this awful task,  
To learn the lore of undeceitful good,           390  
And Truth eternal. Though the poisonous charms  
Of baleful Superstition guide the feet  
Of servile numbers, through a dreary way  
To their abode, through deserts, thorns, and mire;

And leave the wretched pilgrim all forlorn
To muse at last, amid the ghostly gloom
Of graves, and hoary vaults, and cloister'd cells;
To walk with spectres through the midnight shade,
And to the screaming owl's accursed song
Attune the dreadful workings of his heart;      400
Yet be not ye dismay'd.   A gentler star
Your lovely search illumines.   From the grove
Where Wisdom talk'd with her Athenian sons,
Could my ambitious hand entwine a wreath
Of Plato's olive with the Mantuan bay,
Then should my powerful verse at once dispel
Those monkish horrors: then in light divine
Disclose the Elysian prospect, where the steps
Of those whom Nature charms, through blooming
      walks,
Through fragrant mountains and poetic streams,
Amid the train of sages, heroes, bards,
Led by their winged Genius, and the choir
Of laurell'd science and harmonious art,
Proceed exulting to the eternal shrine,
Where Truth conspicuous with her sister-twins,
The undivided partners of her sway,
With good and beauty reigns.   O let not us,
Lull'd by luxurious Pleasure's languid strain,
Or crouching to the frowns of bigot rage,
O let us not a moment pause to join      420
That godlike band.   And if the gracious Power
Who first awaken'd my untutor'd song,
Will to my invocation breathe anew
The tuneful spirit; then through all our paths,
Ne'er shall the sound of this devoted lyre
Be wanting; whether on the rosy mead,
When summer smiles, to warn the melting heart
Of luxury's allurement; whether firm
Against the torrent and the stubborn hill
To urge bold Virtue's unremitted nerve,      430
And wake the strong divinity of soul
That conquers chance and fate; or whether struck

For sounds of triumph, to proclaim her toils
Upon the lofty summit, round her brow
To twine the wreath of incorruptive praise ;
To trace her hallow'd light through future worlds,
And bless Heaven's image in the heart of man.
   Thus with a faithful aim have we presum'd,
Adventurous, to delineate Nature's form ;
Whether in vast, majestic pomp array'd,      440
Or drest for pleasing wonder, or serene
In Beauty's rosy smile.  It now remains,
Through various being's fair proportion'd scale,
To trace the rising lustre of her charms,
From their first twilight, shining forth at length
To full meridian splendour.  Of degree
The least and lowliest, in the effusive warmth
Of colours mingling with a random blaze,
Doth Beauty dwell.  Then higher in the line
And variation of determin'd shape,      450
Where Truth's eternal measures mark the bound
Of circle, cube, or sphere.  The third ascent
Unites this varied symmetry of parts
With colour's bland allurement ; as the pearl
Shines in the concave of its azure bed,
And painted shells indent their speckled wreath.
Then more attractive rise the blooming forms
Through which the breath of Nature has infus'd
Her genial power to draw with pregnant veins
Nutritious moisture from the bounteous earth,  460
In fruit and seed prolific : thus the flowers
Their purple honours with the Spring resume ;
And such the stately tree which Autumn bends
With blushing treasures.  But more lovely still
Is Nature's charm, where to the full consent
Of complicated members, to the bloom
Of colour, and the vital change of growth,
Life's holy flame and piercing sense are given,
And active motion speaks the temper'd soul :
So moves the bird of Juno ; so the steed     470
With rival ardour beats the dusty plain,

And faithful dogs with eager airs of joy
Salute their fellows.   Thus doth Beauty dwell
There most conspicuous, even in outward shape,
Where dawns the high expression of a mind:
By steps conducting our enraptur'd search
To that eternal origin, whose power,
Through all the unbounded symmetry of things,
Like rays effulging from the parent sun,
This endless mixture of her charms diffus'd.     480
Mind, mind alone, (bear witness earth and heaven!)
The living fountains in itself contains
Of beauteous and sublime : here hand in hand,
Sit paramount the Graces; here enthron'd,
Celestial Venus, with divinest airs,
Invites the soul to never fading joy.
Look then abroad through nature, to the range
Of planets, suns, and adamantine spheres
Wheeling unshaken through the void immense;
And speak, O man! does this capacious scene  490
With half that kindling majesty dilate
Thy strong conception, as when Brutus rose
Refulgent from the stroke of Cæsar's fate,
Amid the crowd of patriots ; and his arm
Aloft extending, like eternal Jove
When guilt brings down the thunder, call'd aloud
On Tully's name, and shook his crimson steel,
And bade the father of his country, hail!
For lo! the tyrant prostrate on the dust,
And Rome again is free!   Is aught so fair       500
In all the dewy landscapes of the Spring,
In the bright eye of Hesper, or the morn,
In Nature's fairest forms, is aught so fair
As virtuous friendship ? as the candid blush
Of him who strives with fortune to be just ?
The graceful tear that streams for others' woes ?
Or the mild majesty of private life,
Where Peace with ever blooming olive crowns
The gate; where Honour's liberal hands effuse
Unenvied treasures, and the snowy wings         510

Of Innocence and Love protect the scene?
Once more search, undismay'd, the dark profound
Where Nature works in secret; view the beds
Of mineral treasure, and the eternal vault
That bounds the hoary ocean; trace the forms
Of atoms moving with incessant change
Their elemental round; behold the seeds
Of being, and the energy of life
Kindling the mass with ever active flame:
Then to the secrets of the working mind          520
Attentive turn; from dim oblivion call
Her fleet, ideal band; and bid them, go!
Break through time's barrier, and o'ertake the hour
That saw the heavens created: then declare
If aught were found in those external scenes
To move thy wonder now.   For what are all
The forms which brute, unconscious matter wears,
Greatness of bulk, or symmetry of parts?
Not reaching to the heart, soon feeble grows
The superficial impulse; dull their charms,          530
And satiate soon, and pall the languid eye.
Not so the moral species, nor the powers
Of genius and design; the ambitious mind
There sees herself: by these congenial forms
Touch'd and awaken'd, with intenser act
She bends each nerve, and meditates well pleas'd
Her features in the mirror.   For of all
The inhabitants of earth, to man alone
Creative Wisdom gave to lift his eye
To Truth's eternal measures; thence to frame  540
The sacred laws of action and of will,
Discerning justice from unequal deeds,
And temperance from folly.   But beyond
This energy of Truth, whose dictates bind
Assenting reason, the benignant Sire,
To deck the honour'd paths of just and good,
Has added bright Imagination's rays:
Where Virtue, rising from the awful depth
Of Truth's mysterious bosom, doth forsake

The unadorn'd condition of her birth ;                550
And dress'd by Fancy in ten thousand hues,
Assumes a various feature, to attract,
With charms responsive to each gazer's eye,
The hearts of men.   Amid his rural walk,
The ingenuous youth, whom solitude inspires
With purest wishes, from the pensive shade
Beholds her moving, like a virgin muse
That wakes her lyre to some indulgent theme
Of harmony and wonder : while among
The herd of servile minds, her strenuous form  560
Indignant flashes on the patriot's eye,
And through the rolls of memory appeals
To ancient honour, or in act serene,
Yet watchful, raises the majestic sword
Of public Power, from dark Ambition's reach
To guard the sacred volume of the laws.
   Genius of ancient Greece ! whose faithful steps
Well pleas'd I follow through the sacred paths
Of Nature and of Science ; nurse divine
Of all heroic deeds and fair desires !                570
O ! let the breath of thy extended praise
Inspire my kindling bosom to the height
Of this untempted theme.   Nor be my thoughts
Presumptuous counted, if amid the calm
That soothes this vernal evening into smiles,
I steal impatient from the sordid haunts
Of Strife and low Ambition, to attend
Thy sacred presence in the sylvan shade,
By their malignant footsteps ne'er profan'd.
Descend propitious ! to my favour'd eye ;             580
Such in thy mien, thy warm, exalted air,
As when the Persian tyrant, foil'd and stung
With shame and desperation, gnash'd his teeth
To see thee rend the pageants of his throne ;
And at the lightning of thy lifted spear
Crouch'd like a slave.   Bring all thy martial spoils,
Thy palms, thy laurels, thy triumphal songs,
Thy smiling band of art, thy godlike sires

Of civil wisdom, thy heroic youth
Warm from the schools of glory.  Guide my way
Through fair Lycéum's walk, the green retreats
Of Academus, and the thymy vale,
Where oft enchanted with Socratic sounds,
Ilissus pure devolv'd his tuneful stream
In gentler murmurs.  From the blooming store
Of these auspicious fields, may I unblam'd
Transplant some living blossoms to adorn
My native clime : while far above the flight
Of Fancy's plume aspiring, I unlock
The springs of ancient wisdom! while I join      600
Thy name, thrice honour'd! with the immortal praise
Of Nature; while to my compatriot youth
I point the high example of thy sons,
And tune to Attic themes the British lyre.


## BOOK II.

### ARGUMENT.

THE separation of the works of Imagination from Philosophy,
the cause of their abuse among the moderns.  Prospect of
their re-union under the influence of public Liberty.  Enu-
meration of accidental pleasures, which increase the effect
of objects delightful to the Imagination.  The pleasures of
sense.  Particular circumstances of the mind.  Discovery
of truth.  Perception of contrivance and design.  Emotion
of the passions.  All the natural passions partake of a
pleasing sensation ; with the final cause of this constitution
illustrated by an allegorical vision, and exemplified in sorrow, pity, terror, and indignation.


WHEN shall the laurel and the vocal string
    Resume their honours?  When shall we
        behold
The tuneful tongue, the Promethéan hand
Aspire to ancient praise?  Alas! how faint,

How slow the dawn of Beauty and of Truth
Breaks the reluctant shades of gothic night
Which yet involve the nations! Long they groan'd
Beneath the furies of rapacious force;
Oft as the gloomy north, with iron swarms
Tempestuous pouring from her frozen caves,     10
Blasted the Italian shore, and swept the works
Of Liberty and Wisdom down the gulph
Of all devouring night.  As long immur'd
In noontide darkness by the glimmering lamp,
Each Muse and each fair Science pin'd away
The sordid hours : while foul, barbarian hands
Their mysteries profan'd, unstrung the lyre,
And chain'd the soaring pinion down to earth.
At last the Muses rose, and spurn'd their bonds,
And, wildly warbling, scatter'd, as they flew,     20
Their blooming wreaths from fair Valclusa's bowers
To Arno's myrtle border and the shore
Of soft Parthenopé.  But still the rage
Of dire ambition and gigantic power,
From public aims and from the busy walk
Of civil commerce, drove the bolder train
Of penetrating Science to the cells,
Where studious Ease consumes the silent hour
In shadowy searches and unfruitful care.
Thus from their guardians torn, the tender arts     30
Of mimic fancy and harmonious joy,
To priestly domination and the lust
Of lawless courts, their amiable toil
For three inglorious ages have resign'd,
In vain reluctant : and Torquato's tongue
Was tun'd for slavish pæans at the throne
Of tinsel pomp : and Raphael's magic hand
Effus'd its fair creation to enchant
The fond adoring herd in Latian fanes
To blind belief; while on their prostrate necks     40
The sable tyrant plants his heel secure.
But now, behold! the radiant era dawns,
When freedom's ample fabric, fix'd at length

For endless years on Albion's happy shore
In full proportion, once more shall extend
To all the kindred powers of social bliss
A common mansion, a parental roof.
There shall the Virtues, there shall Wisdom's train,
Their long-lost friends rejoining, as of old,
Embrace the smiling family of Arts,                    50
The Muses and the Graces.   Then no more
Shall Vice, distracting their delicious gifts
To aims abhorr'd, with high distaste and scorn
Turn from their charms the philosophic eye,
The patriot bosom ; then no more the paths
Of public care or intellectual toil,
Alone by footsteps haughty and severe
In gloomy state be trod : the harmonious Muse
And her persuasive sisters then shall plant
Their sheltering laurels o'er the bleak ascent,       60
And scatter flowers along the rugged way.
Arm'd with the lyre, already have we dar'd
To pierce divine Philosophy's retreats,
And teach the Muse her lore ; already strove
Their long divided honours to unite,
While tempering this deep argument we sang
Of Truth and Beauty.   Now the same glad task
Impends ; now urging our ambitious toil,
We hasten to recount the various springs
Of adventitious pleasure, which adjoin                70
Their grateful influence to the prime effect
Of objects grand or beauteous, and enlarge
The complicated joy.   The sweets of sense,
Do they not oft with kind accession flow,
To raise harmonious Fancy's native charm ?
So while we taste the fragrance of the rose,
Glows not her blush the fairer ?   While we view
Amid the noontide walk a limpid rill
Gush through the trickling herbage, to the thirst
Of summer yielding the delicious draught             80
Of cool refreshment ; o'er the mossy brink
Shines not the surface clearer, and the waves

With sweeter music murmur as they flow ?
  Nor this alone ; the various lot of life
Oft from external circumstance assumes
A moment's disposition to rejoice
In those delights which at a different hour
Would pass unheeded.  Fair the face of Spring,
When rural songs and odours wake the morn,
To every eye ; but how much more to his    90
Round whom the bed of sickness long diffus'd
Its melancholy gloom ! how doubly fair,
When first with fresh-born vigour he inhales
The balmy breeze, and feels the blessed sun
Warm at his bosom, from the springs of life
Chasing oppressive damps and languid pain !
  Or shall I mention, where celestial Truth
Her awful light discloses, to bestow
A more majestic pomp on Beauty's frame ?
For man loves knowledge, and the beams of Truth
More welcome touch his understanding's eye,
Than all the blandishments of sound his ear,
Than all of taste his tongue.  Nor ever yet
The melting rainbow's vernal-tinctur'd hues
To me have shown so pleasing, as when first
The hand of Science pointed out the path
In which the sunbeams gleaming from the west
Fall on the watery cloud, whose darksome veil
Involves the orient ; and that trickling shower
Piercing through every crystalline convex    110
Of clustering dewdrops to their flight oppos'd,
Recoil at length where concave all behind
The internal surface of each glassy orb
Repels their forward passage into air ;
That thence direct they seek the radiant goal
From which their course began ; and, as they strike
In different lines the gazer's obvious eye,
Assume a different lustre, through the brede
Of colours changing from the splendid rose
To the pale violet's dejected hue.    120
  Or shall we touch that kind access of joy,

H

That springs to each fair object, while we trace
Through all its fabric, Wisdom's artful aim
Disposing every part, and gaining still
By means proportion'd her benignant end?
Speak ye, the pure delight, whose favour'd steps
The lamp of Science through the jealous maze
Of Nature guides, when haply you reveal
Her secret honours: whether in the sky,
The beauteous laws of light, the central powers
That wheel the pensile planets round the year;
Whether in wonders of the rolling deep,
Or the rich fruits of all-sustaining earth,
Or fine-adjusted springs of life and sense,
Ye scan the counsels of their Author's hand.
   What, when to raise the meditated scene,
The flame of passion, through the struggling soul
Deep-kindled, shows across that sudden blaze
The object of its rapture, vast of size,
With fiercer colours and a night of shade?          140
What? like a storm from their capacious bed
The sounding seas o'erwhelming, when the might
Of these eruptions, working from the depth
Of man's strong apprehension, shakes his frame
Even to the base; from every naked sense
Of pain or pleasure dissipating all
Opinion's feeble coverings, and the veil
Spun from the cobweb fashion of the times
To hide the feeling heart?   Then Nature speaks
Her genuine language, and the words of men,     150
Big with the very motion of their souls,
Declare with what accumulated force,
The impetuous nerve of passion urges on
The native weight and energy of things.
   Yet more: her honours where nor Beauty claims,
Nor shows of good the thirsty sense allure,
From passion's power alone our nature holds
Essential pleasure.   Passion's fierce illapse
Rouses the mind's whole fabric; with supplies
Of daily impulse keeps the elastic powers        160

Intensely pois'd, and polishes anew
By that collision all the fine machine:
Else rust would rise, and foulness, by degrees
Incumbering, choke at last what heaven design'd
For ceaseless motion and a round of toil.
—But say, does every passion thus to man
Administer delight? That name indeed
Becomes the rosy breath of love; becomes
The radiant smiles of joy, the applauding hand
Of admiration: but the bitter shower          170
That sorrow sheds upon a brother's grave;
But the dumb palsy of nocturnal fear,
Or those consuming fires that gnaw the heart
Of panting indignation, find we there
To move delight?—Then listen while my tongue
The unalter'd will of Heaven with faithful awe
Reveals; what old Harmodius wont to teach
My early age; Harmodius, who had weigh'd
Within his learned mind whate'er the schools
Of Wisdom, or thy lonely-whispering voice,     180
O faithful Nature! dictate of the laws
Which govern and support this mighty frame
Of universal being. Oft the hours
From morn to eve have stolen unmark'd away,
While mute attention hung upon his lips,
As thus the sage his awful tale began:
" 'Twas in the windings of an ancient wood,
When spotless youth with solitude resigns
To sweet philosophy the studious day,
What time pale Autumn shades the silent eve,  190
Musing I rov'd. Of good and evil much,
And much of mortal man my thought revolv'd;
When starting full on fancy's gushing eye
The mournful image of Parthenia's fate,
That hour, O long belov'd and long deplor'd!
When blooming youth, nor gentlest wisdom's arts,
Nor Hymen's honours gather'd for thy brow,
Nor all thy lover's, all thy father's tears
Avail'd to snatch thee from the cruel grave;

Thy agonizing looks, thy last farewell          200
Struck to the inmost feeling of my soul
As with the hand of Death.   At once the shade
More horrid nodded o'er me, and the winds
With hoarser murmuring shook the branches.   Dark
As midnight storms, the scene of human things
Appear'd before me ; deserts, burning sands,
Where the parch'd adder dies.; the frozen south,
And desolation blasting all the west
With rapine and with murder : tyrant power
Here sits enthron'd with blood ; the baleful charms
Of superstition there infect the skies,
And turn the sun to horror.   Gracious Heaven !
What is the life of man ?  Or cannot these,
Not these portents thy awful will suffice ?
That, propagated thus beyond their scope,
They rise to act their cruelties anew
In my afflicted bosom, thus decreed
The universal sensitive of pain,
The wretched heir of evils not its own ! "
     Thus I impatient : when, at once effus'd,       220
A flashing torrent of celestial day
Burst through the shadowy void.   With slow descent
A purple cloud came floating through the sky,
And pois'd at length within the circling trees,
Hung obvious to my view ; till opening wide
Its lucid orb, a more than human form
Emerging lean'd majestic o'er my head,
And instant thunder shook the conscious grove.
Then melted into air the liquid cloud,
And all the shining vision stood reveal'd.          230
A wreath of palm his ample forehead bound,
And o'er his shoulder, mantling to his knee,
Flow'd the transparent robe, around his waist
Collected with a radiant zone of gold
Æthereal : there in mystic signs engrav'd,
I read his office high and sacred name,
Genius of human kind !   Appall'd I gaz'd
The godlike presence ; for athwart his brow

Displeasure, temper'd with a mild concern,
Look'd down reluctant on me, and his words     240
Like distant thunders broke the murmuring air.
  " Vain are thy thoughts, O child of mortal birth !
And impotent thy tongue.   Is thy short span
Capacious of this universal frame ?
Thy wisdom all sufficient ? Thou, alas !
Dost thou aspire to judge between the Lord
Of Nature and his works ? to lift thy voice
Against the sovereign order he decreed,
All good and lovely ? to blaspheme the bands
Of tenderness innate and social love,     250
Holiest of things ! by which the general orb
Of being, as by adamantine links,
Was drawn to perfect union and sustain'd
From everlasting ?   Hast thou felt the pangs
Of softening sorrow, of indignant zeal
So grievous to the soul, as thence to wish
The ties of Nature broken from thy frame ;
That so thy selfish, unrelenting heart
Might cease to mourn its lot, no longer then
The wretched heir of evils not its own ?     260
O fair benevolence of generous minds !
O man by Nature form'd for all mankind ! "
  He spoke ; abash'd and silent I remain'd,
As conscious of my tongue's offence, and aw'd
Before his presence, though my secret soul
Disdain'd the imputation.   On the ground
I fix'd my eyes ; till from his airy couch
He stoop'd sublime, and touching with his hand
My dazzling forehead, " Raise thy sight," he cried,
" And let thy sense convince thy erring tongue."
  I look'd, and lo ! the former scene was chang'd ;
For verdant alleys and surrounding trees,
A solitary prospect, wide and wild,
Rush'd on my senses.   'Twas a horrid pile
Of hills with many a shaggy forest mix'd,
With many a sable cliff and glittering stream.
Aloft recumbent o'er the hanging ridge,

The brown woods wav'd; while ever-trickling springs
Wash'd from the naked roots of oak and pine
The crumbling soil; and still at every fall      280
Down the steep windings of the channel'd rock,
Remurmuring rush'd the congregated floods
With hoarser inundation; till at last
They reach'd a grassy plain, which from the skirts
Of that high desert spread her verdant lap,
And drank the gushing moisture, where confin'd
In one smooth current, o'er the lilied vale
Clearer than glass it flow'd.   Autumnal spoils
Luxuriant spreading to the rays of morn,
Blush'd o'er the cliffs, whose half-encircling mound
As in a sylvan theatre enclos'd
That flowery level.   On the river's brink
I spied a fair pavilion, which diffus'd
Its floating umbrage 'mid the silver shade
Of osiers.   Now the western sun reveal'd
Between two parting cliffs his golden orb,
And pour'd across the shadow of the hills,
On rocks and floods, a yellow stream of light
That cheer'd the solemn scene.   My listening powers
Were aw'd, and every thought in silence hung,  300
And wondering expectation.   Then the voice
Of that celestial power, the mystic show
Declaring, thus my deep attention call'd:
   " Inhabitant of earth, to whom is given
The gracious ways of Providence to learn,
Receive my sayings with a steadfast ear—
Know then, the Sovereign Spirit of the world,
Though, self-collected from eternal time,
Within his own deep essence he beheld
The bounds of true felicity complete;      310
Yet by immense benignity inclin'd
To spread around him that primeval joy
Which fill'd himself, he rais'd his plastic arm,
And sounded through the hollow depths of space
The strong, creative mandate.   Straight arose
These heavenly orbs, the glad abodes of life,

Effusive kindled by his breath divine
Through endless forms of being. Each inhal'd
From him its portion of the vital flame,
In measure such, that, from the wide complex  320
Of coexistent orders, one might rise,
One order, all-involving and entire.
He too beholding in the sacred light
Of his essential reason, all the shapes
Of swift contingence, all successive ties
Of action propagated through the sum
Of possible existence, he at once,
Down the long series of eventful time,
So fix'd the dates of being, so dispos'd,
To every living soul of every kind  330
The field of motion and the hour of rest,
That all conspir'd to his supreme design,
To universal good: with full accord
Answering the mighty model he had chose,
The best and fairest of unnumber'd worlds
That lay from everlasting in the store
Of his divine conceptions. Nor content,
By one exertion of creative power
His goodness to reveal; through every age,
Through every moment up the tract of time  340
His parent hand with ever new increase
Of happiness and virtue has adorn'd
The vast harmonious frame: his parent hand,
From the mute shell-fish gasping on the shore,
To men, to angels, to celestial minds
For ever leads the generations on
To higher scenes of being; while supplied
From day to day with his enlivening breath,
Inferior orders in succession rise
To fill the void below. As flame ascends,  350
As bodies to their proper centre move,
As the pois'd ocean to the attracting moon
Obedient swells, and every headlong stream
Devolves its winding waters to the main.;
So all things which have life aspire to God,

The sun of being, boundless, unimpair'd,
Centre of souls ! Nor does the faithful voice
Of Nature cease to prompt their eager steps
Aright ; nor is the care of Heaven withheld
From granting to the task porportion'd aid ;      360
That in their stations all may persevere
To climb the ascent of being, and approach
For ever nearer to the life divine.—
   " That rocky pile thou seest, that verdant lawn
Fresh-water'd from the mountains.   Let the scene
Paint in thy fancy the primeval seat
Of man, and where the Will Supreme ordain'd
His mansion, that pavilion fair-diffus'd
Along the shady brink; in this recess
To wear the appointed season of his youth,      370
Till riper hours should open to his toil
The high communion of superior minds,
Of consecrated heroes and of gods.
Nor did the Sire Omnipotent forget
His tender bloom to cherish; nor withheld
Celestial footsteps from his green abode.
Oft from the radiant honours of his throne,
He sent whom most he lov'd, the sovereign fair,
The effluence of his glory, whom he plac'd
Before his eyes for ever to behold;      380
The goddess from whose inspiration flows
The toil of patriots, the delight of friends ;
Without whose work divine, in heaven or earth,
Nought lovely, nought propitious comes to pass,
Nor hope, nor praise, nor honour.   Her the Sire
Gave it in charge to rear the blooming mind,
The folded powers to open, to direct
The growth luxuriant of his young desires,
And from the laws of this majestic world
To teach him what was good.   As thus the nymph
Her daily care attended, by her side
With constant steps her gay companion stay'd,
The fair Euphrosyné, the gentle queen
Of smiles, and graceful gladness, and delights

That cheer alike the hearts of mortal men
And powers immortal. See the shining pair!
Behold, where from his dwelling now disclos'd
They quit their youthful charge and seek the skies."
   I look'd, and on the flowery turf there stood
Between two radiant forms a smiling youth   400
Whose tender cheeks display'd the vernal flower
Of beauty: sweetest innocence illum'd
His bashful eyes, and on his polish'd brow
Sate young simplicity. With fond regard
He view'd the associates, as their steps they mov'd;
The younger chief his ardent eyes detain'd,
With mild regret invoking her return.
Bright as the star of evening she appear'd
Amid the dusky scene. Eternal youth
O'er all her form its glowing honours breath'd; 410
And smiles eternal from her candid eyes
Flow'd, like the dewy lustre of the morn
Effusive trembling on the placid waves.
The spring of heaven had shed its blushing spoils
To bind her sable tresses: full diffus'd
Her yellow mantle floated in the breeze;
And in her hand she wav'd a living branch
Rich with immortal fruits, of power to calm
The wrathful heart, and from the brightening eyes,
To chase the cloud of sadness. More sublime 420
The heavenly partner mov'd. The prime of age
Compos'd her steps. The presence of a god,
High on the circle of her brow enthron'd,
From each majestic motion darted awe,
Devoted awe! till, cherish'd by her looks
Benevolent and meek, confiding love
To filial rapture soften'd all the soul.
Free in her graceful hand she pois'd the sword
Of chaste dominion. An heroic crown
Display'd the old simplicity of pomp   430
Around her honour'd head. A matron's robe,
White as the sunshine streams through vernal clouds,
Her stately form invested. Hand in hand

The immortal pair forsook the enamel'd green,
Ascending slowly.   Rays of limpid light
Gleam'd round their path; celestial sounds were
        heard,
And through the fragrant air ethereal dews
Distill'd around them; till at once the clouds
Disparting wide in midway sky, withdrew
Their airy veil, and left a bright expanse       440
Of empyrean flame, where spent and drown'd,
Afflicted vision plung'd in vain to scan
What object it involv'd.   My feeble eyes
Endur'd not.   Bending down to earth I stood,
With dumb attention.   Soon a female voice,
As watery murmurs sweet, or warbling shades,
With sacred invocation thus began:
   " Father of gods and mortals! whose right arm
With reins eternal guides the moving heavens,
Bend thy propitious ear.   Behold well pleas'd   450
I seek to finish thy divine decree.
With frequent steps I visit yonder seat
Of man, thy offspring; from the tender seeds
Of justice and of wisdom, to evolve
The latent honours of his generous frame;
Till thy conducting hand shall raise his lot
From earth's dim scene to these ethereal walks,
The temple of thy glory.   But not me,
Not my directing voice he oft requires,
Or hears delighted: this enchanting maid,       460
The associate thou hast given me, her alone
He loves, O Father! absent, her he craves;
And but for her glad presence ever join'd,
Rejoices not in mine: that all my hopes
This thy benignant purpose to fulfil,
I deem uncertain: and my daily cares
Unfruitful all and vain, unless by thee
Still farther aided in the work divine."
   She ceas'd; a voice more awful thus replied:
" O thou! in whom for ever I delight,           470
Fairer than all the inhabitants of Heaven,

Best image of thy Author! far from thee
Be disappointment, or distaste, or blame;
Who soon or late shalt every work fulfil,
And no resistance find. If man refuse
To hearken to thy dictates; or, allur'd
By meaner joys, to any other power
Transfer the honours due to thee alone;
That joy which he pursues he ne'er shall taste,
That power in whom delighteth ne'er behold. 480
Go then, once more, and happy be thy toil;
Go then! but let not this thy smiling friend
Partake thy footsteps. In her stead, behold!
With thee the son of Nemesis I send;
The fiend abhorr'd! whose vengeance takes account
Of sacred order's violated laws.
See where he calls thee, burning to be gone,
Fierce to exhaust the tempest of his wrath
On yon devoted head. But thou, my child,
Control his cruel frenzy, and protect 490
Thy tender charge; that when despair shall grasp
His agonizing bosom, he may learn,
Then he may learn to love the gracious hand
Alone sufficient in the hour of ill,
To save his feeble spirit; then confess
Thy genuine honours, O excelling fair!
When all the plagues that wait the deadly will
Of this avenging demon, all the storms
Of night infernal, serve but to display
The energy of thy superior charms 500
With mildest awe triumphant o'er his rage,
And shining clearer in the horrid gloom."
    Here ceas'd that awful voice, and soon I felt
The cloudy curtain of refreshing eve
Was clos'd once more, from that immortal fire
Sheltering my eye-lids. Looking up, I view'd
A vast gigantic spectre striding on
Thro' murmuring thunders and a waste of clouds,
With dreadful action. Black as night his brow
Relentless frowns involv'd. His savage limbs 510

With sharp impatience violent he writh'd,
As through convulsive anguish ; and his hand,
Arm'd with a scorpion lash, full oft he rais'd
In madness to his bosom ; while his eyes
Rain'd bitter tears, and bellowing loud he shook
The void with horror.   Silent by his side
The virgin came.   No discomposure stirr'd
Her features.  From the glooms which hung around,
No stain of darkness mingled with the beam
Of her divine effulgence.   Now they stoop    520
Upon the river bank ; and now to hail
His wonted guests, with eager steps advanc'd
The unsuspecting inmate of the shade.
    As when a famish'd wolf, that all night long
Had rang'd the Alpine snows, by chance at morn
Sees from a cliff, incumbent o'er the smoke
Of some lone village, a neglected kid
That strays along the wild for herb or spring ;
Down from the winding ridge he sweeps amain,
And thinks he tears him : so with tenfold rage, 530
The monster sprung remorseless on his prey.
Amaz'd the stripling stood : with panting breast
Feebly he pour'd the lamentable wail
Of helpless consternation, struck at once,
And rooted to the ground.   The Queen beheld
His terror, and with looks of tenderest care
Advanc'd to save him.   Soon the tyrant felt
Her awful power.   His keen tempestuous arm
Hung nerveless, nor descended where his rage
Had aim'd the deadly blow : then dumb retir'd 540
With sullen rancour.   Lo! the sovereign maid
Folds with a mother's arms the fainting boy,
Till life rekindles in his rosy cheek ;        [tongue :
Then grasps his hands, and cheers him with her
    " O wake thee, rouse thy spirit! Shall the spite
Of yon tormentor thus appal thy heart,
While I, thy friend and guardian, am at hand
To rescue and to heal?   O let thy soul
Remember, what the will of heaven ordains

Is ever good for all; and if for all, 550
Then good for thee. Nor only by the warmth
And soothing sunshine of delightful things,
Do minds grow up and flourish. Oft misled
By that bland light, the young unpractis'd views
Of reason wander through a fatal road,
Far from their native aim: as if to lie
Inglorious in the fragrant shade, and wait
The soft access of ever circling joys,
Were all the end of being. Ask thyself,
This pleasing error did it never lull 560
Thy wishes? Has thy constant heart refus'd
The silken fetters of delicious ease?
Or when divine Euphrosyné appear'd
Within this dwelling, did not thy desires
Hang far below the measure of thy fate,
Which I reveal'd before thee? and thy eyes,
Impatient of my counsels, turn away
To drink the soft effusion of her smiles?
Know then, for this the everlasting Sire
Deprives thee of her presence, and instead, 570
O wise and still benevolent! ordains
This horrid visage hither to pursue
My steps; that so thy nature may discern
Its real good, and what alone can save
Thy feeble spirit in this hour of ill
From folly and despair. O yet belov'd!
Let not this headlong terror quite o'erwhelm
Thy scatter'd powers; nor fatal deem the rage
Of this tormentor, nor his proud assault,
While I am here to vindicate thy toil, 580
Above the generous question of thy arm.
Brave by thy fears and in thy weakness strong,
This hour he triumphs: but confront his might,
And dare him to the combat, then with ease
Disarm'd and quell'd, his fierceness he resigns
To bondage and to scorn: while thus inur'd
By watchful danger, by unceasing toil,
The immortal mind, superior to his fate,

Amid the outrage of external things,
Firm as the solid base of this great world,        590
Rests on his own foundations.   Blow, ye winds!
Ye waves! ye thunders! roll your tempest on;
Shake, ye old pillars of the marble sky!
Till all its orbs and all its worlds of fire
Be loosen'd from their seats; yet still serene,
The unconquer'd mind looks down upon the wreck;
And ever stronger as the storms advance,
Firm through the closing ruin holds his way,
Where Nature calls him to the destin'd goal."
    So spake the goddess; while through all her frame
Celestial raptures flow'd, in every word,
In every motion kindling warmth divine
To seize who listen'd.   Vehement and swift
As lightning fires the aromatic shade
In Æthiopian fields, the stripling felt
Her inspiration catch his fervid soul,
And starting from his languor thus exclaim'd:
    " Then let the trial come ! and witness thou,
If terror be upon me; if I shrink
To meet the storm, or falter in my strength        610
When hardest it besets me.   Do not think
That I am fearful and infirm of soul,
As late thy eyes beheld: for thou hast chang'd
My nature; thy commanding voice has wak'd
My languid powers to bear me boldly on,
Where'er the will divine my path ordains
Through toil or peril: only do not thou
Forsake me ; O be thou for ever near,
That I may listen to thy sacred voice,
And guide by thy decrees my constant feet.        620
But say, for ever are my eyes bereft ?
Say, shall the fair Euphrosyné not once
Appear again to charm me ?   Thou, in heaven !
O thou eternal arbiter of things !
Be thy great bidding done: for who am I,
To question thy appointment ?   Let the frowns
Of this avenger every morn o'ercast

The cheerful dawn, and every evening damp
With double night my dwelling; I will learn
To hail them both, and unrepining bear    630
His hateful presence: but permit my tongue
One glad request, and if my deeds may find
Thy awful eye propitious, O restore
The rosy-featured maid; again to cheer
This lonely seat, and bless me with her smiles."

He spoke; when instant through the sable glooms
With which that furious presence had involv'd
The ambient air, a flood of radiance came
Swift as the lightning flash; the melting clouds
Flew diverse, and amid the blue serene    640
Euphrosyné appear'd. With sprightly step
The nymph alighted on the irriguous lawn,
And to her wondering audience thus began:

"Lo! I am here to answer to your vows,
And be the meeting fortunate! I come
With joyful tidings; we shall part no more—
Hark! how the gentle echo from her cell
Talks through the cliffs, and murmuring o'er the
      stream
Repeats the accents; we shall part no more.—
O my delightful friends! well pleas'd on high    650
The Father has beheld you, while the might
Of that stern foe with bitter trial prov'd
Your equal doings: then for ever spake
The high decree; that thou, celestial maid!
Howe'er that grisly phantom on thy steps
May sometimes dare intrude, yet never more
Shalt thou, descending to the abode of man,
Alone endure the rancour of his arm,
Or leave thy lov'd Euphrosyné behind."

She ended; and the whole romantic scene    660
Immediate vanish'd; rocks, and woods, and rills,
The mantling tent, and each mysterious form
Flew like the pictures of a morning dream,
When sunshine fills the bed. Awhile I stood
Perplex'd and giddy; till the radiant power

Who bade the visionary landscape rise,
As up to him I turn'd, with gentlest looks
Preventing my enquiry, thus began:
  " There let thy soul acknowledge its complaint
How blind, how impious!   There behold the ways
Of Heaven's eternal destiny to man,
For ever just, benevolent, and wise:
That Virtue's awful steps, howe'er pursu'd
By vexing fortune and intrusive pain,
Should never be divided from her chaste,
Her fair attendant, Pleasure.   Need I urge
Thy tardy thought through all the various round
Of this existence, that thy softening soul
At length may learn what energy the hand
Of virtue mingles in the bitter tide                680
Of passion swelling with distress and pain,
To mitigate the sharp with gracious drops
Of cordial pleasure?   Ask the faithful youth,
Why the cold urn of her whom long he lov'd
So often fills his arms; so often draws
His lonely footsteps at the silent hour,
To pay the mournful tribute of his tears?
O! he will tell thee, that the wealth of worlds
Should ne'er seduce his bosom to forego
That sacred hour, when, stealing from the noise
Of care and envy, sweet remembrance soothes
With virtue's kindest looks his aching breast,
And turns his tears to rapture.—Ask the crowd
Which flies impatient from the village walk
To climb the neighbouring cliffs, when far below
The cruel winds have hurl'd upon the coast
Some helpless bark; while sacred Pity melts
The general eye, or Terror's icy hand
Smites their distorted limbs and horrent hair;
While every mother closer to her breast          700
Catches her child, and pointing where the waves
Foam through the shatter'd vessel, shrieks aloud
As one poor wretch that spreads his piteous arms
For succour, swallow'd by the roaring surge,

As now another, dash'd against the rock,
Drops lifeless down: O! deemest thou indeed
No kind endearment here by Nature given
To mutual terror and compassion's tears?
No sweetly melting softness which attracts,
O'er all that edge of pain, the social powers          710
To this their proper action and their end?
—Ask thy own heart; when at the midnight hour,
Slow through that studious gloom thy pausing eye
Led by the glimmering taper moves around
The sacred volumes of the dead, the songs
Of Grecian bards, and records writ by Fame
For Grecian heroes, where the present power
Of heaven and earth surveys the immortal page,
Even as a father blessing, while he reads
The praises of his son.  If then thy soul,          720
Spurning the yoke of these inglorious days,
Mix in their deeds, and kindle with their flame;
Say, when the prospect blackens on thy view,
When rooted from the base, heroic states
Mourn in the dust, and tremble at the frown
Of curst ambition; when the pious band
Of youths who fought for freedom and their sires,
Lie side by side in gore; when ruffian pride
Usurps the throne of Justice, turns the pomp
Of public power, the majesty of rule,          730
The sword, the laurel, and the purple robe,
To slavish empty pageants, to adorn
A tyrant's walk, and glitter in the eyes
Of such as bow the knee; when honour'd urns
Of patriots and of chiefs, the awful bust
And storied arch, to glut the coward rage
Of regal envy, strew the public way
With hallow'd ruins; when the Muse's haunt,
The marble porch where Wisdom wont to talk
With Socrates or Tully, hears no more,          740
Save the hoarse jargon of contentious monks,
Or female Superstition's midnight prayer;
When ruthless Rapine from the hand of Time

I

Tears the destroying scythe, with surer blow
To sweep the works of glory from their base;
Till Desolation o'er the grass-grown street
Expands his raven wings, and up the wall,
Where senates once the price of monarchs doom'd,
Hisses the gliding snake through hoary weeds
That clasp the mouldering column; thus defac'd,
Thus widely mournful when the prospect thrills
Thy beating bosom, when the patriot's tear
Starts from thine eye, and thy extended arm
In fancy hurls the thunderbolt of Jove
To fire the impious wreath on Philip's brow,
Or dash Octavius from the trophied car;
Say, does thy secret soul repine to taste
The big distress? Or would'st thou then exchange
Those heart-ennobling sorrows for the lot
Of him who sits amid the gaudy herd            760
Of mute barbarians bending to his nod,
And bears aloft his gold-invested front,
And says within himself, 'I am a king,
And wherefore should the clamorous voice of woe
Intrude upon mine ear?'—The baleful dregs
Of these late ages, this inglorious draught
Of servitude and folly, have not yet,
Blest be the eternal Ruler of the world!
Defil'd to such a depth of sordid shame
The native honours of the human soul,          770
Nor so effac'd the image of its Sire."

# BOOK III.

WHAT wonder therefore, since the endearing
      ties
Of passion link the universal kind
Of man so close, what wonder if to search
This common nature through the various change
Of sex, and age, and fortune, and the frame
Of each peculiar, draw the busy mind
With unresisted charms?   The spacious west,
And all the teeming regions of the south,
Hold not a quarry, to the curious flight
Of Knowledge, half so tempting or so fair,    10
As man to man.   Nor only where the smiles
Of Love invite; nor only where the applause
Of cordial Honour turns the attentive eye
On Virtue's graceful deeds.   For since the course
Of things external acts in different ways
On human apprehensions, as the hand
Of Nature temper'd to a different frame
Peculiar minds; so haply where the powers

Of Fancy neither lessen nor enlarge
The images of things, but paint in all              20
Their genuine hues, the features which they wore
In Nature ; there Opinion will be true,
And Action right.    For Action treads the path
In which Opinion says he follows good,
Or flies from evil ; and Opinion gives
Report of good or evil, as the scene
Was drawn by Fancy, lovely or deform'd :
Thus her report can never there be true
Where Fancy cheats the intellectual eye,
With glaring colours and distorted lines.           30
Is there a man, who at the sound of death
Sees ghastly shapes of terror conjur'd up,
And black before him ; nought but deathbed groans
And fearful prayers, and plunging from the brink
Of light and being, down the gloomy air,
An unknown depth ?    Alas ! in such a mind,
If no bright forms of excellence attend
The image of his country ; nor the pomp
Of sacred senates, nor the guardian voice
Of Justice on her throne, nor aught that wakes   40
The conscious bosom with a patriot's flame ;
Will not Opinion tell him, that to die,
Or stand the hazard, is a greater ill
Than to betray his country ?    And in act
Will he not choose to be a wretch and live ?
Here vice begins then.    From the enchanting cup
Which Fancy holds to all, the unwary thirst
Of youth oft swallows a Circæan draught,
That sheds a baleful tincture o'er the eye
Of Reason, till no longer he discerns,              50
And only guides to err.    Then revel forth
A furious band that spurn him from the throne ;
And all is uproar.    Thus ambition grasps
The empire of the soul : thus pale Revenge
Unsheaths her murderous dagger ; and the hands
Of Lust and Rapine, with unholy arts,
Watch to o'erturn the barrier of the laws

That keeps them from their prey : thus all the
    plagues
The wicked bear, or o'er the trembling scene
The tragic Muse discloses, under shapes     60
Of honour, safety, pleasure, ease, or pomp,
Stole first into the mind.  Yet not by all
Those lying forms which Fancy in the brain
Engenders, are the kindling passions driven
To guilty deeds; nor Reason bound in chains,
That Vice alone may lord it : oft adorn'd
With solemn pageants, Folly mounts the throne,
And plays her idiot antics, like a queen.
A thousand garbs she wears ; a thousand ways
She wheels her giddy empire.—Lo ! thus far   70
With bold adventure, to the Mantuan lyre
I sing of Nature's charms, and touch well pleas'd
A stricter note : now haply must my song
Unbend her serious measure, and reveal
In lighter strains, how Folly's awkward arts
Excite impetuous Laughter's gay rebuke ;
The sportive province of the comic Muse.
    See ! in what crowds the uncouth forms advance :
Each would outstrip the other, each prevent
Our careful search, and offer to your gaze,   80
Unask'd, his motley features.  Wait awhile,
My curious friends ! and let us first arrange
In proper order your promiscuous throng.
    Behold the foremost band ; of slender thought,
And easy faith ; whom flattering Fancy soothes
With lying spectres, in themselves to view
Illustrious forms of excellence and good,
That scorn the mansion.  With exulting hearts
They spread their spurious treasures to the sun,
And bid the world admire ! but chief the glance
Of wishful Envy draws their joy-bright eyes,
And lifts with self-applause each lordly brow.
In number boundless as the blooms of Spring,
Behold their glaring idols, empty shades
By Fancy gilded o'er, and then set up

For adoration.   Some in Learning's garb,
With formal band, and sable-cinctur'd gown,
And rags of mouldy volumes.   Some elate
With martial splendour, steely pikes and swords
Of costly frame, and gay Phœnician robes      100
Inwrought with flowery gold, assume the port
Of stately Valour : listening by his side
There stands a female form ; to her, with looks
Of earnest import, pregnant with amaze,
He talks of deadly deeds, of breaches, storms,
And sulphurous mines, and ambush : then at once
Breaks off, and smiles to see her look so pale,
And asks some wondering question of her fears.
Others of graver mien ; behold, adorn'd
With holy ensigns, how sublime they move,      110
And bending oft their sanctimonious eyes
Take homage of the simple-minded throng ;
Ambassadors of Heaven !   Nor much unlike
Is he whose visage in the lazy mist
That mantles every feature, hides a brood
Of politic conceits ; of whispers, nods,
And hints deep omen'd with unwieldy schemes,
And dark portents of state.   Ten thousand more,
Prodigious habits and tumultuous tongues,
Pour dauntless in and swell the boastful band.   120
   Then comes the second order ; all who seek
The debt of praise, where watchful Unbelief
Darts through the thin pretence her squinting eye
On some retir'd appearance which belies
The boasted virtue, or annuls the applause
That justice else would pay.   Here side by side
I see two leaders of the solemn train
Approaching : one a female old and gray,
With eyes demure, and wrinkle-furrow'd brow,
Pale as the cheeks of death ; yet still she stuns   130
The sickening audience with a nauseous tale ;
How many youths her myrtle chains have worn,
How many virgins at her triumphs pin'd !
Yet how resolv'd she guards her cautious heart ;

Such is her terror at the risks of love,
And man's seducing tongue! The other seems
A bearded sage, ungentle in his mien,
And sordid all his habit; peevish Want
Grins at his heels, while down the gazing throng
He stalks, resounding in magnific praise     140
The vanity of riches, the contempt
Of pomp and power. Be prudent in your zeal,
Ye grave associates! let the silent grace
Of her who blushes at the fond regard
Her charms inspire, more eloquent unfold
The praise of spotless honour: let the man
Whose eye regards not his illustrious pomp
And ample store, but as indulgent streams
To cheer the barren soil and spread the fruits
Of joy, let him by juster measures fix     150
The price of riches and the end of power.
    Another tribe succeeds; deluded long
By Fancy's dazzling optics, these behold
The images of some peculiar things
With brighter hues resplendent, and portray'd
With features nobler far than e'er adorn'd
Their genuine objects. Hence the fever'd heart
Pants with delirious hope for tinsel charms;
Hence oft obtrusive on the eye of scorn,
Untimely zeal her witless pride betrays!     160
And serious manhood from the towering aim
Of wisdom, stoops to emulate the boast
Of childish toil. Behold yon mystic form,
Bedeck'd with feathers, insects, weeds, and shells!
Not with intenser view the Samian sage
Bent his fix'd eye on heaven's intenser fires,
When first the order of that radiant scene
Swell'd his exulting thought, than this surveys
A muckworm's entrails or a spider's fang.
Next him a youth, with flowers and myrtles crown'd,
Attends that virgin form, and blushing kneels,
With fondest gesture and a suppliant's tongue,
To win her coy regard: adieu, for him,

The dull engagements of the bustling world!
Adieu the sick impertinence of praise!
And hope, and action! for with her alone,
By streams and shades, to steal these sighing hours,
Is all he asks, and all that fate can give!
Thee too, facetious Momion, wandering here,
Thee, dreaded censor, oft have I beheld          180
Bewilder'd unawares: alas! too long
Flush'd with thy comic triumphs and the spoils
Of sly derision! till on every side
Hurling thy random bolts, offended Truth
Assign'd thee here thy station with the slaves
Of Folly.  Thy once formidable name
Shall grace her humble records, and be heard
In scoffs and mockery bandied from the lips
Of all the vengeful brotherhood around,
So oft the patient victims of thy scorn.          190
    But now, ye gay! to whom indulgent fate,
Of all the Muse's empire hath assign'd
The fields of folly, hither each advance
Your sickles; here the teeming soil affords
Its richest growth.  A favourite brood appears;
In whom the demon, with a mother's joy,
Views all her charms reflected, all her cares
At full repaid.  Ye most illustrious band!
Who, scorning Reason's tame, pedantic rules,
And Order's vulgar bondage, never meant          200
For souls sublime as yours, with generous zeal
Pay Vice the reverence Virtue long usurp'd,
And yield Deformity the fond applause
Which Beauty wont to claim; forgive my song,
That for the blushing diffidence of youth,
It shuns the unequal province of your praise.
    Thus far triumphant in the pleasing guile
Of bland Imagination, Folly's train
Have dar'd our search: but now a dastard kind
Advance reluctant, and with faltering feet          210
Shrink from the gazer's eye: enfeebled hearts
Whom Fancy chills with visionary fears,

Or bends to servile tameness with conceits
Of shame, of evil, or of base defect,
Fantastic and delusive.   Here the slave
Who droops abash'd when sullen Pomp surveys
His humbler habit; here the trembling wretch
Unnerv'd and struck with Terror's icy bolts,
Spent in weak wailings, drown'd in shameful tears,
At every dream of danger : here subdued        220
By frontless laughter and the hardy scorn
Of old, unfeeling vice, the abject soul,
Who blushing half resigns the candid praise
Of Temperance and Honour ; half disowns
A freeman's hatred of tyrannic pride ;
And hears with sickly smiles the venal mouth
With foulest license mock the patriot's name.
    Last of the motley bands on whom the power
Of gay Derision bends her hostile aim,
Is that where shameful Ignorance presides.        230
Beneath her sordid banners, lo ! they march
Like blind and lame.  Whate'er their doubtful hands
Attempt, Confusion straight appears behind,
And troubles all the work.   Thro' many a maze,
Perplex'd they struggle, changing every path,
O'erturning every purpose ; then at last
Sit down dismay'd, and leave the entangled scene
For Scorn to sport with.   Such then is the abode
Of Folly in the mind ; and such the shapes
In which she governs her obsequious train.        240
    Through every scene of ridicule in things
To lead the tenor of my devious lay ;
Through every swift occasion, which the hand
Of Laughter points at, when the mirthful sting
Distends her sallying nerves and chokes her tongue ;
What were it but to count each crystal drop
Which Morning's dewy fingers on the blooms
Of May distill ?   Suffice it to have said,
Where'er the power of Ridicule displays
Her quaint ey'd visage, some incongruous form,
Some stubborn dissonance of things combin'd

Strikes on the quick observer : whether Pomp,
Or Praise, or Beauty, mix their partial claim
Where sordid fashions, where ignoble deeds,
Where foul Deformity are wont to dwell ;
Or whether these with violation loath'd,
Invade resplendent Pomp's imperious mien,
The charms of Beauty, or the boast of Praise.
  Ask we for what fair end, the Almighty Sire
In mortal bosoms wakes this gay contempt,       260
These grateful stings of laughter, from disgust
Educing pleasure ?   Wherefore, but to aid
The tardy steps of Reason, and at once
By this prompt impulse urge us to depress
The giddy aims of Folly ?   Though the light
Of Truth slow dawning on the enquiring mind,
At length unfolds, through many a subtile tie,
How these uncouth disorders end at last
In public evil ! yet benignant Heaven,
Conscious how dim the dawn of truth appears   270
To thousands ; conscious what a scanty pause
From labours and from care, the wider lot
Of humble life affords for studious thought
To scan the maze of Nature ; therefore stamp'd
The glaring scenes with characters of scorn,
As broad, as obvious, to the passing clown,
As to the letter'd sage's curious eye.
  Such are the various aspects of the mind—
Some heavenly genius, whose unclouded thoughts
Attain that secret harmony which blends       280
The etherial spirit with its mould of clay ;
O ! teach me to reveal the grateful charm
That searchless Nature o'er the sense of man
Diffuses, to behold, in lifeless things,
The inexpressive semblance of himself,
Of thought and passion.   Mark the sable woods
That shade sublime yon mountain's nodding brow ;
With what religious awe the solemn scene
Commands your steps ! as if the reverend form
Of Minos or of Numa should forsake       290

The Elysian seats, and down the embowering glade
Move to your pausing eye! Behold the expanse
Of yon gay landscape, where the silver clouds
Flit o'er the heavens before the sprightly breeze :
Now their gray cincture skirts the doubtful sun ;
Now streams of splendour, thro' their opening veil
Effulgent, sweep from off the gilded lawn
The aërial shadows ; on the curling brook,
And on the shady margin's quivering leaves
With quickest lustre glancing; while you view    300
The prospect, say, within your cheerful breast
Plays not the lively sense of winning mirth
With clouds and sunshine chequer'd, while the round
Of social converse, to the inspiring tongue
Of some gay nymph amid her subject train,
Moves all obsequious ?   Whence is this effect,
This kindred power of such discordant things ?
Or flows their semblance from that mystic tone
To which the new-born mind's harmonious powers
At first were strung ?   Or rather from the links
Which artful custom twines around her frame ?
  For when the different images of things,
By chance combin'd, have struck the attentive soul
With deeper impulse, or connected long,
Have drawn her frequent eye; howe'er distinct
The external scenes, yet oft the ideas gain
From that conjunction an eternal tie,
And sympathy unbroken.   Let the mind
Recall one partner of the various league,
Immediate, lo! the firm confederates rise,    320
And each his former station straight resumes :
One movement governs the consenting throng,
And all at once with rosy pleasure shine,
Or all are sadden'd with the glooms of care.
'Twas thus, if ancient fame the truth unfold,
Two faithful needles, from the informing touch
Of the same parent stone, together drew
Its mystic virtue, and at first conspir'd
With fatal impulse quivering to the pole :

Then, tho' disjoin'd by kingdoms, tho' the main
Roll'd its broad surge betwixt, and different stars
Beheld their wakeful motions, yet preserv'd
The former friendship, and remember'd still
The alliance of their birth : whate'er the line
Which one possess'd, nor pause, nor quiet knew
The sure associate, ere with trembling speed
He found its path and fix'd unerring there.
Such is the secret union, when we feel
A song, a flower, a name, at once restore
Those long connected scenes where first they mov'd
The attention : backward thro' her mazy walks
Guiding the wanton fancy to her scope,
To temples, courts or fields ; with all the band
Of painted forms, of passions and designs
Attendant : whence, if pleasing in itself,
The prospect from that sweet accession gains
Redoubled influence o'er the listening mind.
   By these mysterious ties, the busy power
Of Memory her ideal train preserves
Entire ; or when they would elude her watch,     350
Reclaims their fleeting footsteps from the waste
Of dark oblivion ; thus collecting all
The various forms of being to present,
Before the curious aim of mimic art,
Their largest choice : like Spring's unfolded blooms
Exhaling sweetness, that the skilful bee
May taste at will, from their selected spoils
To work her dulcet food.   For not the expanse
Of living lakes in Summer's noontide calm,
Reflects the bordering shade, and sun-bright heavens
With fairer semblance ; not the sculptur'd gold
More faithful keeps the graver's lively trace,
Than he whose birth the sister powers of art
Propitious view'd, and from his genial star
Shed influence to the seeds of fancy kind ;
Than his attemper'd bosom must preserve
The seal of Nature.   There alone unchang'd,
Her form remains.   The balmy walks of May

There breathe perennial sweets : the trembling chord
Resounds for ever in the abstracted ear,                370
Melodious : and the virgin's radiant eye,
Superior to disease, to grief, and time,
Shines with unbating lustre.   Thus at length
Endow'd with all that nature can bestow,
The child of Fancy oft in silence bends
O'er these mixt treasures of his pregnant breast,
With conscious pride.   From them he oft resolves
To frame he knows not what excelling things ;
And win he knows not what sublime reward
Of praise and wonder.   By degrees, the mind   380
Feels her young nerves dilate : the plastic powers
Labour for action : blind emotions heave
His bosom ; and with loveliest frenzy caught,
From earth to heaven he rolls his daring eye,
From heaven to earth.   Anon ten thousand shapes,
Like spectres trooping to the wizard's call,
Flit swift before him.   From the womb of earth,
From ocean's bed they come : the eternal heavens
Disclose their splendours, and the dark abyss
Pours out her births unknown.   With fixed gaze
He marks the rising phantoms.   Now compares
Their different forms ; now blends them, now divides,
Enlarges and extenuates by turns ;
Opposes, ranges in fantastic bands,
And infinitely varies.   Hither now,
Now thither fluctuates his inconstant aim,
With endless choice perplex'd.   At length his plan
Begins to open.   Lucid order dawns ;
And as from Chaos old the jarring seeds
Of Nature at the voice divine repair'd                400
Each to its place, till rosy earth unveil'd
Her fragrant bosom, and the joyful sun
Sprung up the blue serene ; by swift degrees
Thus disentangled, his entire design
Emerges.   Colours mingle, features join,
And lines converge : the fainter parts retire ;
The fairer eminent in light advance ;

And every image on its neighbour smiles.
Awhile he stands, and with a father's joy
Contemplates.　Then with Promethéan art,　410
Into its proper vehicle he breathes
The fair conception; which, embodied thus,
And permanent, becomes to eyes or ears
An object ascertain'd: while thus inform'd,
The various organs of his mimic skill,
The consonance of sounds, the featur'd rock,
The shadowy picture and impassion'd verse,
Beyond their proper powers attract the soul
By that expressive semblance, while in sight
Of Nature's great original we scan　　　420
The lively child of Art; while line by line,
And feature after feature we refer
To that sublime exemplar whence it stole
Those animating charms.　Thus Beauty's palm
Betwixt them wavering hangs : applauding Love
Doubts where to choose; and mortal man aspires
To tempt creative praise.　As when a cloud
Of gathering hail with limpid crusts of ice
Inclos'd and obvious to the beaming sun,
Collects his large effulgence ; straight the heavens
With equal flames present on either hand
The radiant visage: Persia stands at gaze,
Appall'd ; and on the brink of Ganges doubts
The snowy-vested seer, in Mithra's name,
To which the fragrance of the south shall burn,
To which his warbled orisons ascend.
　　Such various bliss the well-tun'd heart enjoys,
Favour'd of Heaven ! while plung'd in sordid cares,
The unfeeling vulgar mocks the boon divine :
And harsh Austerity, from whose rebuke　　440
Young Love and smiling Wonder shrink away
Abash'd and chill of heart, with sager frowns
Condemns the fair enchantment.　On my strain,
Perhaps even now, some cold, fastidious judge
Casts a disdainful eye ; and calls my toil,
And calls the love and beauty which I sing,

The dream of folly.   Thou, grave censor! say,
Is Beauty then a dream, because the glooms
Of dulness hang too heavy on thy sense,
To let her shine upon thee ?   So the man      450
Whose eye ne'er open'd on the light of heaven,
Might smile with scorn while raptur'd vision tells
Of the gay-colour'd radiance flushing bright
O'er all creation.   From the wise be far
Such gross unhallow'd pride ; nor needs my song
Descend so low; but rather now unfold,
If human thought could reach, or words unfold,
By what mysterious fabric of the mind,
The deep-felt joys and harmony of sound
Result from airy motion ; and from shape      460
The lovely phantoms of sublime and fair.
By what fine ties hath God connected things
When present in the mind, which in themselves
Have no connection ?   Sure the rising sun
O'er the cerulean convex of the sea,
With equal brightness and with equal warmth
Might roll his fiery orb ; nor yet the soul
Thus feel her frame expanded, and her powers
Exulting in the splendour she beholds ;
Like a young conqueror moving through the pomp
Of some triumphal day.   When join'd at eve,
Soft murmuring streams and gales of gentlest breath
Melodius Philomela's wakeful strain
Attemper, could not man's discerning ear
Through all its tones the sympathy pursue ;
Nor yet this breath divine of nameless joy
Steal thro' his veins and fan the awaken'd heart,
Mild as the breeze, yet rapturous as the song.
But were not Nature still endow'd at large
With all which life requires, tho' unadorn'd      480
With such enchantment ? Wherefore then her form
So exquisitely fair ? her breath perfum'd
With such ethereal sweetness ? whence her voice
Inform'd at will to raise or to depress
The impassion'd soul ? and whence the robes of light

Which thus invest her with more lovely pomp
Than Fancy can describe? Whence but from Thee,
O source divine of ever-flowing love,
And thy unmeasur'd goodness?   Not content
With every food of life to nourish man,          490
By kind illusions of the wondering sense
Thou mak'st all Nature beauty to his eye,
Or music to his ear: well-pleas'd he scans
The goodly prospect; and with inward smiles
Treads the gay verdure of the painted plain;
Beholds the azure canopy of heaven,
And living lamps that over-arch his head
With more than regal splendour; bends his ears
To the full choir of water, air, and earth;
Nor heeds the pleasing error of his thought,     500
Nor doubts the painted green or azure arch,
Nor questions more the music's mingling sounds,
Than space, or motion, or eternal time;
So sweet he feels their influence to attract
The fixed soul; to brighten the dull glooms
Of care, and make the destin'd road of life
Delightful to his feet.   So fables tell,
The adventurous hero, bound on hard exploits,
Beholds with glad surprise, by secret spells
Of some kind sage, the patron of his toils,      510
A visionary paradise disclos'd
Amid the dubious wild: with streams, and shades,
And airy songs, the enchanted landscape smiles,
Cheers his long labours and renews his frame.
     What then is taste, but these internal powers
Active, and strong, and feelingly alive
To each fine impulse? a discerning sense
Of decent and sublime, with quick disgust
From things deform'd, or disarrang'd, or gross
In species? This, nor gems, nor stores of gold,  520
Nor purple state, nor culture can bestow;
But God alone, when first his active hand
Imprints the secret bias of the soul.
He, mighty Parent! wise and just in all,

Free as the vital breeze or light of heaven,
Reveals the charms of Nature.   Ask the swain
Who journeys homeward from a summer day's
Long labour, why, forgetful of his toils
And due repose, he loiters to behold
The sunshine gleaming as thro' amber clouds,   530
O'er all the western sky; full soon, I ween,
His rude expression and untutor'd airs,
Beyond the power of language, will unfold
The form of beauty, smiling at his heart,
How lovely! how commanding! But tho' Heaven
In every breast hath sown these early seeds
Of love and admiration, yet in vain,
Without fair culture's kind parental aid,
Without enlivening suns, and genial showers,
And shelter from the blast, in vain we hope   540
The tender plant should rear its blooming head,
Or yield the harvest promis'd in its spring.
Nor yet will every soil with equal stores
Repay the tiller's labour ; or attend
His will, obsequious, whether to produce
The olive or the laurel.   Different minds
Incline to different objects ; one pursues
The vast alone, the wonderful, the wild ;
Another sighs for harmony, and grace,
And gentlest beauty.   Hence when lightning fires
The arch of heaven, and thunders rock the ground,
When furious whirlwinds rend the howling air,
And ocean, groaning from his lowest bed,
Heaves his tempestuous billows to the sky ;
Amid the mighty uproar, while below
The nations tremble, Shakespeare looks abroad
From some high cliff, superior, and enjoys
The elemental war.   But Waller longs,
All on the margin of some flowery stream
To spread his careless limbs amid the cool   560
Of plantane shades, and to the listening deer
The tale of slighted vows and love's disdain
Resound soft-warbling all the livelong day :

K

Consenting Zephyr sighs ; the weeping rill
Joins in his plaint, melodious ; mute the groves ;
And hill and dale with all their echoes mourn.
Such and so various are the tastes of men.
   Oh! blest of Heaven, whom not the languid songs
Of Luxury, the Siren ! not the bribes
Of sordid Wealth, nor all the gaudy spoils    570
Of pageant Honour can seduce to leave
Those ever-blooming sweets, which from the store
Of Nature fair Imagination culls
To charm the enliven'd soul !   What tho' not all
Of mortal offspring can attain the heights
Of envied life ; though only few possess
Patrician treasures or imperial state ;
Yet Nature's care, to all her children just,
With richer treasures and an ampler state,
Endows at large whatever happy man    580
Will deign to use them.   His the city's pomp,
The rural honours his.   Whate'er adorns
The princely dome, the column and the arch,
The breathing marbles and the sculptur'd gold,
Beyond the proud possessor's narrow claim,
His tuneful breast enjoys.   For him, the Spring
Distills her dews, and from the silken gem
Its lucid leaves unfolds : for him, the hand
Of Autumn tinges every fertile branch
With blooming gold and blushes like the morn.    590
Each passing Hour sheds tribute from her wings ;
And still new beauties meet his lonely walk,
And loves unfelt attract him.   Not a breeze
Flies o'er the meadow, not a cloud imbibes
The setting sun's effulgence, not a strain
From all the tenants of the warbling shade
Ascends, but whence his bosom can partake
Fresh pleasure, unreprov'd.   Nor thence partakes
Fresh pleasure only : for the attentive mind,
By this harmonious action on her powers    600
Becomes herself harmonious : wont so oft
In outward things to meditate the charm

Of sacred order, soon she seeks at home
To find a kindred order, to exert
Within herself this elegance of love,
This fair-inspir'd delight : her temper'd powers
Refine at length, and every passion wears
A chaster, milder, more attractive mien.
But if to ampler prospects, if to gaze
On Nature's form, where, negligent of all          610
These lesser graces, she assumes the port
Of that Eternal Majesty that weigh'd
The world's foundations, if to these the mind
Exalts her daring eye; then mightier far
Will be the change, and nobler.  Would the forms
Of servile custom cramp her generous powers ?
Would sordid policies, the barbarous growth
Of ignorance and rapine, bow her down
To tame pursuits, to indolence and fear?
Lo ! she appeals to Nature, to the winds          620
And rolling waves, the sun's unwearied course,
The elements and seasons : all declare
For what the Eternal Maker has ordain'd
The powers of man : we feel within ourselves
His energy divine : he tells the heart,
He meant, he made us to behold and love
What he beholds and loves, the general orb
Of life and being ; to be great like him,
Beneficent and active.  Thus the men
Whom Nature's works can charm, with God himself
Hold converse ; grow familiar, day by day,
With his conceptions, act upon his plan ;
And form to his, the relish of their souls.

## NOTES ON BOOK I.

Ver. 151. *Say why was man*, &c.] In apologizing for the frequent negligences of the sublimest authors of Greece, " Those god-like geniuses," says Longinus, " were well assured, that Nature had not intended man for a low-spirited or ignoble being : but bringing us into life and the midst of this wide universe, as before a multitude assembled at some heroic solemnity, that we might be spectators of all her magnificence, and candidates high in emulation for the prize of glory; she has therefore implanted in our souls an inextinguishable love of every thing great and exalted, of every thing which appears divine beyond our comprehension. Whence it comes to pass, that even the whole world is not an object sufficient for the depth and rapidity of human imagination, which often sallies forth beyond the limits of all that surrounds us. Let any man cast his eye through the whole circle of our existence, and consider how especially it abounds in excellent and grand objects, he will soon acknowledge for what enjoyments and pursuits we were destined. Thus by the very propensity of nature we are led to admire, not little springs or shallow rivulets, however clear and delicious, but the Nile, the Rhine, the Danube, and, much more than all, the Ocean," &c. Dionys. Longin. de Sublim. § xxiv.

Ver. 202. *The empyreal waste.*] " Ne se peut-il point qu'il y a un grand espace au dela de la region des etoiles ? Que ce soit le ciel empyrée, ou non, toujours cet espace immense qui environne toute cette region, pourra etre rempli de bonheur et de gloire. Il pourra etre conçu comme l'ocean, où se rendent les fleuves de toutes les creatures bien-heureuses, quand elles seront venues à leur perfection dans le systeme des etoiles." Leibnitz dans la Theodicee, part. i. § 19.

Ver. 204. *Whose unfading light*, &c.] It was a notion of the great Mr. Huygens, that there may be fixed stars at such a distance from our solar system, as that their light should not have had time to reach us, even from the creation of the world to this day.

Ver. 234. ——————— *the neglect*
        *Of all familiar prospects*, &c.] It is here said,

that in consequence of the love of novelty, objects which at first were highly delightful to the mind, lose that effect by repeated attention to them. But the instance of habit is opposed to this observation; for there, objects at first distasteful are in time rendered entirely agreeable by repeated attention.

The difficulty in this case will be removed, if we consider, that, when objects at first agreeable, lose that influence by frequently recurring, the mind is wholly passive, and the perception involuntary; but habit, on the other hand, generally supposes choice and activity accompanying it: so that the pleasure arises here not from the object, but from the mind's conscious determination of its own activity; and consequently increases in proportion to the frequency of that determination.

It will still be urged perhaps, that a familiarity with disagreeable objects renders them at length acceptable, even when there is no room for the mind to resolve or act at all. In this case, the appearance must be accounted for one of these ways.

The pleasure from habit may be merely negative. The object at first gave uneasiness: this uneasiness gradually wears off as the object grows familiar: and the mind, finding it at last entirely removed, reckons its situation really pleasurable, compared with what it had experienced before.

The dislike conceived of the object at first, might be owing to prejudice or want of attention. Consequently the mind being necessitated to review it often, may at length perceive its own mistake, and be reconciled to what it had looked on with aversion. In which case, a sort of instinctive justice naturally leads it to make amends for the injury, by running toward the other extreme of fondness and attachment.

Or lastly, though the object itself should always continue disagreeable, yet circumstances of pleasure or good fortune may occur along with it. Thus an association may arise in the mind, and the object never be remembered without those pleasing circumstances attending it; by which means the disagreeable impression which it at first occasioned will in time be quite obliterated.

Ver. 240. ——————— *this desire*
*Of objects new and strange*—.] These two ideas are oft confounded; though it is evident the mere novelty of an object makes it agreeable, even where the mind is not affected with the least degree of wonder: whereas wonder indeed always implies novelty, being never excited by common or well-known appearances. But the pleasure in both cases is explicable from the same final cause, the acquisi-

tion of knowledge and enlargement of our views of nature: on this account, it is natural to treat of them together.

Ver. 374. —— *Truth and good are one,*
                    *And beauty dwells in them,* &c.] " Do you imagine," says Socrates to Aristippus, " that what is good is not beautiful? Have you not observed that these appearances always coincide? Virtue, for instance, in the same respect as to which we call it good, is ever acknowledged to be beautiful also. In the characters of men we always* join the two denominations together. The beauty of human bodies corresponds, in like manner, with that economy of parts which constitutes them good ; and in every circumstance of life, the same object is constantly accounted both beautiful and good, inasmuch as it answers the purposes for which it was designed." Xenophont. Memorab. Socrat. l. iii. c. 8.

This excellent observation has been illustrated and extended by the noble restorer of ancient philosophy ; see the Characteristics, vol. ii. pp. 339 and 422, and vol. iii. p. 181. And another ingenious author has particularly shown, that it holds in the general laws of nature, in the works of art, and the conduct of the sciences. Inquiry into the original of our ideas of beauty and virtue, Treat. i. § 8. As to the connection between beauty and truth, there are two opinions concerning it. Some philosophers assert an independent and invariable law in nature, in consequence of which all rational beings must alike perceive beauty in some certain proportions, and deformity in the contrary. And this necessity being supposed the same with that which commands the assent or dissent of the understanding, it follows of course that beauty is founded on the universal and unchangeable law of truth.

But others there are, who believe beauty to be merely a relative and arbitrary thing ; that indeed it was a benevolent provision in nature to annex so delightful a sensation to those objects which are best and most perfect in themselves, that so we might be engaged to the choice of them at once and without staying to infer their usefulness from their structure and effects; but that it is not impossible, in a physical sense, that two beings, of equal capacities for truth, should perceive, one of them beauty, and the other deformity, in the same proportions. And upon this supposition, by that truth which is always connected with beauty, nothing more can be meant than the conformity of

---

* This the Athenians did in a peculiar manner, by the words καλοκάγαθὸς and καλοκἀγαθία.

any object to those proportions upon which, after careful examination, the beauty of that species is found to depend. Polycletus, for instance, a famous ancient sculptor, from an accurate mensuration of the several parts of the most perfect human bodies, deduced a canon or system of proportions, which was the rule of all succeeding artists. Suppose a statue modelled according to this: a man of mere natural taste, upon looking at it, without entering into its proportions, confesses and admires its beauty; whereas a professor of the art applies his measures to the head, the neck, or the hand, and, without attending to its beauty, pronounces the workmanship to be just and true.

Ver. 492. *As when Brutus rose,* &c.] Cicero himself describes this fact—" Cæsare interfecto—statim cruentum altè extollens M. Brutus pugionem, Ciceronem nominatim exclamavit, atque ei recuperatam libertatem est gratulatus." Cic. Philipp. ii. 12.

Ver. 548. *Where virtue rising from the awful depth*
        *Of truth's mysterious bosom,* &c.] According to the opinion of those who assert moral obligation to be founded on an immutable and universal law; and that which is usually called the moral sense, to be determined by the peculiar temper of the imagination and the earliest associations of ideas.

Ver. 591. *Lyceum.*] The school of Aristotle.

Ver. 592. *Academus.*] The school of Plato.

Ver. 594. *Ilissus.*] One of the rivers on which Athens was situated. Plato, in some of his finest dialogues, lays the scene of the conversation with Socrates on its banks.


## NOTES ON BOOK II.


Ver. 19. *At last the Muses rose,* &c.] About the age of Hugh Capet, founder of the third race of French kings, the poets of Province were in high reputation; a sort of strolling bards or rhapsodists, who went about the courts of princes and noblemen, entertaining them at festivals with music and poetry. They attempted both the epic, ode, and satire; and abounded in a wild and fantastic vein of fable, partly allegorical, and partly founded on traditionary legends of the Saracen wars. These were the rudiments of Italian poetry. But their taste and composition must have been extremely barbarous, as we may judge by those who followed the turn of their fable in much politer times; such as Boiardo, Bernardo, Tasso, Ariosto, &c.

Ver. 21. *Valclusa.*] The famous retreat of Francisco Petrarcha, the father of Italian poetry, and his mistress Laura, a lady of Avignon.

Ver. 22. *Arno.*] The river which runs by Florence, the birth-place of Dante and Boccaccio.

Ver. 23. *Parthenope.*] Or Naples, the birth-place of Sannazaro. The great Torquato Tasso was born at Sorento in the kingdom of Naples.

Ibid. —— *the rage*

*Of dire ambition,* &c.] This relates to the cruel wars among the republics of Italy, and abominable politics of its little princes, about the fifteenth century. These, at last, in conjunction with the papal power, entirely extinguished the spirit of liberty in that country, and established that abuse of the fine arts which has been since propagated over all Europe.

Ver. 30. *Thus from their guardians torn, the tender arts,* &c.] Nor were they only losers by the separation. For philosophy itself, to use the words of a noble philosopher, " being thus severed by the sprightly arts and sciences, must consequently grow dronish, insipid, pedantic, useless, and directly opposite to the real knowledge and practice of the world." Insomuch that " a gentleman," says another excellent writer, " cannot easily bring himself to like so austere and ungainly a form : so greatly is it changed from what was once the delight of the finest gentlemen of antiquity, and their recreation after the hurry of public affairs !" From this condition it cannot be recovered but by uniting it once more with the works of imagination ; and we have had the pleasure of observing a very great progress made towards their union in England within these few years. It is hardly possible to conceive them at a greater distance from each other than at the Revolution, when Locke stood at the head of one party, and Dryden of the other. But the general spirit of liberty, which has ever since been growing, naturally invited our men of wit and genius to improve that influence which the arts of persuasion gave them with the people, by applying them to subjects of importance to society. Thus poetry and eloquence became considerable ; and philosophy is now of course obliged to borrow of their embellishments, in order even to gain audience with the public.

Ver. 157. *From passion's power alone,* &c.] This very mysterious kind of pleasure which is often found in the exercise of passions generally counted painful, has been taken notice of by several authors. Lucretius resolves it into self-love :

Suave mari magno, &c. lib. ii. 1.

As if a man was never pleased in being moved at the distress of a tragedy, without a cool reflection that though these fictitious personages were so unhappy, yet he himself was perfectly at ease and in safety. The ingenious author of the " Reflections Critiques sur la Poesie et sur la Peinture," accounts for it by the general delight which the mind takes in its own activity, and the abhorrence it feels of an indolent and inattentive state : and this, joined with the moral approbation of its own temper, which attends these emotions when natural and just, is certainly the true foundation of the pleasure, which, as it is the origin and basis of tragedy and epic, deserved a very particular consideration in this poem.

Ver. 304. *Inhabitant of earth*, &c.] The account of the economy of providence here introduced, as the most proper to calm and satisfy the mind when under the compunction of private evils, seems to have come originally from the Pythagorean school : but of the ancient philosophers, Plato has most largely insisted upon it, has established it with all the strength of his capacious understanding, and ennobled it with all the magnificence of his divine imagination. He has one passage so full and clear on this head, that I am persuaded the reader will be pleased to see it here, though somewhat long. Addressing himself to such as are not satisfied concerning divine Providence : " The Being who presides over the whole," says he, " has disposed and complicated all things for the happiness and virtue of the whole, every part of which, according to the extent of its influence, does and suffers what is fit and proper. One of these parts is yours, O unhappy man, which though in itself most inconsiderable and minute, yet being connected with the universe, ever seeks to co-operate with that supreme order. You in the mean time are ignorant of the very end for which all particular natures are brought into existence, that the all-comprehending nature of the whole may be perfect and happy ; existing, as it does, not for your sake, but the cause and reason of your existence, which, as in the symmetry of every artificial work, must of necessity concur with the general design of the artist, and be subservient to the whole of which it is a part. Your complaint therefore is ignorant and groundless ; since, according to the various energy of creation, and the common laws of nature, there is a constant provision of that which is best at the same time for you and for the whole.—For the governing intelligence clearly beholding all the actions of animated and self-moving creatures, and that mixture of good and evil which diversifies them, considered first of all by what disposition of things, and by what situation of each individual in the general system, vice might be depressed and subdued, and virtue made secure of victory and happiness with the greatest facility and in the highest degree possible. In this manner he ordered through the entire circle of being, the internal constitution of every mind, where should be its station in the universal fabric, and through what variety of circumstances it should proceed in the whole tenor of its existence." He goes on in his sublime manner to assert a future state of retribution, " as well for those who, by the exercise of good dispositions being harmonized and assimilated into the divine virtue, are consequently removed to a place of unblemished sanctity and happiness; as of those who by the most flagitious arts have risen from contemptible beginnings to the greatest affluence and power, and whom you therefore look upon as unanswerable instances of negligence in the gods, because you are ignorant of the purposes to which they are subservient, and in what manner they contribute to that supreme intention of good to the whole." Plato de Leg. x. 16.

This theory has been delivered of late, especially abroad, in a manner which subverts the freedom of human actions; whereas Plato appears very careful to preserve it, and has been in that respect imitated by the best of his followers.

Ver. 321. —— *one might rise,*
*One order,* &c.] See the Meditations of Antoninus and the Characteristics, passim.

Ver. 355. *The best and fairest,* &c.] This opinion is so old, that Timæus Locrus calls the Supreme Being δημιϑργὸς τϑ βελτίονος, the artificer of that which is best; and represents him as resolving in the beginning to produce the most excellent work, and as copying the world most exactly from his own intelligible and essential idea; " so that it yet remains, as it was at first, perfect in beauty, and will never stand in need of any correction or improvement." There can be no room for a caution here, to understand the expressions, not of any particular circumstances of human life separately considered, but of the sum or universal system of life and being. See also the vision at the end of the Theodicée of Leibnitz.

Ver. 350. *As flame ascends,* &c.] This opinion, though not held by Plato nor any of the ancients, is yet a very natural consequence of his principles. But the disquisition is too complex and extensive to be entered upon here.

Ver. 755. *Philip.*] The Macedonian.

## NOTES ON BOOK III.

Ver. 18. ———— *where the powers*
*Of fancy*, &c ] The influence of the imagination on the conduct of life, is one of the most important points in moral philosophy. It were easy by an induction of facts to prove that the imagination directs almost all the passions, and mixes with almost every circumstance of action or pleasure. Let any man, even of the coldest head and soberest industry, analyse the idea of what he calls his interest; he will find, that it consists chiefly of certain degrees of decency, beauty, and order, variously combined into one system, the idol which he seeks to enjoy by labour, hazard, and self-denial. It is on this account of the last consequence to regulate these images by the standard of nature and the general good; otherwise the imagination, by heightening some objects beyond their real excellence and beauty, or by representing others in a more odious or terrible shape than they deserve, may of course engage us in pursuits utterly inconsistent with the moral order of things.

If it be objected that this account of things supposes the passions to be merely accidental, whereas there appears in some a natural and hereditary disposition to certain passions prior to all circumstances of education or fortune; it may be answered, that though no man is born ambitious or a miser, yet he may inherit from his parents a peculiar temper or complexion of mind, which shall render his imagination more liable to be struck with some particular objects, consequently dispose him to form opinions of good and ill, and entertain passions of a particular turn. Some men, for instance, by the original frame of their minds, are more delighted with the vast and magnificent, others on the contrary with the elegant and gentle aspects of nature. And it is very remarkable, that the disposition of the moral powers is always similar to this of the imagination; that those who are most inclined to admire prodigious and sublime objects in the physical world, are also most inclined to applaud examples of fortitude and heroic virtue in the moral. While those who are charmed rather with the delicacy and sweetness of colours, and forms, and sounds, never fail in like manner to yield the preference to the softer scenes of virtue' and the sympathies of a domestic life. And this is sufficient to account for the objection.

Among the ancient philosophers, though we have several hints concerning this influence of the imagination upon morals among the remains of the Socratic school, yet the Stoics were the first who paid it a due attention. Zeno, their founder, thought it impossible to preserve any tolerable regularity in life, without frequently inspecting those pictures or appearances of things, which the imagination offers to the mind (Diog. Laërt. l. vii.). The meditations of M. Aurelius, and the discourses of Epictetus, are full of the same sentiment; insomuch that the latter makes the Χρῆσις οἵα δεῖ, φαντασιῶν, or right management of the fancies, the only thing for which we are accountable to providence, and without which a man is no other than stupid or frantic. Arrian. l. i. c. 12. and l. ii. c. 22. See also the Characteristics, vol. i. from p. 313 to 321, where this Stoical doctrine is embellished with all the elegance and graces of Plato.

Ver. 75. —— *how Folly's awkward arts*, &c.] Notwithstanding the general influence of ridicule on private and civil life, as well as on learning and the sciences, it has been almost constantly neglected or misrepresented, by divines especially. The manner of treating these subjects in the science of human nature, should be precisely the same as in natural philosophy; from particular facts to investigate the stated order in which they appear, and then apply the general law, thus discovered, to the explication of other appearances and the improvement of useful arts.

Ver. 84. *Behold the foremost band*, &c.] The first and most general source of ridicule in the characters of men, is vanity, or self applause for some desirable quality or possession which evidently does not belong to those who assume it.

Ver. 121. *Then comes the second order*, &c.] Ridicule from the same vanity, where, though the possession be real, yet no merit can arise from it, because of some particular circumstances, which, though obvious to the spectator, are yet overlooked by the ridiculous character.

Ver. 152. *Another tribe succeeds*, &c.] Ridicule from a notion of excellence in particular objects disproportioned to their intrinsic value, and inconsistent with the order of nature.

Ver. 191. *But now, ye gay*, &c.] Ridicule from a notion of excellence, when the object is absolutely odious or contemptible. This is the highest degree of the ridiculous; as in the affectation of diseases or vices.

Ver. 207. *Thus far triumphant*, &c.] Ridicule from false shame or groundless fear.

Ver. 228. *Last of the*, &c.] Ridicule from the ignorance of such things as our circumstances require us to know.

Ver. 248. — *Suffice it to have said*, &c.] By comparing these general sources of ridicule with each other, and examining the ridiculous in other objects, we may obtain a general definition of it, equally applicable to every species. The most important circumstance of this definition is laid down in the lines referred to; but others more minute we shall subjoin here. Aristotle's account of the matter seems both imperfect and false; τὸ γὰρ γελοῖον, says he, ἐςὶν ἁμάρτημά τι ὴ αἶσχος, ἀνώδυνον ὴ ε᾽ φθαρτικόν: " the ridiculous is some certain fault or turpitude without pain, and not destructive to its subject," (Poët. c. 5.) For allowing it to be true, as it is not, that the ridiculous is never accompanied with pain, yet we might produce many instances of such a fault or turpitude which cannot with any tolerable propriety be called ridiculous. So that the definition does not distinguish the thing designed. Nay farther; even when we perceive the turpitude tending to the destruction of its subject, we may still be sensible of a ridiculous appearance, till the ruin become imminent, and the keener sensations of pity or terror banish the ludicrous apprehension from our minds. For the sensation of ridicule is not a bare perception of the agreement or disagreement of ideas; but a passion or emotion of the mind consequential to that perception. So that the mind may perceive the agreement or disagreement, and yet not feel the ridiculous, because it is engrossed by a more violent emotion. Thus it happens that some men think those objects ridiculous, to which others cannot endure to apply the name; because in them they excite a much intenser and more important feeling. And this difference, among other causes, has brought a good deal of confusion into this question.

" That which makes objects ridiculous, is some ground of admiration or esteem connected with other more general circumstances comparatively worthless or deformed; or it is some circumstance of turpitude or deformity connected with what is in general excellent or beautiful : the inconsistent properties existing either in the objects themselves, or in the apprehension of the person to whom they relate; belonging always to the same order or class of being ; implying sentiment or design ; and exciting no acute or vehement emotion of the heart."

To prove the several parts of this definition : " The appearance of excellence or beauty connected with a general condition comparatively sordid or deformed," is ridiculous : for instance, pompous pretensions of wisdom joined with ignorance or folly in the Socrates of Aristophanes ; and the ostentations of military glory with cowardice and stupidity in the Thraso of Terence.

" The appearance of deformity or turpitude in conjunction with what is in general excellent or venerable," is also ridiculous : for instance, the personal weaknesses of a magistrate appearing in the solemn and public functions of his station.

" The incongruous properties may either exist in the objects themselves, or in apprehension of the person to whom they relate :" in the last-mentioned instance, they both exist in the objects ; in the instances from Aristophanes and Terence, one of them is objective and real, the other only founded in the apprehension of the ridiculous character.

" The inconsistent properties must belong to the same order or class of being." A coxcomb in fine clothes, bedaubed by accident in foul weather, is a ridiculous object ; because his general apprehension of excellence and esteem is referred to the splendour and expense of his dress. A man of sense and merit, in the same circumstances, is not counted ridiculous ; because the general ground of excellence and esteem in him is, both in fact and in his own apprehension, of a very different species.

" Every ridiculous object implies sentiment or design." A column placèd by an architect without a capital or base, is laughed at : the same column in a ruin causes a very different sensation.

And lastly, " the occurrence must excite no acute or vehement emotion of the heart," such as terror, pity, or indignation ; for in that case, as was observed above, the mind is not at leisure to contemplate the ridiculous.

Whether any appearance not ridiculous be involved in this description, and whether it comprehend every species and form of the ridiculous, must be determined by repeated applications of it to particular instances.

Ver. 259. *Ask we for what fair end,* &c.] Since it is beyond all contradiction evident that we have a natural sense or feeling of the ridiculous, and since so good a reason may be assigned to justify the supreme Being for bestowing it ; one cannot, without astonishment, reflect on the conduct of those men who imagine it is for the service of true religion to vilify and blacken it without distinction, and endeavour to persuade us that it is never applied but in a bad cause. Ridicule is not concerned with mere speculative truth or falsehood. It is not in abstract propositions or theorems, but in actions and passions, good and evil, beauty and deformity, that we find materials for it ; and all these terms are relative, implying approbation or blame. To ask them whether ridicule be a test of truth, is, in other words, to ask whether that which is ridiculous can be morally true, can be just and becoming; or whether that which is just and becoming, can be ridiculous. A question that does not deserve a serious answer. For it is most evident, that, as in a metaphysical proposition offered to the understanding for its assent, the faculty of reason examines the terms of the proposition, and finding one idea, which was supposed equal to another, to be in fact unequal, of consequence rejects the proposition as a falsehood; so, in objects offered to the mind for its esteem or applause, the faculty of ridicule, finding an incongruity in the claim, urges the mind to reject it with laughter and contempt. When, therefore, we observe such a claim obtruded upon mankind, and the inconsistent circumstances carefully concealed from the eye of the public, it is our business, if the matter be of importance to society, to drag out those latent circumstances, and, by setting them in full view, to convince the world how ridiculous the claim is: and thus a double advantage is gained; for we both detect the moral falsehood sooner than in the way of speculative enquiry, and impress the minds of men with a stronger sense of the vanity and error of its authors. And this and no more is meant by the application of ridicule.

But it is said, the practice is dangerous, and may be inconsistent with the regard we owe to objects of real dignity and excellence. I answer, the practice fairly managed can never be dangerous; men may be dishonest in obtruding circumstances foreign to the object, and we may be inadvertent in allowing those circumstances to impose upon us: but the sense of ridicule always judges right. The Socrates of Aristophanes is as truly ridiculous a character as ever was drawn:—true; but it is not the character of Socrates, the divine moralist and father of ancient wisdom. What then? did the ridicule of the poet hinder the philosopher from detecting and disclaiming those foreign circumstances which he had falsely introduced into his character, and thus rendered the satirist doubly ridiculous in his turn? No; but it nevertheless had an ill influence on the minds of the people. And so has the reasoning of Spinoza made many atheists: he has founded it indeed on suppositions utterly false; but allow him these, and his conclusions are unavoidably true. And if we must reject the use of ridicule, because, by the imposition of false circumstances, things may be made to seem ridiculous, which are not so in themselves; why we ought not in the same manner to reject the use of reason, because, by proceeding on false principles, conclusions will appear true which are impossible in nature, let the vehement and obstinate declaimers against ridicule determine.

Ver. 285. *The inexpressive semblance,* &c.] This simi-
litude is the foundation of almost all the ornaments of
poetic diction.

Ver. 326. *Two faithful needles,* &c.] See the elegant
poem recited by Cardinal Bembo in the character of Lucretius; Strada Prolus. vi. Academ. 2. c. v.

Ver. 348. *By these mysterious ties,* &c.] The act of re-
membering seems almost wholly to depend on the association of ideas.

Ver. 411. *Into its proper vehicle,* &c.] This relates to
the different sorts of corporeal mediums, by which the ideas
of the artists are rendered palpable to the senses; as by
sounds, in music; by lines and shadows, in painting; by
diction, in poetry, &c.

Ver 547. —— *One pursues*
               *The vast alone,* &c.]    See the note to ver. 18
of this book.

Ver. 558. *Waller longs,* &c.]
          O! how I long my careless limbs to lay
          Under the plantane shade; and all the day
          With amorous airs my fancy entertain, &c.

          WALLER, Battle of the Summer-Islands, Canto I.
And again,
          While in the park I sing, the list'ning deer
          Attend my passion, and forget to fear, &c.
                                        At Pens-hurst.

Ver. 593.—*Not a breeze,* &c.] That this account may
not appear rather poetically extravagant than just in philosophy, it may be proper to produce the sentiment of
one of the greatest, wisest, and best of men on this head;
one so little to be suspected of partiality in the case, that
he reckons it among those favours for which he was
especially thankful to the gods, that they had not suffered
him to make any great proficiency in the arts of eloquence
and poetry, lest by that means he should have been
diverted from pursuits of more importance to his high
station. Speaking of the beauty of universal nature, he
observes, that there " is a pleasing and graceful aspect in
every object we perceive," when once we consider its connection with that general order. He instances in many
things which at first sight would be thought rather defor-
mities; and then adds, " that a man who enjoys a sensibility
of temper with a just comprehension of the universal order
—will discern many amiable things, not credible to every
mind, but to those alone who have entered into an honourable familiarity with nature and her works."
                                        M. Antonin. iii, 2.

# THE

# PLEASURES OF THE IMAGINATION.

## A POEM.

### GENERAL ARGUMENT.

THE pleasures of the imagination proceed either from natural objects, as from a flourishing grove, a clear and murmuring fountain, a calm sea by moonlight; or from works of art, such as a noble edifice, a musical tune, a statue, a picture, a poem. In treating of these pleasures, we must begin with the former class; they being original to the other; and nothing more being necessary, in order to explain them, than a view of our natural inclination toward greatness and beauty, and of those appearances, in the world around us, to which that inclination is adapted. This is the subject of the first book of the following poem.

But the pleasures which we receive from the elegant arts, from music, sculpture, painting, and poetry, are much more various and complicated. In them (besides greatness and beauty, or forms proper to the imagination) we find interwoven frequent representations of truth, of virtue and vice, of circumstances proper to move us with laughter, or to excite in us pity, fear, and the other passions. These moral and intellectual objects are described in the second book; to which the third properly belongs as an episode, though too large to have been included in it.

With the above-mentioned causes of pleasure, which are universal in the course of human life, and appertain to our higher faculties, many others do generally occur, more limited in their operation, or of an inferior origin: such are the novelty of objects, the association of ideas, affections of the bodily senses, influences of education, national habits, and the like. To illustrate these, and from the whole to determine the character of a perfect taste, is the argument of the fourth book.

Hitherto the pleasures of the imagination belong to the human species in general. But there are certain particular men whose imagination is endowed with powers, and sus-

L

ceptible of pleasures, which the generality of mankind
never participate. These are the men of genius, destined
by nature to excel in one or other of the arts already mentioned. It is proposed therefore, in the last place, to delineate that genius which in some degree appears common
to them all; yet with a more peculiar consideration of
poetry : inasmuch as poetry is the most extensive of those
arts, the most philosophical, and the most useful.

## BOOK I. 1757.

### ARGUMENT.

THE subject proposed. Dedication. The ideas of the Supreme Being, the exemplars of all things. The variety of
constitution in the minds of men ; with its final cause. The
general character of a fine imagination. All the immediate
pleasures of the human imagination proceed either from
Greatness or Beauty in external objects. The pleasure
from Greatness ; with its final cause. The natural connection of Beauty with truth* and good. The different
orders of Beauty in different objects. The infinite and all-
comprehending form of Beauty, which belongs to the Divine
Mind. The partial and artificial forms of Beauty, which
belong to inferior intellectual beings. The origin and general conduct of beauty in man. The subordination of local
beauties to the beauty of the Universe. Conclusion.

WITH what enchantment Nature's goodly
        scene
Attracts the sense of mortals ; how the mind
For its own eye doth objects nobler still
Prepare; how men by various lessons learn
To judge of Beauty's praise; what raptures fill
The breast with fancy's native arts endow'd,
And what true culture guides it to renown ;
My verse unfolds. Ye gods, or godlike powers,

* Truth is here taken, not in a logical, but in a mixed
and popular sense, or for what has been called the truth of
things; denoting as well their natural and regular condition,
as a proper estimate or judgment concerning them.

Ye guardians of the sacred task, attend
Propitious.   Hand in hand around your bard     10
Move in majestic measures, leading on
His doubtful step through many a solemn path,
Conscious of secrets which to human sight
Ye only can reveal.   Be great in him :
And let your favour make him wise to speak
Of all your wondrous empire ; with a voice
So temper'd to his theme, that those, who hear,
May yield perpetual homage to yourselves.
Thou chief, O daughter of eternal Love,
Whate'er thy name ; or Muse, or Grace, ador'd 20
By Grecian prophets ; to the sons of Heaven
Known, while with deep amazement thou dost there
The perfect counsels read, the ideas old,
Of thine omniscient Father ; known on earth
By the still horror and the blissful tear
With which thou seizest on the soul of man ;
Thou chief, Poetic Spirit, from the banks
Of Avon, whence thy holy fingers cull
Fresh flowers and dews to sprinkle on the turf
Where Shakespeare lies, be present.   And with thee
Let Fiction come ; on her aërial wings
Wafting ten thousand colours ; which in sport,
By the light glances of her magic eye,
She blends and shifts at will thro' countless forms,
Her wild creation.   Goddess of the lyre,
Whose awful tones control the moving sphere,
Wilt thou, eternal Harmony, descend,
And join this happy train ? for with thee comes
The guide, the guardian of their mystic rites,
Wise Order : and, where Order deigns to come, 40
Her sister, Liberty, will not be far.
Be present all ye Genii, who conduct
Of youthful bards the lonely wandering step    [ear
New to your springs and shades ; who touch their
With finer sounds, and heighten to their eye
The pomp of nature, and before them place
The fairest, loftiest countenance of things.

Nor thou, my Dyson, to the lay refuse
Thy wonted partial audience.  What, though first
In years unseason'd, haply ere the sports          50
Of childhood yet were o'er, the adventurous lay
With many splendid prospects, many charms,
Allur'd my heart, nor conscious whence they sprung,
Nor heedful of their end ?  yet serious Truth
Her empire o'er the calm, sequester'd theme
Asserted soon; while Falsehood's evil brood,
Vice and deceitful Pleasure, she at once
Excluded, and my fancy's careless toil
Drew to the better cause.   Maturer aid
Thy friendship added, in the paths of life,          60
The busy paths, my unaccustom'd feet
Preserving : nor to Truth's recess divine,
Through this wide argument's unbeaten space,
Withholding surer guidance ; while by turns
We trac'd the sages old, or while the queen
Of sciences (whom manners and the mind
Acknowledge) to my true companion's voice
Not unattentive, o'er the wintry lamp
Inclin'd her sceptre, favouring.   Now the fates
Have other tasks impos'd :—to thee, my friend,  70
The ministry of freedom and the faith
Of popular decrees, in early youth,
Not vainly they committed : me they sent
To wait on pain ; and silent arts to urge,
Inglorious : not ignoble ; if my cares,
To such as languish on a grievous bed,
Ease and the sweet forgetfulness of ill
Conciliate : nor delightless ; if the Muse,
Her shades to visit and to taste her springs,
If some distinguish'd hours the bounteous Muse 80
Impart, and grant (what she and she alone
Can grant to mortals) that my hand those wreaths
Of fame and honest favour, which the bless'd
Wear in Elysium, and which never felt
The breath of envy or malignant tongues,
That these my hand for thee and for myself

May gather.   Meanwhile, O my faithful friend,
O early chosen, ever found the same,
And trusted and belov'd; once more the verse
Long destin'd, always obvious to thine ear,       90
Attend, indulgent : so in latest years,
When time thy head with honours shall have cloth'd
Sacred to even virtue, may thy mind,
Amid the calm review of seasons past,
Fair offices of friendship or kind peace
Or public zeal, may then thy mind well-pleas'd
Recall these happy studies of our prime.
     From Heaven my strains begin: from Heaven
          descends
The flame of genius to the chosen breast,
And beauty with poetic wonder join'd,            100
And inspiration.   Ere the rising sun
Shone o'er the deep, or 'mid the vault of night
The moon her silver lamp suspended : ere
The vales with springs were water'd, or with groves
Of oak or pine the ancient hills were crown'd;
Then the Great Spirit, whom his works adore,
Within his own deep essence view'd the forms,
The forms eternal of created things :
The radiant sun; the moon's nocturnal lamp ;
The mountains and the streams; the ample stores
Of earth, of heaven, of nature.   From the first,
On that full scene his love divine he fix'd,
His admiration : till, in time complete,
What he admir'd and lov'd his vital power
Unfolded into being.   Hence the breath
Of life informing each organic frame :
Hence the green earth, and wild-resounding waves :
Hence light and shade, alternate ; warmth and cold ;
And bright autumnal skies, and vernal showers,
And all the fair variety of things.              120
     But not alike to every mortal eye
Is this great scene unveil'd.   For while the claims
Of social life to different labours urge
The active powers of man, with wisest care

Hath Nature on the multitude of minds
Impress'd a various bias; and to each
Decreed its province in the common toil.
To some she taught the fabric of the sphere,
The changeful moon, the circuit of the stars,
The golden zones of heaven : to some she gave
To search the story of eternal thought;
Of space, and time ; of fate's unbroken chain,
And will's quick movement : others by the hand
She led o'er vales and mountains, to explore
What healing virtue dwells in every vein
Of herbs or trees.   But some to nobler hopes
Were destin'd : some within a finer mould
She wrought, and temper'd with a purer flame.
To these the Sire Omnipotent unfolds,
In fuller aspects and with fairer lights,              140
This picture of the world.   Through every part
They trace the lofty sketches of his hand :
In earth, or air, the meadow's flowery store,
The moon's mild radiance, or the virgin's mien
Dress'd in attractive smiles, they see portray'd
(As far as mortal eyes the portrait scan)
Those lineaments of beauty which delight
The Mind Supreme.   They also feel their force,
Enamour'd : they partake the eternal joy.
     For as old Memnon's image long renown'd    150
Through fabling Egypt, at the genial touch
Of morning, from its inmost frame sent forth
Spontaneous music ; so doth Nature's hand,
To certain attributes which matter claims,
Adapt the finer organs of the mind :
So the glad impulse of those kindred powers
(Of form, of colour's cheerful pomp, of sound
Melodious, or of motion aptly sped)
Detains the enliven'd sense ; till soon the soul
Feels the deep concord and assents through all
Her functions.   Then the charm by fate prepar'd
Diffuseth its enchantment.   Fancy dreams,
Rapt into high discourse with prophets old,

And wandering through Elysium, Fancy dreams
Of sacred fountains, of o'ershadowing groves,
Whose walks with godlike harmony resound:
Fountains, which Homer visits; happy groves,
Where Milton dwells: the intellectual power,
On the mind's throne, suspends his graver cares,
And smiles: the passions, to divine repose,     170
Persuaded yield: and love and joy alone
Are waking: love and joy, such as await
An angel's meditation. O! attend,
Whoe'er thou art whom these delights can touch;
Whom Nature's aspect, Nature's simple garb
Can thus command; O! listen to my song;
And I will guide thee to her blissful walks,
And teach thy solitude her voice to hear,
And point her gracious features to thy view.
    Know then, whate'er of the world's ancient store,
Whate'er of mimic Art's reflected scenes,
With love and admiration thus inspire
Attentive Fancy, her delighted sons
In two illustrious orders comprehend,
Self-taught: from him whose rustic toil the lark
Cheers warbling, to the bard whose daring thoughts
Range the full orb of being, still the form,
Which fancy worships, or sublime or fair
Her votaries proclaim. I see them dawn:
I see the radiant visions where they rise,     190
More lovely than when Lucifer displays
His glittering forehead through the gates of morn,
To lead the train of Phœbus and the Spring.
    Say, why was man so eminently rais'd
Amid the vast creation; why impower'd
Through life and death to dart his watchful eye,
With thoughts beyond the limit of his frame;
But that the Omnipotent might send him forth,
In sight of angels and immortal minds,
As on an ample theatre to join     200
In contest with his equals, who shall best
The task achieve, the course of noble toils,

By wisdom and by mercy preordain'd?
Might send him forth the sovereign good to learn;
To chase each meaner purpose from his breast;
And through the mists of passion and of sense,
And thro' the pelting storms of chance and pain,
To hold straight on with constant heart and eye
Still fix'd upon his everlasting palm,          [burns
The approving smile of Heaven?   Else wherefore
In mortal bosoms this unquenched hope,
That seeks from day to day sublimer ends;
Happy, though restless?  Why departs the soul
Wide from the track and journey of her times,
To grasp the good she knows not?   In the field
Of things which may be, in the spacious field
Of science, potent arts, or dreadful arms,
To raise up scenes in which her own desires
Contented may repose; when things, which are,
Pall on her temper, like a twice-told tale:      220
Her temper, still demanding to be free;
Spurning the rude control of wilful might;
Proud of her dangers brav'd, her griefs endur'd,
Her strength severely prov'd?  To these high aims,
Which reason and affection prompt in man,
Not adverse nor unapt hath Nature fram'd
His bold imagination.   For, amid
The various forms which this full world presents
Like rivals to his choice, what human breast
E'er doubts, before the transient and minute,     230
To prize the vast, the stable, the sublime?
Who, that from heights aërial sends his eye
Around a wild horizon, and surveys
Indus or Ganges rolling his broad wave
Through mountains, plains, thro' spacious cities old,
And regions dark with woods; will turn away
To mark the path of some penurious rill
Which murmureth at his feet?  Where does the soul
Consent her soaring fancy to restrain,
Which bears her up, as on an eagle's wings,       240
Destin'd for highest heaven; or which of fate's

Tremendous barriers shall confine her flight
To any humbler quarry ?  The rich earth
Cannot detain her; nor the ambient air
With all its changes.  For a while with joy
She hovers o'er the sun, and views the small
Attendant orbs, beneath his sacred beam,
Emerging from the deep, like cluster'd isles
Whose rocky shores to the glad sailor's eye
Reflect the gleams of morning : for a while      250
With pride she sees his firm, paternal sway
Bend the reluctant planets to move each
Round its perpetual year.  But soon she quits
That prospect : meditating loftier views,
She darts adventurous up the long career
Of comets ; through the constellations holds
Her course, and now looks back on all the stars
Whose blended flames as with a milky stream
Part the blue region.  Empyréan tracts,
Where happy souls beyond this concave heaven
Abide, she then explores, whence purer light
For countless ages travels through the abyss,
Nor hath in sight of mortals yet arriv'd.
Upon the wide creation's utmost shore
At length she stands, and the dread space beyond
Contemplates, half-recoiling : nathless down
The gloomy void, astonish'd, yet unquell'd,
She plungeth ; down the unfathomable gulf
Where God alone hath being.  There her hopes
Rest at the fated goal.  For, from the birth      270
Of human kind, the Sovereign Maker said
That not in humble, nor in brief delight,
Not in the fleeting echoes of renown,
Power's purple robes, nor Pleasure's flowery lap,
The soul should find contentment; but, from these
Turning disdainful to an equal good,
Through Nature's opening walks enlarge her aim,
Till every bound at length should disappear,
And infinite perfection fill the scene.
  But lo, where Beauty, dress'd in gentler pomp,

With comely steps advancing, claims the verse
Her charms inspire.    O Beauty, source of praise,
Of honour, ev'n to mute and lifeless things ;
O thou that kindlest in each human heart
Love, and the wish of poets, when their tongue
Would teach to other bosoms what so charms
Their own ; O child of Nature and the soul,
In happiest hour brought forth ; the doubtful garb
Of words, of earthly language, all too mean,
Too lowly I account, in which to clothe            290
Thy form divine : for thee the mind alone
Beholds ; nor half thy brightness can reveal
Through those dim organs, whose corporeal touch
O'ershadoweth thy pure essence.    Yet, my Muse
If Fortune call thee to the task, wait thou
Thy favourable seasons : then, while fear
And doubt are absent, thro' wide nature's bounds
Expatiate with glad step, and choose at will
Whate'er bright spoils the florid earth contains,
Whate'er the waters, or the liquid air,            300
To manifest unblemish'd Beauty's praise,
And o'er the breasts of mortals to extend
Her gracious empire.    Wilt thou to the isles
Atlantic, to the rich Hesperian clime,
Fly in the train of Autumn ; and look on,
And learn from him ; while, as he roves around,
Where'er his fingers touch the fruitful grove,
The branches bloom with gold ; where'er his foot
Imprints the soil, the ripening clusters swell,
Turning aside their foliage, and come forth        310
In purple lights, till every hillock glows
As with the blushes of an evening sky ?
Or wilt thou that Thessalian landscape trace,
Where slow Penéus his clear glassy tide
Draws smooth along, between the winding cliffs
Of Ossa and the pathless woods unshorn
That wave o'er huge Olympus ? Down the stream,
Look how the mountains with their double range
Embrace the vale of Tempé : from each side

Ascending steep to heaven, a rocky mound 320
Cover'd with ivy and the laurel boughs
That crown'd young Phœbus for the Python slain.
Fair Tempé! on whose primrose banks the morn
Awoke most fragrant, and the noon repos'd
In pomp of lights and shadows most sublime:
Whose lawns, whose glades, ere human footsteps yet
Had trac'd an entrance, were the hallow'd haunt
Of silvan powers immortal: where they sate
Oft in the golden age, the Nymphs and Fauns,
Beneath some arbour branching o'er the flood, 330
And leaning round hung on the instructive lips
Of hoary Pan, or o'er some open dale
Danc'd in light measures to his sevenfold pipe,
While Zephyr's wanton hand along their path
Flung showers of painted blossoms, fertile dews,
And one perpetual spring. But if our task
More lofty rites demand, with all good vows
Then let us hasten to the rural haunt
Where young Melissa dwells. Nor thou refuse
The voice which calls thee from thy lov'd retreat,
But hither, gentle maid, thy footsteps turn:
Here, to thy own unquestionable theme,
O fair, O graceful, bend thy polish'd brow,
Assenting; and the gladness of thy eyes
Impart to me, like morning's wished light
Seen through the vernal air. By yonder stream,
Where beech and elm along the bordering mead
Send forth wild melody from every bough,
Together let us wander; where the hills
Cover'd with fleeces to the lowing vale 350
Reply; where tidings of content and peace
Each echo brings. Lo, how the western sun
O'er fields and floods, o'er every living soul,
Diffuseth glad repose! There while I speak
Of Beauty's honours, thou, Melissa, thou
Shalt hearken, not unconscious, while I tell
How first from Heaven she came: how after all
The works of life, the elemental scenes,

The hours, the seasons, she had oft explor'd,
At length her favourite mansion and her throne
She fix'd in woman's form : what pleasing ties
To virtue bind her ; what effectual aid
They lend each other's power ; and how divine
Their union, should some unambitious maid,
To all the enchantment of the Idalian queen,
Add sanctity and wisdom : while my tongue
Prolongs the tale, Melissa, thou may'st feign
To wonder whence my rapture is inspir'd ;
But soon the smile which dawns upon thy lip
Shall tell it, and the tenderer bloom o'er all    370
That soft cheek springing to the marble neck,
Which bends aside in vain, revealing more
What it would thus keep silent, and in vain
The sense of praise dissembling.   Then my song
Great Nature's winning arts, which thus inform
With joy and love the rugged breast of man,
Should sound in numbers worthy such a theme :
While all whose souls have ever felt the force
Of those enchanting passions, to my lyre
Should throng attentive, and receive once more
Their influence, unobscur'd by any cloud
Of vulgar care, and purer than the hand
Of Fortune can bestow : nor, to confirm
Their sway, should awful Contemplation scorn
To join his dictates to the genuine strain
Of Pleasure's tongue ; nor yet should Pleasure's ear
Be much averse.   Ye chiefly, gentle band
Of youths and virgins, who through many a wish
And many a fond pursuit, as in some scene
Of magic bright and fleeting, are allur'd    390
By various Beauty ; if the pleasing toil
Can yield a moment's respite, hither turn
Your favourable ear, and trust my words.
I do not mean, on bless'd Religion's seat
Presenting Superstition's gloomy form,
To dash your soothing hopes : I do not mean
To bid the jealous thunderer fire the heavens,

Or shapes infernal rend the groaning earth,
And scare you from your joys.  My cheerful song
With happier omens calls you to the field,  400
Pleas'd with your generous ardour in the chase,
And warm like you.  Then tell me (for ye know)
Doth Beauty ever deign to dwell where use
And aptitude are strangers ? is her praise
Confess'd in aught whose most peculiar ends
Are lame and fruitless ? or did Nature mean
This pleasing call the herald of a lie,
To hide the shame of discord and disease,
And win each fond admirer into snares,
Foil'd, baffled ? No :—with better providence  410
The general mother, conscious how infirm
Her offspring tread the paths of good and ill,
Thus, to the choice of credulous desire,
Doth objects the completest of their tribe
Distinguish and commend.  Yon flowery bank
Cloth'd in the soft magnificence of Spring,
Will not the flocks approve it ? will they ask
The reedy fen for pasture ?  That clear rill
Which trickleth murmuring from the mossy rock,
Yields it less wholesome beverage to the worn  420
And thirsty traveller, than the standing pool
With muddy weeds o'ergrown ?  Yon ragged vine
Whose lean and sullen clusters mourn the rage
Of Eurus, will the wine-press or the bowl
Report of her, as of the swelling grape
Which glitters through the tendrils, like a gem
When first it meets the sun ?  Or what are all
The various charms to life and sense adjoin'd ?
Are they not pledges of a state entire,
Where native order reigns, with every part  430
In health, and every function well perform'd ?
    Thus then at first was Beauty sent from Heaven,
The lovely ministress of Truth and Good
In this dark world : for Truth and Good are one ;
And Beauty dwells in them, and they in her,
With like participation.  Wherefore then,

O sons of earth, would ye dissolve the tie?
O ! wherefore with a rash and greedy aim
Seek ye to rove through every flattering scene
Which Beauty seems to deck, nor once inquire
Where is the suffrage of eternal Truth,
Or where the seal of undeceitful good,
To save your search from folly?   Wanting these,
Lo, Beauty withers in your void embrace ;
And with the glittering of an idiot's toy
Did fancy mock your vows.   Nor yet let hope,
That kindliest inmate of the youthful breast,
Be hence appall'd ; be turn'd to coward sloth
Sitting in silence, with dejected eyes
Incurious and with folded hands : far less          450
Let scorn of wild fantastic folly's dreams,
Or hatred of the bigot's savage pride
Persuade you e'er that Beauty, or the love
Which waits on Beauty, may not brook to hear
The sacred lore of undeceitful good
And Truth eternal.   From the vulgar crowd
Though Superstition, tyranness abhorr'd,
The reverence due to this majestic pair
With threats and execration still demands ;
Though the tame wretch, who asks of her the way
To their celestial dwelling, she constrains
To quench or set at nought the lamp of God
Within his frame ; through many a cheerless wild
Though forth she leads him credulous and dark
And aw'd with dubious notion ; though at length
Haply she plunge him into cloister'd cells
And mansions unrelenting as the grave,
But void of quiet, there to watch the hours
Of midnight ; there, amid the screaming owl's
Dire song, with spectres or with guilty shades  470
To talk of pangs and everlasting woe ;
Yet be not ye dismay'd.   A gentler star
Presides o'er your adventure.   From the bower
Where Wisdom sat with her Athenian sons,
Could but my happy hand entwine a wreath

Of Plato's olive with the Mantuan bay,
Then (for what need of cruel fear to you,
To you whom godlike love can well command?)
Then should my powerful voice at once dispel
Those monkish horrors; should in words divine
Relate how favour'd minds like you inspir'd,
And taught their inspiration to conduct
By ruling Heaven's decree, through various walks
And prospects various, but delightful all,
Move onward; while now myrtle groves appear,
Now arms and radiant trophies, now the rods
Of empire with the curule throne, or now
The domes of contemplation and the Muse.
Led by that hope sublime, whose cloudless eye
Through the fair toils and ornaments of earth   490
Discerns the nobler life reserv'd for heaven,
Favour'd alike they worship round the shrine
Where Truth conspicuous with her sister-twins,
The undivided partners of her sway,
With Good and Beauty reigns. O! let not us
By Pleasure's lying blandishments detain'd,
Or crouching to the frowns of bigot rage,
O! let not us one moment pause to join
That chosen band. And if the gracious Power,
Who first awaken'd my untutor'd song,         500
Will to my invocation grant anew
The tuneful spirit, then through all our paths
Ne'er shall the sound of this devoted lyre
Be wanting; whether on the rosy mead
When Summer smiles, to warn the melting heart
Of Luxury's allurement; whether firm
Against the torrent and the stubborn hill
To urge free Virtue's steps, and to her side
Summon that strong divinity of soul
Which conquers Chance and Fate: or on the height,
The goal assign'd her, haply to proclaim
Her triumph; on her brow to place the crown
Of uncorrupted praise; through future worlds
To follow her interminated way,

And bless Heaven's image in the heart of man.
　　Such is the worth of Beauty: such her power,
So blameless, so rever'd.　It now remains,
In just gradation through the various ranks
Of being, to contemplate how her gifts
Rise in due measure, watchful to attend　　　520
The steps of rising Nature.　Last and least,
In colours mingling with a random blaze,
Doth Beauty dwell.　Then higher in the forms
Of simplest, easiest measure ; in the bounds
Of circle, cube, or sphere.　The third ascent
To symmetry adds colour: thus the pearl
Shines in the concave of its purple bed,
And painted shells along some winding shore
Catch with indented folds the glancing sun.
Next, as we rise, appear the blooming tribes　[her
Which clothe the fragrant earth; which draw from
Their own nutrition ; which are born and die ;
Yet, in their seed, immortal : such the flowers
With which young Maia pays the village-maids
That hail her natal morn ; and such the groves
Which blithe Pomona rears on Vaga's bank,
To feed the bowl of Ariconian swains
Who quaff beneath her branches.　Nobler still
Is Beauty's name where, to the full consent
Of members and of features, to the pride　　　540
Of colour, and the vital change of growth,
Life's holy flame with piercing sense is given,
While active motion speaks the temper'd soul:
So moves the bird of Juno: so the steed
With rival swiftness beats the dusty plain,
And faithful dogs with eager airs of joy
Salute their fellows.　What sublimer pomp
Adorns the seat where Virtue dwells on earth,
And Truth's eternal day-light shines around ;
What palm belongs to man's imperial front,　　550
And woman powerful with becoming smiles,
Chief of terrestrial natures ; need we now
Strive to inculcate ?　Thus hath Beauty there

Her most conspicuous praise to matter lent,
Where most conspicuous through that shadowy veil
Breaks forth the bright expression of a mind :
By steps directing our enraptur'd search
To Him, the first of minds ; the chief ; the sole ;
From whom, through this wide, complicated world,
Did all her various lineaments begin ;          560
To whom alone, consenting and entire,
At once their mutual influence all display.
He, God most high (bear witness, Earth and Heaven)
The living fountains in himself contains
Of beauteous and sublime : with him enthron'd
Ere days or years trod their ethereal way,
In his supreme intelligence enthron'd,
The queen of love holds her unclouded state,
Urania.   Thee, O Father ! this extent
Of matter ; thee the sluggish earth and tract   570
Of seas, the heavens and heavenly splendours feel
Pervading, quickening, moving.   From the depth
Of thy great essence, forth didst thou conduct
Eternal Form ; and there, where Chaos reign'd,
Gav'st her dominion to erect her seat,
And sanctify the mansion.   All her works
Well-pleas'd thou didst behold : the gloomy fires
Of storm or earthquake, and the purest light
Of summer ; soft Campania's new-born rose,
And the slow weed which pines on Russian hills,
Comely alike to thy full vision stand :
To thy surrounding vision, which unites
All essences and powers of the great world
In one sole order, fair alike they stand,
As features well consenting, and alike
Requir'd by Nature ere she could attain
Her just resemblance to the perfect shape
Of universal Beauty, which with thee
Dwelt from the first.   Thou also, ancient Mind,
Whom love and free beneficence await        590
In all thy doings ; to inferior minds,
Thy offspring, and to man, thy youngest son,

M

Refusing no convenient gift nor good;
Their eyes did'st open, in this earth, yon heaven,
Those starry worlds, the .countenance divine
Of Beauty to behold.    But not to them
Did'st thou her awful magnitude reveal
Such as before thine own unbounded sight
She stands, (for never shall created soul
Conceive that object) nor, to all their kinds,    600
The same in shape or features didst thou frame
Her image.  Measuring well their different spheres
Of sense and action, thy paternal hand
Hath for each race prepar'd a different test
Of Beauty, own'd and reverenc'd as their guide
Most apt, most faithful.  Thence inform'd, they scan
The objects that surround them; and select,
Since the great whole disclaims their scanty view,
Each for himself selects peculiar parts
Of Nature; what the standard fix'd by Heaven
Within his breast approves: acquiring thus
A partial Beauty, which becomes his lot;
A Beauty which his eye may comprehend,
His hand may copy: leaving, O Supreme,
O thou whom none hath utter'd, leaving all
To thee that infinite, consummate form,
Which the great powers, the gods around thy throne
And nearest to thy counsels, know with thee
For ever to have been; but who she is,
Or what her likeness, know not.   Man surveys
A narrower scene, where, by the mix'd effect
Of things corporeal on his passive mind,
He judgeth what is fair.   Corporeal things
The mind of man impel with various powers,
And various features to his eye disclose.
The powers which move his sense with instant joy,
The features which attract his heart to love,
He marks, combines, reposits.   Other powers
And features of the selfsame thing (unless
The beauteous form, the creature of his mind,    630
Request their close alliance) he o'erlooks

Forgotten; or with self-beguiling zeal,
Whene'er his passions mingle in the work,
Half alters, half disowns.   The tribes of men
Thus from their different functions and the shapes
Familiar to their eye, with art obtain,
Unconscious of their purpose, yet with art
Obtain the Beauty fitting man to love:
Whose proud desires from Nature's homely toil
Oft turn away, fastidious: asking still          640
His mind's high aid, to purify the form
From matter's gross communion; to secure
For ever, from the meddling hand of Change
Or rude Decay, her features; and to add
Whatever ornaments may suit her mien,
Where'er he finds them scatter'd thro' the paths
Of Nature or of Fortune.   Then he seats
The accomplish'd image deep within his breast,
Reviews it, and accounts it good and fair.

 Thus the one Beauty of the world entire,      650
The universal Venus, far beyond
The keenest effort of created eyes,
And their most wide horizon, dwells enthron'd
In ancient silence.   At her footstool stands
An altar burning with eternal fire
Unsullied, unconsum'd.   Here every hour,
Here every moment, in their turns arrive
Her offspring; an innumerable band
Of sisters, comely all! but differing far
In age, in stature, and expressive mien,         660
More than bright Helen from her new born babe.
To this maternal shrine in turns they come,
Each with her sacred lamp; that from the source
Of living flame, which here immortal flows,
Their portions of its lustre they may draw
For days, or months, or years; for ages, some;
As their great parent's discipline requires.
Then to their several mansions they depart,
In stars, in planets, through the unknown shores
Of yon ethereal ocean.   Who can tell,           670

Even on the surface of this rolling earth,
How many make abode? The fields, the groves,
The winding rivers and the azure main,
Are render'd solemn by their frequent feet,
Their rites sublime. There each her destin'd home
Informs with that pure radiance from the skies
Brought down, and shines throughout her little
    sphere,
Exulting. Straight, as travellers by night
Turn toward a distant flame, so some fit eye,
Among the various tenants of the scene,     680
Discerns the heaven-born phantom seated there,
And owns her charms. Hence the wide universe,
Through all the seasons of revolving worlds,
Bears witness with its people, gods and men,
To Beauty's blissful power, and with the voice
Of grateful admiration still resounds:
That voice, to which is Beauty's frame divine
As is the cunning of the master's hand
To the sweet accent of the well-tun'd lyre.
    Genius of ancient Greece, whose faithful steps
Have led us to these awful solitudes
Of Nature and of Science; nurse rever'd
Of generous counsels and heroic deeds;
O! let some portion of thy matchless praise
Dwell in my breast, and teach me to adorn
This unattempted theme. Nor be my thoughts
Presumptuous counted, if amid the calm
Which Hesper sheds along the vernal heaven,
If I, from vulgar Superstition's walk,
Impatient steal, and from the unseemly rites     700
Of splendid Adulation, to attend
With hymns thy presence in the sylvan shade,
By their malignant footsteps unprofan'd.
Come, O renowned power; thy glowing mien
Such, and so elevated all thy form,
As when the great barbaric lord, again
And yet again diminish'd, hid his face
Among the herd of satraps and of kings;

And, at the lightning of thy lifted spear,
Crouch'd like a slave. Bring all thy martial spoils,
Thy palms, thy laurels, thy triumphal songs,
Thy smiling band of Arts, thy godlike sires
Of civil wisdom, thy unconquer'd youth
After some glorious day rejoicing round
Their new-erected trophy. Guide my feet
Through fair Lycéum's walk, the olive shades
Of Academus, and the sacred vale
Haunted by steps divine, where once beneath
That ever living platane's ample boughs
Ilissus, by Socratic sounds detain'd,      720
On his neglected urn attentive lay;
While Boreas, lingering on the neighbouring steep
With beauteous Orithyia, his love tale
In silent awe suspended. There let me
With blameless hand, from thy unenvious fields,
Transplant some living blossoms, to adorn
My native clime: while, far beyond the meed
Of Fancy's toil aspiring, I unlock
The springs of ancient wisdom: while I add
(What cannot be disjoin'd from Beauty's praise)
Thy name and native dress, thy works belov'd
And honour'd: while to my compatriot youth
I point the great example of thy sons,
And tune to Attic themes the British lyre.

## BOOK II.  1765.

INTRODUCTION to this more difficult part of the subject.  Of
Truth and its three classes, matter of fact, experimental
or scientifical truth, (contradistinguished from opinion)
and universal truth ; which last is either metaphysical or
geometrical, either purely intellectual or perfectly abstracted.  On the power of discerning truth depends that
of acting with the view of an end ; a circumstance essential to virtue.  Of Virtue, considered in the divine mind
as a perpetual and universal beneficence.  Of human virtue, considered as a system of particular sentiments and
actions, suitable to the design of Providence and the condition of man; to whom it constitutes the chief good and
the first beauty.  Of Vice and its origin.  Of Ridicule :
Its general nature and final cause.  Of the Passions ; particularly of those which relate to evil natural or moral,
and which are generally accounted painful, though not always unattended with pleasure.

THUS far of Beauty and the pleasing forms
　　　Which man's untutor'd fancy, from the scenes
Imperfect of this ever changing world,
Creates ; and views, enamour'd.   Now my song
Severer themes demand: mysterious Truth ;
And Virtue, sovereign good : the spells, the trains,
The progeny of Error ; the dread sway
Of Passion ; and whatever hidden stores
From her own lofty deeds and from herself
The mind acquires.   Severer argument:　　　　10
Not less attractive ; nor deserving less
A constant ear.   For what are all the forms
Educ'd by fancy from corporeal things,
Greatness, or pomp, or symmetry of parts ?
Not tending to the heart, soon feeble grows,
As the blunt arrow 'gainst the knotty trunk,
Their impulse on the sense : while the pall'd eye

Expects in vain its tribute; asks in vain,
Where are the ornaments it once admir'd?
Not so the moral species, nor the powers      20
Of Passion and of Thought.   The ambitious mind
With objects boundless as her own desires
Can there converse: by these unfading forms
Touch'd and awaken'd still, with eager act
She bends each nerve, and meditates well pleas'd
Her gifts, her godlike fortune.   Such the scenes
Now opening round us.   May the destin'd verse
Maintain its equal tenor, though in tracts
Obscure and arduous!   May the source of light,
All-present, all-sufficient, guide our steps      30
Through every maze! and whom in childish years
From the loud throng, the beaten paths of wealth
And power, thou didst apart send forth to speak
In tuneful words concerning highest things,
Him still do thou, O Father, at those hours
Of pensive freedom, when the human soul
Shuts out the rumour of the world, him still
Touch thou with secret lessons: call thou back
Each erring thought; and let the yielding strains
From his full bosom, like a welcome rill      40
Spontaneous from its healthy fountain, flow!
    But from what name, what favourable sign,
What heavenly auspice, rather shall I date
My perilous excursion, than from Truth,
That nearest inmate of the human soul;
Estrang'd from whom, the countenance divine
Of man disfigur'd and dishonour'd, sinks
Among inferior things?   For to the brutes
Perception and the transient boons of sense
Hath Fate imparted: but to man alone      50
Of sublunary beings was it given
Each fleeting impulse on the sensual powers
At leisure to review; with equal eye
To scan the passion of the stricken nerve,
Or the vague object striking: to conduct
From sense, the portal turbulent and loud,

Into the mind's wide palace one by one
The frequent, pressing, fluctuating forms,
And question and compare them.  Thus he learns
Their birth and fortunes; how allied they haunt
The avenues of sense; what laws direct
Their union; and what various discords rise,
Or fixed or casual: which when his clear thought
Retains and when his faithful words express,
That living image of the external scene,
As in a polish'd mirror held to view,
Is Truth: where'er it varies from the shape
And hue of its exemplar, in that part
Dim Error lurks.  Moreover, from without
When oft the same society of forms                    70
In the same order have approach'd his mind,
He deigns no more their steps with curious heed
To trace;  no more their features or their garb
He now examines; but of them and their
Condition, as with some diviner's tongue,
Affirms what Heaven in every distant place,
Through every future season, will decree.
This too is Truth: where'er his prudent lips
Wait till experience diligent and slow
Has authoriz'd their sentence, this is Truth;       80
A second, higher kind: the parent this
Of Science; or the lofty power herself,
Science herself: on whom the wants and cares
Of social life depend; the substitute
Of God's own wisdom in this toilsome world;
The providence of man.  Yet oft in vain,
To earn her aid, with fix'd and anxious eye
He looks on Nature's and on Fortune's course:
Too much in vain.  His duller visual ray
The stillness and the persevering acts               90
Of Nature oft elude; and Fortune oft     .
With step fantastic from her wonted walk
Turns into mazes dim: his sight is foil'd;
And the crude sentence of his faltering tongue
Is but opinion's verdict, half believed

And prone to change. Here thou, who feel'st thine ear
Congenial to my lyre's profounder tone,
Pause, and be watchful.  Hitherto the stores,
Which feed thy mind and exercise her powers,
Partake the relish of their native soil,          100
Their parent earth.  But know, a nobler dower
Her Sire at birth decreed her; purer gifts
From his own treasure; forms which never deign'd
In eyes or ears to dwell, within the sense
Of earthly organs; but sublime were plac'd
In his essential reason, leading there
That vast ideal host which all his works
Through endless ages never will reveal.
Thus then endow'd, the feeble creature man,
The slave of hunger and the prey of death,        110
Even now, even here, in earth's dim prison bound,
The language of intelligence divine
Attains; repeating oft concerning one
And many, pass'd and present, parts and whole,
Those sovereign dictates which in farthest heaven,
Where no orb rolls, Eternity's fix'd ear
Hears from coëval Truth, when Chance nor Change,
Nature's loud progeny, nor Nature's self
Dares intermeddle or approach her throne.
Ere long, o'er this corporeal world he learns      120
To extend her sway; while calling from the deep,
From earth and air, their multitudes untold
Of figures and of motions round his walk,
For each wide family some single birth
He sets in view, the impartial type of all
Its brethren; suffering it to claim, beyond
Their common heritage, no private gift,
No proper fortune.  Then whate'er his eye
In this discerns, his bold unerring tongue
Pronounceth of the kindred, without bound,         130
Without condition.  Such the rise of forms
Sequester'd far from sense and every spot
Peculiar in the realms of space or time:
Such is the throne which man for Truth amid

The paths of mutability hath built
Secure, unshaken, still; and whence he views,
In matter's mouldering structures, the pure forms
Of triangle or circle, cube or cone,
Impassive all; whose attributes nor force
Nor fate can alter.   There he first conceives    140
True being, and an intellectual world
The same this hour and ever.   Thence he deems
Of his own lot; above the painted shapes
That fleeting move o'er this terrestrial scene
Looks up; beyond the adamantine gates
Of death expatiates; as his birthright claims
Inheritance in all the works of God;
Prepares for endless time his plan of life,
And counts the universe itself his home.

Whence also but from Truth, the light of minds,
Is human fortune gladden'd with the rays
Of Virtue? with the moral colours thrown
On every walk of this our social scene,
Adorning for the eye of gods and men
The passions, actions, habitudes of life,
And rendering earth like heaven, a sacred place
Where Love and Praise may take delight to dwell?
Let none with heedless tongue from Truth disjoin
The reign of Virtue.   Ere the dayspring flow'd,
Like sisters link'd in Concord's golden chain,    160
They stood before the great Eternal Mind,
Their common parent; and by him were both
Sent forth among his creatures, hand in hand,
Inseparably join'd: nor e'er did Truth
Find an apt ear to listen to her lore,        [Truth's
Which knew not Virtue's voice; nor, save where
Majestic words are heard and understood,
Doth Virtue deign to inhabit.   Go, inquire
Of Nature: not among Tartarian rocks,
Whither the hungry vulture with its prey        170
Returns: not where the lion's sullen roar
At noon resounds along the lonely banks
Of ancient Tigris: but her gentler scenes,

The dovecote and the shepherd's fold at morn,
Consult; or by the meadow's fragrant hedge,
In spring-time when the woodlands first are green,
Attend the linnet singing to his mate
Couch'd o'er their tender young. To this fond care
Thou dost not Virtue's honourable name
Attribute; wherefore, save that not one gleam  180
Of Truth did e'er discover to themselves
Their little hearts, or teach them, by the effects
Of that parental love, the love itself
To judge, and measure its officious deeds?
But man, whose eyelids Truth has fill'd with day,
Discerns how skilfully to bounteous ends
His wise affections move; with free accord
Adopts their guidance; yields himself secure
To Nature's prudent impulse; and converts
Instinct to duty and to sacred law.          190
Hence Right and Fit on earth: while thus to man
The Almighty Legislator hath explain'd
The springs of action fix'd within his breast;
Hath given him power to slacken or restrain
Their effort; and hath shown him how they join
Their partial movements with the master-wheel
Of the great world, and serve that sacred end
Which he, the unerring reason, keeps in view.
    For (if a mortal tongue may speak of him
And his dread ways) even as his boundless eye,  200
Connecting every form and every change,
Beholds the perfect Beauty; so his will,
Through every hour producing good to all
The family of creatures, is itself
The perfect Virtue.  Let the grateful swain
Remember this, as oft with joy and praise
He looks upon the falling dews which clothe
His lawns with verdure, and the tender seed
Nourish within his furrows: when between
Dead seas and burning skies, where long unmov'd
The bark had languish'd, now a rustling gale
Lifts o'er the fickle waves her dancing prow,

Let the glad pilot, bursting out in thanks,
Remember this : lest blind o'erweening pride
Pollute their offerings : lest their selfish heart
Say to the heavenly ·ruler, " At our call
Relents thy power : by us thy arm is mov'd."
Fools ! who of God as of each other deem :
Who his invariable acts deduce
From sudden counsels transient as their own ;    220
Nor farther of his bounty, than the event
Which haply meets their loud and eager prayer,
Acknowledge ; nor, beyond the drop minute
Which haply they have tasted, heed the source
That flows for all ; the fountain of his love
Which, from the summit where he sits enthron'd,
Pours health and joy, unfailing streams, throughout
The spacious region flourishing in view,
The goodly work of his eternal day,
His own fair universe ; on which alone    230
His counsels fix, and whence alone his will
Assumes her strong direction.   Such is now
His sovereign purpose : such it was before
All multitude of years.   For his right arm
Was never idle : his bestowing love
Knew no beginning ; was not as a change
Of mood that woke at last and started up
After a deep and solitary sloth
Of boundless ages.   No : he now is good,
He ever was.   The feet of hoary Time    240
Through their eternal course have travell'd o'er
No speechless, lifeless desert ; but through scenes
Cheerful with bounty still ; among a pomp
Of worlds, for gladness round the Maker's throne
Loud-shouting, or, in many dialects
Of hope and filial trust, imploring thence
The fortunes of their people : where so fix'd
Were all the dates of being, so dispos'd
To every living soul of every kind
The field of motion and the hour of rest,    250
That each the general happiness might serve ;

And, by the discipline of laws divine
Convinc'd of folly or chastis'd from guilt,
Each might at length be happy. What remains
Shall be like what is pass'd; but fairer still,
And still increasing in the godlike gifts
Of Life and Truth. The same paternal hand,
From the mute shell-fish gasping on the shore,
To men, to angels, to celestial minds,
Will ever lead the generations on                       260
Through higher scenes of being: while, supplied
From day to day by his enlivening breath,
Inferior orders in succession rise
To fill the void below. As flame ascends,
As vapours to the earth in showers return,
As the pois'd ocean toward the attracting moon
Swells, and the ever-listening planets charm'd
By the sun's call their onward pace incline,
So all things which have life aspire to God,
Exhaustless fount of intellectual day!                  270
Centre of souls! Nor doth the mastering voice
Of Nature cease within to prompt aright
Their steps; nor is the care of Heaven withheld
From sending to the toil external aid;
That in their stations all may persevere
To climb the ascent of being, and approach
For ever nearer to the Life divine.
    But this eternal fabric was not rais'd
For man's inspection. Though to some be given
To catch a transient visionary glimpse                  280
Of that majestic scene which boundless power
Prepares for perfect goodness, yet in vain
Would human life her faculties expand
To embosom such an object. Nor could e'er
Virtue or praise have touch'd the hearts of men,
Had not the Sovereign Guide, through every stage
Of this their various journey, pointed out
New hopes, new toils, which to their humble sphere
Of sight and strength might such importance hold
As doth the wide creation to his own.                   290

Hence all the little charities of life,
With all their duties : hence that favourite palm
Of human will, when duty is suffic'd,
And still the liberal soul in ampler deeds
Would manifest herself; that sacred sign
Of her rever'd affinity to Him
Whose bounties are his own ; to whom none said,
" Create the wisest, fullest, fairest world,
And make its offspring happy ;" who, intent
Some likeness of Himself among his works        300
To view, hath pour'd into the human breast
A ray of knowledge and of love, which guides
Earth's feeble race to act their Maker's part,
Self-judging, self-oblig'd : while, from before
That god-like function, the gigantic power
Necessity, though wont to curb the force
Of Chaos and the savage elements,
Retires abash'd, as from a scene too high
For her brute tyranny, and with her bears
Her scorned followers, Terror, and base Awe      310
Who blinds herself, and that ill-suited pair,
Obedience link'd with Hatred.   Then the soul
Arises in her strength ; and, looking round
Her busy sphere, whatever work she views,
Whatever counsel bearing any trace
Of her Creator's likeness, whether apt
To aid her fellows or preserve herself
In her superior functions unimpair'd,
Thither she turns exulting : that she claims
As her peculiar good: on that, through all        320
The fickle seasons of the day, she looks
With reverence still : to that, as to a fence
Against affliction and the darts of pain,
Her drooping hopes repair : and, once oppos'd
To that, all other pleasure, other wealth,
Vile, as the dross upon the molten gold,
Appears, and loathsome as the briny sea
To him who languishes with thirst and sighs
For some known fountain pure.  For what can strive

With Virtue? Which of Nature's regions vast 330
Can in so many forms produce to sight
Such powerful Beauty? Beauty, which the eye
Of Hatred cannot look upon secure:
Which Envy's self contemplates, and is turn'd
Ere long to tenderness, to infant smiles,
Or tears of humblest love. Is aught so fair
In all the dewy landscapes of the Spring,
The Summer's noontide groves, the purple eve
At harvest-home, or in the frosty moon
Glittering on some smooth sea; is aught so fair
As virtuous friendship? as the honour'd roof
Whither from highest heaven immortal Love
His torch ethereal and his golden bow
Propitious brings, and there a temple holds
To whose unspotted service gladly vow'd
The social band of parent, brother, child,
With smiles and sweet discourse and gentle deeds
Adore his power? What gift of richest clime
E'er drew such eager eyes, or prompted such
Deep wishes, as the zeal that snatcheth back 350
From Slander's poisonous tooth a foe's renown;
Or crosseth danger in his lion walk,
A rival's life to rescue? as the young
Athenian warrior sitting down in bonds,
That his great father's body might not want
A peaceful, humble tomb? the Roman wife
Teaching her lord how harmless was the wound
Of death, how impotent the tyrant's rage,
Who nothing more could threaten to afflict
Their faithful love? Or is there in the abyss, 360
Is there, among the adamantine spheres
Wheeling unshaken through the boundless void,
Aught that with half such majesty can fill
The human bosom, as when Brutus rose
Refulgent from the stroke of Cæsar's fate
Amid the crowd of patriots; and, his arm
Aloft extending like eternal Jove
When guilt brings down the thunder, call'd aloud

On Tully's name, and shook the crimson sword
Of justice in his rapt astonish'd eye,                    370
And bade the father of his country hail,
For lo, the tyrant prostrate on the dust,
And Rome again is free?    Thus, thro' the paths
Of human life, in various pomp array'd
Walks the wise daughter of the judge of heaven,
Fair Virtue; from her father's throne supreme
Sent down to utter laws, such as on earth
Most apt he knew, most powerful to promote
The weal of all his works, the gracious end
Of his dread empire.    And tho' haply man's          380
Obscurer sight, so far beyond himself
And the brief labours of his little home,
Extends not; yet, by the bright presence won
Of this divine instructress, to her sway
Pleas'd he assents, nor heeds the distant goal
To which her voice conducts him.    Thus hath God,
Still looking toward his own high purpose, fix'd
The virtues of his creatures; thus he rules
The parent's fondness and the patriot's zeal;
Thus the warm sense of honour and of shame;    390
The vows of gratitude, the faith of love;
And all the comely intercourse of praise,
The joy of human life, the earthly heaven!
     How far unlike them must the lot of guilt
Be found?    Or what terrestrial woe can match
The self-convicted bosom, which hath wrought
The bane of others or enslaved itself
With shackles vile?    Not poison, nor sharp fire,
Nor the worst pangs that ever monkish hate
Suggested, or despotic rage impos'd,                     400
Were at that season an unwish'd exchange:
When the soul loathes herself: when, flying thence
To crowds, on every brow she sees portray'd
Fell demons, Hate or Scorn, which drive her back
To solitude, her judge's voice divine
To hear in secret, haply sounding through
The troubled dreams of midnight, and still, still

Demanding for his violated laws
Fit recompense, or charging her own tongue
To speak the award of justice on herself. 410
For well she knows what faithful hints within
Were whisper'd, to beware the lying forms
Which turn'd her footsteps from the safer way,
What cautions to suspect their painted dress,
And look with steady eyelid on their smiles,
Their frowns, their tears. In vain : the dazzling hues
Of Fancy, and Opinion's eager voice,
Too much prevail'd. For mortals tread the path
In which Opinion says they follow good
Or fly from evil : and Opinion gives 420
Report of good or evil, as the scene
Was drawn by Fancy, pleasing or deform'd :
Thus her report can never there be true
Where Fancy cheats the intellectual eye
With glaring colours and distorted lines.
Is there a man to whom the name of death
Brings terror's ghastly pageants conjur'd up
Before him, death-bed groans, and dismal vows,
And the frail soul plung'd headlong from the brink
Of life and daylight down the gloomy air, 430
An unknown depth, to gulfs of torturing fire
Unvisited by mercy ? Then what hand
Can snatch this dreamer from the fatal toils
Which Fancy and Opinion thus conspire
To twine around his heart ? Or who shall hush
Their clamour, when they tell him that to die,
To risk those horrors, is a direr curse
Than basest life can bring ? Tho' Love with prayers
Most tender, with affliction's sacred tears,
Beseech his aid ; though Gratitude and Faith 440
Condemn each step which loiters ; yet let none
Make answer for him that if any frown
Of Danger thwart his path, he will not stay
Content, and be a wretch to be secure.
Here Vice begins then : at the gate of life,
Ere the young multitude to diverse roads

N

Part, like fond pilgrims on a journey unknown,
Sits Fancy, deep enchantress; and to each
With kind maternal looks presents her bowl,
A potent beverage.   Heedless they comply :    450
Till the whole soul from that mysterious draught
Is ting'd, and every transient thought imbibes
Of gladness or disgust, desire or fear,
One homebred colour : which not all the lights
Of Science e'er shall change ; not all the storms
Of adverse Fortune wash away, nor yet
The robe of purest Virtue quite conceal.
Thence on they pass, where meeting frequent shapes
Of good and evil, cunning phantoms apt
To fire or freeze the breast, with them they join
In dangerous parley ; listening oft, and oft
Gazing with reckless passion, while its garb
The spectre heightens, and its pompous tale
Repeats with some new circumstance to suit
That early tincture of the hearer's soul.
And should the guardian, Reason, but for one
Short moment yield to this illusive scene
His ear and eye, the intoxicating charm
Involves him, till no longer he discerns,
Or only guides to err.   Then revel forth    470
A furious band that spurn him from the throne,
And all is uproar.   Hence Ambition climbs
With sliding feet and hands impure, to grasp
Those solemn toys which glitter in his view
On Fortune's rugged steep : hence pale Revenge
Unsheaths her murderous dagger : Rapine hence
And envious Lust, by venal fraud upborne,
Surmount the reverend barrier of the laws
Which kept them from their prey : hence all the
        crimes
That e'er defil'd the earth, and all the plagues    480
That follow them for vengeance, in the guise
Of Honour, Safety, Pleasure, Ease, or Pomp,
Stole first into the fond believing mind.
    Yet not by Fancy's witchcraft on the brain

Are always the tumultuous passions driven
To guilty deeds, nor Reason bound in chains
That Vice alone may lord it. Oft adorn'd
With motley pageants, Folly mounts his throne,
And plays her idiot antics, like a queen.
A thousand garbs she wears: a thousand ways
She whirls her giddy empire. Lo, thus far
With bold adventure\to the Mantuan lyre
I sing for contemplation link'd with love,
A pensive theme. Now haply should my song
Unbend that serious countenance, and learn
Thalia's tripping gait, her shrill-ton'd voice,
Her wiles familiar: whether scorn she darts
In wanton ambush from her lip or eye,
Or whether with a sad disguise of care
O'ermantling her gay brow, she acts in sport   500
The deeds of Folly, and from all sides round
Calls forth impetuous Laughter's gay rebuke;
Her province. But through every comic scene
To lead my Muse with her light pencil arm'd;
Through every swift occasion which the hand
Of Laughter points at, when the mirthful sting
Distends her labouring sides and chokes her tongue;
Were endless as to sound each grating note
With which the rooks, and chattering daws, and
Unwieldy inmates of the village pond,   [grave
The changing seasons of the sky proclaim;
Sun, cloud, or shower. Suffice it to have said,
Where'er the power of Ridicule displays
Her quaint-ey'd visage, some incongruous form,
Some stubborn dissonance of things combin'd,
Strikes on her quick perception: whether Pomp,
Or Praise, or Beauty be dragg'd in and shown
Where sordid fashions, where ignoble deeds,
Where foul Deformity is wont to dwell;
Or whether these with shrewd and wayward spite
Invade resplendent Pomp's imperious mien,
The charms of Beauty, or the boast of Praise.
   Ask we for what fair end the Almighty Sire

In mortal bosoms stirs this gay contempt,
These grateful pangs of laughter; from disgust
Educing pleasure?   Wherefore, but to aid
The tardy steps of Reason, and at once
By this prompt impulse urge us to depress
Wild Folly's aims?   For though the sober light
Of Truth slow dawning on the watchful mind     530
At length unfolds, through many a subtile tie,
How these uncouth disorders end at last
In public evil; yet benignant Heaven,
Conscious how dim the dawn of Truth appears
To thousands, conscious what a scanty pause
From labour and from care the wider lot
Of humble life affords for studious thought
To scan the maze of Nature, therefore stamp'd
These glaring scenes with characters of scorn,
As broad, as obvious to the passing clown     540
As to the letter'd sage's curious eye.
     But other evils o'er the steps of man
Thro' all his walks impend ; against whose might
The slender darts of Laughter nought avail :
A trivial warfare.   Some, like cruel guards,
On Nature's ever moving throne attend;
With mischief arm'd for him whoe'er shall thwart
The path of her inexorable wheels,
While she pursues the work that must be done
Thro' ocean, earth, and air.   Hence, frequent forms
Of woe; the merchant, with his wealthy bark,
Buried by dashing waves; the traveller
Pierc'd by the pointed lightning in his haste;
And the poor husbandman, with folded arms,
Surveying his lost labours, and a heap
Of blasted chaff the product of the field
Whence he expected bread.   But worse than these
I deem, far worse, that other race of ills
Which human kind rear up among themselves;
That horrid offspring which misgovern'd Will     560
Bears to fantastic Error; vices, crimes,
Furies that curse the earth, and make the blows,

The heaviest blows, of Nature's innocent hand
Seem sport : which are indeed but as the care
Of a wise parent, who solicits good
To all her house, though haply at the price
Of tears and froward wailing and reproach
From some unthinking child, 'whom not the less
Its mother destines to be happy still.

   These sources then of pain, this double lot   570
Of evil in the inheritance of man,
Requir'd for his protection no slight force,
No careless watch ; and therefore was his breast
Fenc'd round with passions quick to be alarm'd,
Or stubborn to oppose ; with Fear, more swift
Than beacons catching flame from hill to hill,
Where armies land ; with Anger, uncontrol'd
As the young lion bounding on his prey ;
With Sorrow, that locks up the struggling heart,
And Shame, that overcasts the drooping eye   580
As with a cloud of lightning.  These the part
Perform of eager monitors, and goad
The soul more sharply than with points of steel,
Her enemies to shun or to resist.
And as those passions, that converse with good,
Are good themselves ; as Hope and Love and Joy,
Among the fairest and the sweetest boons
Of life, we rightly count : so these, which guard
Against invading evil, still excite
Some pain, some tumult : these, within the mind
Too oft admitted or too long retain'd,
Shock their frail seat, and by their uncurb'd rage
To savages more fell than Libya breeds
Transform themselves : till human thought becomes
A gloomy ruin, haunt of shapes unbless'd,
Of self-tormenting fiends ; Horror, Despair,
Hatred, and wicked Envy : foes to all
The works of Nature and the gifts of Heaven.

   But when thro' blameless paths to righteous ends
Those keener passions urge the awaken'd soul,
I would not, as ungracious violence,

Their sway describe, nor from their free career
The fellowship of Pleasure quite exclude.
For what can render, to the self-approv'd,
Their temper void of comfort, though in pain?
Who knows not with what majesty divine
The forms of Truth and Justice to the mind
Appear, ennobling oft the sharpest woe
With triumph and rejoicing?   Who, that bears
A human bosom, hath not often felt          610
How dear are all those ties which bind our race
In gentleness together, and how sweet
Their force, let Fortune's wayward hand the while
Be kind or cruel?   Ask the faithful youth
Why the cold urn, of her whom long he lov'd,
So often fills his arms; so often draws
His lonely footsteps, silent and unseen,
To pay the mournful tribute of his tears?
Oh! he will tell thee that the wealth of worlds
Should ne'er seduce his bosom to forego        620
Those sacred hours when, stealing from the noise
Of care and envy, sweet remembrance soothes
With Virtue's kindest looks his aching breast,
And turns his tears to rapture?   Ask the crowd,
Which flies impatient from the village walk
To climb the neighbouring cliffs, when far below
The savage winds have hurl'd upon the coast
Some helpless bark; while holy Pity melts
The general eye, or Terror's icy hand
Smites their distorted limbs and horrent hair;   630
While every mother closer to her breast
Catcheth her child, and, pointing where the waves
Foam through the shatter'd vessel, shrieks aloud
As one poor wretch, who spreads his piteous arms
For succour, swallow'd by the roaring surge,
As now another, dash'd against the rock,
Drops lifeless down.   O! deemest thou indeed
No pleasing influence here by Nature given
To mutual terror and compassion's tears?
No tender charm mysterious, which attracts    640

O'er all that edge of pain the social powers
To this their proper action and their end?
Ask thy own heart; when, at the midnight hour,
Slow through that pensive gloom thy pausing eye,
Led by the glimmering taper, moves around
The reverend volumes of the dead, the songs
Of Grecian bards, and records writ by fame
For Grecian heroes, where the Sovran Power
Of heaven and earth surveys the immortal page
Even as a father meditating all                           650
The praises of his son, and bids the rest
Of mankind there the fairest model learn
Of their own nature, and the noblest deeds
Which yet the world hath seen.  If then thy soul
Join in the lot of those diviner men;
Say, when the prospect darkens on thy view;
When, sunk by many a wound, heroic states
Mourn in the dust and tremble at the frown
Of hard Ambition; when the generous band
Of youths who fought for freedom and their sires
Lie side by side in death; when brutal Force
Usurps the throne of Justice, turns the pomp
Of guardian power, the majesty of rule,
The sword, the laurel, and the purple robe,
To poor dishonest pageants, to adorn
A robber's walk, and glitter in the eyes
Of such as bow the knee; when beauteous works,
Rewards of virtue, sculptur'd forms which deck'd
With more than human grace the warrior's arch
Or patriot's tomb, now victims to appease          670
Tyrannic envy, strew the common path
With awful ruins; when the Muse's haunt,
The marble porch where Wisdom wont to talk
With Socrates or Tully, hears no more
Save the hoarse jargon of contentious monks,
Or female Superstition's midnight prayer;
When ruthless Havoc from the hand of Time
Tears the destroying scythe, with surer stroke
To mow the monuments of Glory down;

Till Desolation o'er the grass-grown street    680
Expands her raven wings, and, from the gate
Where senates once the weal of nations plann'd
Hisseth the gliding snake through hoary weeds
That clasp the mouldering column : thus when all
The widely-mournful scene is fix'd within
Thy throbbing bosom ; when the patriot's tear
Starts from thine eye, and thy extended arm
In fancy hurls the thunderbolt of Jove
To fire the impious wreath on Philip's brow,
Or dash Octavius from the trophied car ;    690
Say, doth thy secret soul repine to taste
The big distress ? or wouldst thou then exchange
Those heart-ennobling sorrows for the lot
Of him who sits amid the gaudy herd
Of silent flatterers bending to his nod ;
And o'er them, like a giant, casts his eye,
And says within himself, " I am a King,
And wherefore should the clamorous voice of woe
Intrude upon mine ear ?"    The dregs corrupt
Of barbarous ages, that Circæan draught    700
Of servitude and folly, have not yet,
Bless'd be the Eternal Ruler of the world !
Yet have not so dishonour'd, so deform'd
The native judgment of the human soul,
Nor so effac'd the image of her Sire.


BOOK III. 1770.


WHAT tongue then may explain the various
        fate
Which reigns o'er earth ? or who to mortal eyes
Illustrate this perplexing labyrinth
Of joy and woe through which the feet of man
Are doom'd to wander ?    That Eternal Mind
From passions, wants, and envy far estrang'd,
Who built the spacious universe, and deck'd

Each part so richly with whate'er pertains
To life, to health, to pleasure; why bade he
The viper Evil, creeping in, pollute      10
The goodly scene, and with insidious rage,
While the poor inmate looks around and smiles,
Dart her fell sting with poison to his soul?
Hard is the question, and from ancient days
Hath still oppress'd with care the sage's thought;
Hath drawn forth accents from the poet's lyre
Too sad, too deeply plaintive: nor did e'er
Those chiefs of human kind, from whom the light
Of heavenly truth first gleam'd on barbarous lands,
Forget this dreadful secret when they told      20
What wondrous things had to their favour'd eyes
And ears on cloudy mountain been reveal'd,
Or in deep cave by nymph or power divine,
Portentous oft and wild. Yet one I know,
Could I the speech of lawgivers assume,
One old and splendid tale I would record
With which the Muse of Solon in sweet strains
Adorn'd this theme profound, and render'd all
Its darkness, all its terrors, bright as noon,
Or gentle as the golden star of eve.      30
Who knows not Solon? last, and wisest far,
Of those whom Greece triumphant in the height
Of glory, styl'd her fathers? him whose voice
Through Athens hush'd the storm of civil wrath;
Taught envious Want and cruel Wealth to join
In friendship; and, with sweet compulsion, tam'd
Minerva's eager people to his laws,
Which their own goddess in his breast inspir'd?
   'Twas now the time when his heroic task
Seem'd but perform'd in vain: when sooth'd by years
Of flattering service, the fond multitude
Hung with their sudden counsels on the breath
Of great Pisistratus: that chief renown'd,
Whom Hermes and the Idalian queen had train'd
Even from his birth to every powerful art
Of pleasing and persuading: from whose lips

Flow'd eloquence which like the vows of love
Could steal away suspicion from the hearts
Of all who listen'd.   Thus from day to day
He won the general suffrage, and beheld          50
Each rival overshadow'd and depress'd
Beneath his ampler state: yet oft complain'd,
As one less kindly treated, who had hop'd
To merit favour, but submits perforce
To find another's services preferr'd,
Nor yet relaxeth aught of faith or zeal.
Then tales were scatter'd of his envious foes,
Of snares that watch'd his fame, of daggers aim'd
Against his life.   At last with trembling limbs,
His hair diffus'd and wild, his garments loose,   60
And stain'd with blood from self-inflicted wounds,
He burst into the public place, as there,
There only, were his refuge; and declar'd
In broken words, with sighs of deep regret,
The mortal danger he had scarce repell'd.
Fir'd with his tragic tale, the indignant crowd
To guard his steps, forthwith a menial band,
Array'd beneath his eye for deeds of war,
Decree.   O still too liberal of their trust,
And oft betray'd by over-grateful love,          70
The generous people !   Now behold him fenc'd
By mercenary weapons, like a king,
Forth issuing from the city-gate at eve
To seek his rural mansion, and with pomp
Crowding the public road.   The swain stops short,
And sighs: the officious townsmen stand at gaze,
And shrinking give the sullen pageant room.
Yet not the less obsequious was his brow;
Nor less profuse of courteous words his tongue,
Of gracious gifts his hand: the while by stealth,
Like a small torrent fed with evening showers,
His train increas'd; till, at that fatal time
Just as the public eye, with doubt and shame
Startled, began to question what it saw,
Swift as the sound of earthquakes rush'd a voice

Through Athens, that Pisistratus had fill'd
The rocky citadel with hostile arms,
Had barr'd the steep ascent, and sate within
Amid his hirelings, meditating death
To all whose stubborn necks his yoke refus'd.     90
Where then was Solon?   After ten long years
Of absence, full of haste from foreign shores
The sage, the lawgiver had now arriv'd:
Arriv'd, alas! to sèe that Athens, that
Fair temple rais'd by him and sacred call'd
To Liberty and Concord, now profan'd
By savage hate, or sunk into a den
Of slaves who crouch beneath the master's scourge,
And deprecate his wrath and court his chains.
Yet did not the wise patriot's grief impede     100
His virtuous will, nor was his heart inclin'd
One moment with such woman-like distress
To view the transient storms of civil war,
As thence to yield his country and her hopes
To all-devouring bondage.   His bright helm,
Even while the traitor's impious act is told,
He buckles on his hoary head: he girds
With mail his stooping breast: the shield, the spear
He snatcheth; and with swift indignant strides
The assembled people seeks: proclaims aloud   110
It was no time for counsel: in their spears
Lay all their prudence now: the tyrant yet
Was not so firmly seated on his throne,
But that one shock of their united force
Would dash him from the summit of his pride
Headlong and groveling in the dust.   "What else
Can re-assert the lost Athenian name
So cheaply to the laughter of the world
Betray'd; by guile beneath an infant's faith
So mock'd and scorn'd? Away, then: Freedom now
And Safety dwell not but with Fame in Arms:
Myself will show you where their mansion lies,
And through the walks of Danger or of Death
Conduct you to them." While he spake, through all

Their crowded ranks his quick sagacious eye
He darted; where no cheerful voice was heard
Of social daring; no stretch'd arm was seen
Hastening their common task: but pale mistrust
Wrinkled each brow: they shook their head, and
      down               [doubts
Their slack hands hung: cold sighs and whisper'd
From breath to breath stole round.   The sage
      meantime
Look'd speechless on, while his big bosom heav'd
Struggling with shame and sorrow: till at last
A tear broke forth; and, " O immortal shades,
O Theseus," he exclaim'd, " O Codrus, where,
Where are ye now? behold for what ye toil'd
Through life! behold for whom ye chose to die."
No more he added; but with lonely steps
Weary and slow, his silver beard depress'd,
And his stern eyes bent heedless on the ground,
Back to his silent dwelling he repair'd.
There o'er the gate, his armour, as a man
Whom from the service of the war his chief
Dismisseth after no inglorious toil,
He fix'd in general view.   One wishful look
He sent, unconscious, toward the public place
At parting: then beneath his quiet roof
Without a word, without a sigh, retir'd.
   Scarce had the morrow's sun his golden rays
From sweet Hymettus darted o'er the fanes    150
Of Cecrops to the Salaminian shores,
When, lo, on Solon's threshold met the feet
Of four Athenians by the same sad care
Conducted all: than whom the state beheld
None nobler.   First came Megacles, the son
Of great Alcmæon, whom the Lydian king,
The mild, unhappy Crœsus, in his days
Of glory had with costly gifts adorn'd,
Fair vessels, splendid garments, tinctur'd webs
And heaps of treasur'd gold, beyond the lot    160
Of many sovereigns; thus requiting well

That hospitable favour which erewhile
Alcmæon to his messengers had shown,
Whom he with offerings worthy of the god
Sent from his throne in Sardis to revere
Apollo's Delphic shrine.  With Megacles
Approach'd his son, whom Agarista bore,
The virtuous child of Clisthenes whose hand
Of Grecian sceptres the most ancient far
In Sicyon sway'd : but greater fame he drew    170
From arms control'd by justice, from the love
Of the wise Muses, and the unenvied wreath
Which glad Olympia gave.  For thither once
His warlike steeds the hero led, and there
Contended through the tumult of the course
With skilful wheels.  Then victor at the goal,
Amid the applauses of assembled Greece,
High on his car he stood and wav'd his arm.
Silence ensued : when straight the herald's voice
Was heard, inviting every Grecian youth,    180
Whom Clisthenes content might call his son,
To visit, ere twice thirty days were pass'd,
The towers of Sicyon.  There the chief decreed,
Within the circuit of the following year,
To join at Hymen's altar, hand in hand
With his fair daughter, him among the guests
Whom worthiest he should deem.  Forthwith from
        all
The bounds of Greece the ambitious wooers came :
From rich Hesperia ; from the Illyrian shore
Where Epidamnus over Adria's surge    190
Looks on the setting sun ; from those brave tribes
Chaonian or Molossian whom the race
Of great Achilles governs, glorying still
In Troy o'erthrown ; from rough Ætolia, nurse
Of men who first among the Greeks threw off
The yoke of kings, to commerce and to arms
Devoted ; from Thessalia's fertile meads,
Where flows Penéus near the lofty walls
Of Cranon old ; from strong Eretria, queen

Of all Eubœan cities, who, sublime          200
On the steep margin of Euripus, views
Across the tide the Marathonian plain,
Not yet the haunt of glory. Athens too,
Minerva's care, among her graceful sons
Found equal lovers for the princely maid:
Nor was proud Argos wanting; nor the domes
Of sacred Elis; nor the Arcadian groves
That overshade Alphéus, echoing oft
Some shepherd's song. But thro' the illustrious band
Was none who might with Megacles compare   210
In all the honours of unblemish'd youth.
His was the beauteous bride: and now their son
Young Clisthenes, betimes, at Solon's gate
Stood anxious; leaning forward on the arm
Of his great sire, with earnest eyes that ask'd
When the slow hinge would turn, with restless feet,
And cheeks now pale, now glowing: for his heart
Throbb'd full of bursting passions, anger, grief
With scorn imbitter'd, by the generous boy
Scarce understood, but which, like noble seeds,
Are destin'd for his country and himself
In riper years to bring forth fruits divine
Of liberty and glory. Next appear'd
Two brave companions whom one mother bore
To different lords; but whom the better ties
Of firm esteem and friendship render'd more
Than brothers: first Miltiades, who drew
From godlike Æacus his ancient line;
That Æacus whose unimpeach'd renown
For sanctity and justice won the lyre          230
Of elder bards to celebrate him thron'd
In Hades o'er the dead, where his decrees
The guilty soul within the burning gates
Of Tartarus compel, or send the good
To inhabit with eternal health and peace
The valleys of Elysium. From a stem
So sacred, ne'er could worthier scion spring
Than this Miltiades; whose aid ere long

The chiefs of Thrace, already on their ways
Sent by the inspir'd foreknowing maid who sits
Upon the Delphic tripod, shall implore
To wield their sceptre, and the rural wealth
Of fruitful Chersonesus to protect
With arms and laws.  But, nothing careful now
Save for his injur'd country, here he stands
In deep solicitude with Cimon join'd:
Unconscious both what widely different lots
Await them, taught by nature as they are
To know one common good, one common ill.
For Cimon, not his valour, not his birth        250
Deriv'd from Codrus, not a thousand gifts
Dealt round him with a wise, benignant hand ;
No, not the Olympic olive by himself
From his own brow transferr'd to soothe the mind
Of this Pisistratus, can long preserve
From the fell envy of the tyrant's sons,
And their assassin dagger.  But if death
Obscure upon his gentle steps attend,
Yet fate an ample recompense prepares
In his victorious son, that other great        260
Miltiades, who o'er the very throne
Of Glory shall with Time's assiduous hand
In adamantine characters engrave
The name of Athens ; and, by Freedom arm'd
'Gainst the gigantic pride of Asia's king,
Shall all the achievements of the heroes old
Surmount, of Hercules, of all who sail'd
From Thessaly with Jason, all who fought
For empire or for fame at Thebes or Troy.
   Such were the patriots who within the porch
Of Solon had assembled.  But the gate
Now opens, and across the ample floor
Straight they proceed into an open space
Bright with the beams of morn : a verdant spot,
Where stands a rural altar, pil'd with sods
Cut from the grassy turf and girt with wreaths
Of branching palm.  Here Solon's self they found

Clad in a robe of purple pure, and deck'd
With leaves of olive on his reverend brow.
He bow'd before the altar, and o'er cakes    280
Of barley from two earthen vessels pour'd
Of honey and of milk a plenteous stream;
Calling meantime the Muses to accept
His simple offering, by no victim ting'd
With blood, nor sullied by destroying fire,
But such as for himself Apollo claims
In his own Delos, where his favourite haunt
Is thence the Altar of the Pious nam'd.
Unseen the guests drew near, and silent view'd
That worship; till the hero-priest his eye    290
Turn'd toward a seat on which prepar'd there lay
A branch of laurel.   Then his friends confess'd
Before him stood.   Backward his step he drew,
As loth that care or tumult should approach
Those early rights divine: but soon their looks,
So anxious, and their hands, held forth with such
Desponding gesture, bring him on perforce
To speak to their affliction.   " Are ye come,"
He cried, " to mourn with me this common shame?
Or ask ye some new effort which may break    300
Our fetters?   Know then, of the public cause
Not for yon traitor's cunning or his might
Do I despair: nor could I wish from Jove
Aught dearer, than at this late hour of life,
As once by laws, so now by strenuous arms,
From impious violation to assert
The rights our fathers left us.   But, alas!
What arms? or who shall wield them?   Ye beheld
The Athenian people.   Many bitter days
Must pass, and many wounds from cruel pride    310
Be felt, ere yet their partial hearts find room
For just resentment, or their hands indure
To smite this tyrant brood, so near to all
Their hopes, so oft admir'd, so long belov'd.
That time will come, however.   Be it yours
To watch its fair approach, and urge it on

With honest prudence : me it ill beseems
Again to supplicate the unwilling crowd
To rescue from a vile deceiver's hold
That envied power which once with eager zeal  320
They offer'd to myself; nor can I plunge
In counsels deep and various, nor prepare
For distant wars, thus faltering as I tread
On life's last verge, ere long to join the shades
Of Minos and Lycurgus.   But behold
What care employs me now.   My vows I pay
To the sweet Muses, teachers of my youth
And solace of my age.   If right I deem
Of the still voice that whispers at my heart,
The immortal sisters have not quite withdrawn  330
Their old harmonious influence.   Let your tongues
With sacred silence favour what I speak,
And haply shall my faithful lips be taught
To unfold celestial counsels, which may arm
As with impenetrable steel your breasts
For the long strife before you, and repel
The darts of adverse fate."   He said, and snatch'd
The laurel bough, and sate in silence down,
Fix'd, wrapp'd in solemn musing, full before
The sun, who now from all his radiant orb  340
Drove the gray clouds, and pour'd his genial light
Upon the breast of Solon.   Solon rais'd
Aloft the leafy rod, and thus began :
  " Ye beauteous offspring of Olympian Jove
And Memory divine, Pierian maids,
Hear me, propitious.   In the morn of life,
When hope shone bright and all the prospect smil'd,
To your sequester'd mansion oft my steps
Were turn'd, O Muses, and within your gate
My offerings paid. Ye taught me then with strains
Of flowing harmony to soften war's
Dire voice, or in fair colours, thát might charm
The public eye, to clothe the form austere
Of civil counsel.   Now my feeble age
Neglected, and supplanted of the hope

o

On which it lean'd, yet sinks not, but to you,
To your mild wisdom flies, refuge belov'd
Of solitude and silence.  Ye can teach
The visions of my bed whate'er the gods
In the rude ages of the world inspir'd,                    360
Or the first heroes acted: ye can make
The morning light more gladsome to my sense
Than ever it appear'd to active youth
Pursuing careless pleasure: ye can give
To this long leisure, these unheeded hours,
A labour as sublime, as when the sons
Of Athens throng'd and speechless round me stood
To hear pronounc'd for all their future deeds
The bounds of right and wrong.  Celestial powers!
I feel that ye are near me: and behold,                    370
To meet your energy divine, I bring
A high and sacred theme; not less than those
Which to the eternal custody of Fame
Your lips intrusted, when of old ye deign'd
With Orpheus or with Homer to frequent
The groves of Hæmus or the Chian shore.
  " Ye know, harmonious maids, (for what of all
My various life was e'er from you estrang'd?)
Oft hath my solitary song to you
Reveal'd that duteous pride which turn'd my steps
To willing exile; earnest to withdraw
From envy and the disappointed thirst
Of lucre, lest the bold familiar strife,
Which in the eye of Athens they upheld
Against her legislator, should impair
With trivial doubt the reverence of his laws.
To Egypt therefore through the Ægean isles
My course I steer'd, and by the banks of Nile
Dwelt in Canopus.  Thence the hallow'd domes
Of Saïs, and the rites to Isis paid,                       390
I sought, and in her temple's silent courts,
Through many changing moons, attentive heard
The venerable Sonchis, while his tongue
At morn or midnight the deep story told

Of her who represents whate'er has been,
Or is, or shall be; whose mysterious veil
No mortal hand hath ever yet remov'd.
By him exhorted, southward to the walls
Of On I pass'd, the city of the sun,
The ever-youthful god. 'Twas there amid   400
His priests and sages, who the livelong night
Watch the dread movements of the starry sphere,
Or who in wondrous fables half disclose
The secrets of the elements, 'twas there
That great Psenophis taught my raptur'd ears
The fame of old Atlantis, of her chiefs,
And her pure laws, the first which earth obey'd.
Deep in my bosom sunk the noble tale;
And often, while I listen'd, did my mind
Foretell with what delight her own free lyre   410
Should sometime for an Attic audience raise
Anew that lofty scene, and from their tombs
Call forth those ancient demigods to speak
Of Justice and the hidden Providence
That walks among mankind. But yet meantime
The mystic pomp of Ammon's gloomy sons
Became less pleasing. With contempt I gaz'd
On that tame garb and those unvarying paths
To which the double yoke of king and priest
Had cramp'd the sullen race. At last with hymns
Invoking our own Pallas and the gods
Of cheerful Greece, a glad farewell I gave
To Egypt, and before the southern wind
Spread my full sails. What climes I then survey'd,
What fortunes I encounter'd in the realm
Of Crœsus or upon the Cyprian shore,
The Muse, who prompts my bosom, doth not now
Consent that I reveal. But when at length
Ten times the sun returning from the south
Had strow'd with flowers the verdant earth and fill'd
The groves with music, pleas'd I then beheld
The term of those long errors drawing nigh.
' Nor yet,' I said, ' will I sit down within

The walls of Athens, till my feet have trod
The Cretan soil, have pierc'd those reverend haunts
Whence Law and Civil Concord issued forth
As from their ancient home, and still to Greece
Their wisest, loftiest discipline proclaim.'
Straight where Amnisus, mart of wealthy ships,
Appears beneath fam'd Cnossus and her towers,
Like the fair handmaid of a stately queen,
I check'd my prow, and thence with eager steps
The city of Minos enter'd.   O ye gods,
Who taught the leaders of the simpler time
By written words to curb the untoward will
Of mortals, how within that generous isle
Have ye the triumphs of your power display'd
Munificent!   Those splendid merchants, lords
Of traffic and the sea, with what delight
I saw them at their public meal, like sons         450
Of the same household, join the plainer sort
Whose wealth was only freedom! whence to these
Vile envy, and to those fantastic pride,
Alike was strange; but noble concord still
Cherish'd the strength untam'd, the rustic faith,
Of their first fathers.   Then the growing race,
How pleasing to behold them in their schools,
Their sports, their labours, ever plac'd within,
O shade of Minos! thy controlling eye.
Here was a docile band in tuneful tones         460
Thy laws pronouncing, or with lofty hymns
Praising the bounteous gods, or, to preserve
Their country's heroes from oblivious night,
Resounding what the Muse inspir'd of old;
There, on the verge of manhood, others met,
In heavy armour through the heats of noon
To march, the rugged mountain's height to climb
With measur'd swiftness, from the hard-bent bow
To send resistless arrows to their mark,
Or for the fame of prowess to contend,         470
Now wrestling, now with fists and staves oppos'd,
Now with the biting falchion, and the fence

Of brazen shields; while still the warbling flute
Presided o'er the combat, breathing strains
Grave, solemn, soft; and changing headlong spite
To thoughtful resolution cool and clear.
Such I beheld those islanders renown'd,
So tutor'd from their birth to meet in war
Each bold invader, and in peace to guard
That living flame of reverence for their laws    480
Which nor the storms of fortune, nor the flood
Of foreign wealth diffus'd o'er all the land,
Could quench or slacken. First of human names
In every Cretan's heart was Minos still;
And holiest far, of what the sun surveys
Thro' his whole course, were those primeval seats
Which with religious footsteps he had taught
Their sires to approach; the wild Dictæan cave
Where Jove was born; the ever verdant meads
Of Ida, and the spacious grotto, where    490
His active youth he pass'd, and where his throne
Yet stands mysterious; whither Minos came
Each ninth returning year, the king of gods
And mortals there in secret to consult
On justice, and the tables of his law
To inscribe anew. Oft also with like zeal
Great Rhea's mansion from the Cnossian gates
Men visit; nor less oft the antique fane
Built on that sacred spot, along the banks
Of shady Theron, where benignant Jove    500
And his majestic consort join'd their hands
And spoke their nuptial vows. Alas, 'twas there
That the dire fame of Athens sunk in bonds
I first receiv'd; what time an annual feast
Had summon d all the genial country round,
By sacrifice and pomp to bring to mind
That first great spousal; while the enamour'd youths
And virgins, with the priest before the shrine,
Observe the same pure ritual and invoke
The same glad omens. There, among the crowd
Of strangers from those naval cities drawn

Which deck, like gems, the island's northern shore,
A merchant of Ægina I descried,
My ancient host; but, forward as I sprung
To meet him, he, with dark dejected brow,
Stopp'd half averse; and, ' O Athenian guest,'
He said, 'art thou in Crete; these joyful rites
Partaking?   Know thy laws are blotted out:
Thy country kneels before a tyrant's throne.'
He added names of men, with hostile deeds     520
Disastrous; which obscure and indistinct
I heard: for, while he spake, my heart grew cold
And my eyes dim: the altars and their train
No more were present to me: how I far'd,
Or whither turn'd, I know not; nor recall
Aught of those moments other than the sense
Of one who struggles in oppressive sleep,
And, from the toils of some distressful dream
To break away, with palpitating heart,
Weak limbs, and temples bath'd in death-like dew,
Makes many a painful effort.   When at last
The sun and nature's face again appear'd,
Not far I found me; where the public path,
Winding thro' cypress groves and swelling meads,
From Cnossus to the cave of Jove ascends.
Heedless I follow'd on; till soon the skirts
Of Ida rose before me, and the vault
Wide opening pierc'd the mountain's rocky side.
Entering within the threshold, on the ground
I flung me, sad, faint, overworn with toil."     540
*          *          *          *

THE BEGINNING OF THE

FOURTH BOOK OF THE PLEASURES OF

THE IMAGINATION. 1770.

ONE effort more, one cheerful sally more,
   Our destin'd course will finish; and in peace
Then, for an offering sacred to the powers
Who lent us gracious guidance, we will then
Inscribe a monument of deathless praise,
O my adventurous song! With steady speed
Long hast thou, on an untried voyage bound,
Sail'd between earth and heaven: hast now sur-
   vey'd,
Stretch'd out beneath thee, all the mazy tracts
Of Passion and Opinion; like a waste    10
Of sands and flowery lawns and tangling woods,
Where mortals roam bewilder'd: and hast now
Exulting soar'd among the worlds above,
Or hover'd near the eternal gates of heaven,
If haply the discourses of the gods,
A curious, but an unpresuming guest,
Thou might'st partake, and carry back some strain
Of divine wisdom, lawful to repeat,
And apt to be conceiv'd of man below.
A different task remains; the secret paths    20
Of early genius to explore: to trace
Those haunts where Fancy her predestin'd sons,
Like to the demigods of old, doth nurse
Remote from eyes profane. Ye happy souls
Who now her tender discipline obey,
Where dwell ye? What wild river's brink at eve
Imprint your steps? What solemn groves at noon
Use ye to visit, often breaking forth
In rapture 'mid your dilatory walk,
Or musing, as in slumber, on the green?    30

—Would I again were with you!—O ye dales
Of Tyne, and ye most ancient woodlands ; where
Oft as the giant flood obliquely strides,
And his banks open, and his lawns extend,
Stops short the pleased traveller to view
Presiding o'er the scene some rustic tower
Founded by Norman or by Saxon hands :
O ye Northumbrian shades, which overlook
The rocky pavement and the mossy falls
Of solitary Wensbeck's limpid stream ;                    40
How gladly I recall your well-known seats
Belov'd of old, and that delightful time
When all alone, for many a summer's day,
I wander'd through your calm recesses, led
In silence by some powerful hand unseen.

   Nor will I e'er forget you ; nor shall e'er
The graver tasks of manhood, or the advice
Of vulgar wisdom, move me to disclaim
Those studies which possessed me in the dawn
Of life, and fix'd the colour of my mind        50
For every future year : whence even now
From sleep I rescue the clear hours of morn,
And, while the world around lies overwhelm'd
In idle darkness, am alive to thoughts
Of honourable fame, of truth divine
Or moral, and of minds to virtue won
By the sweet magic of harmonious verse ;
The themes which now expect us.   For thus far
On general habits, and on arts which grow
Spontaneous in the minds of all mankind,        60
Hath dwelt our argument ; and how self-taught,
Though seldom conscious of their own employ,
In Nature's or in Fortune's changeful scene
Men learn to judge of Beauty, and acquire
Those forms set up, as idols in the soul
For love and zealous praise.   Yet indistinct,
In vulgar bosoms, and unnotic'd lie
These pleasing stores, unless the casual force
Of things external prompt the heedless mind

To recognize her wealth.   But some there are   70
Conscious of Nature, and the rule which man
O'er Nature holds : some who, within themselves
Retiring from the trivial scenes of chance
And momentary passion, can at will
Call up these fair exemplars of the mind ;
Review their features ; scan the secret laws
Which bind them to each other : and display
By forms, or sounds, or colours, to the sense
Of all the world their latent charms display :
Even as in Nature's frame (if such a word,        80
If such a word, so bold, may from the lips
Of man proceed) as in this outward frame
Of things, the great Artificer portrays
His own immense idea.   Various names
These among mortals bear, as various signs
They use, and by peculiar organs speak
To human sense.   There are who by the flight
Of air through tubes with moving stops distinct,
Or by extended chords in measure taught
To vibrate, can assemble powerful sounds        90
Expressing every temper of the mind
From every cause, and charming all the soul
With passion void of care.   Others mean time
The rugged mass of metal, wood, or stone,
Patiently taming ; or with easier hand
Describing lines, and with more ample scope
Uniting colours ; can to general sight
Produce those permanent and perfect forms,
Those characters of heroes and of gods,
Which from the crude materials of the world,   100
Their own high minds created.   But the chief
Are poets ; eloquent men, who dwell on earth
To clothe whate'er the soul admires or loves
With language and with numbers.   Hence to these
A field is open'd wide as Nature's sphere ;
Nay, wider : various as the sudden acts
Of human wit, and vast as the demands
Of human will.   The bard nor length, nor depth,

Nor place, nor form controls.   To eyes, to ears,
To every organ of the copious mind,                    110
He offereth all its treasures.   Him the hours,
The seasons him obey : and changeful Time
Sees him at will keep measure with his flight,
At will outstrip it.   To enhance his toil,
He summoneth from the uttermost extent
Of things which God hath taught him every form
Auxiliar, every power ; and all beside
Excludes imperious.   His prevailing hand
Gives, to corporeal essence, life and sense
And every stately function of the soul.                120
The soul itself to him obsequious lies,
Like matter's passive heap ; and as he wills,
To reason and affection he assigns
Their just alliances, their just degrees :
Whence his peculiar honours : whence the race
Of men who people his delightful world,
Men genuine and according to themselves,
Transcend as far the uncertain sons of earth,
As earth itself to his delightful world,
The palm of spotless Beauty doth resign.               130
          *          *          *          *

# ODES ON SEVERAL SUBJECTS.

## IN TWO BOOKS.  BOOK I.

## ODE I.

### I.

ON yonder verdant hillock laid,
    Where oaks and elms, a friendly shade,
    O'erlook the falling stream,
O master of the Latin lyre,
Awhile with thee will I retire
    From summer's noontide beam.

### II.

And, lo, within my lonely bower,
The industrious bee from many a flower
    Collects her balmy dews:
" For me," she sings, " the gems are born,
For me their silken robe adorn,
    Their fragrant breath diffuse."

### III.

Sweet murmurer! may no rude storm
This hospitable scene deform,
    Nor check thy gladsome toils;
Still may the buds unsullied spring,
Still showers and sunshine court thy wing
    To these ambrosial spoils.

### IV.

Nor shall my Muse hereafter fail
Her fellow labourer thee to hail;
    And lucky be the strains!
For long ago did Nature frame
Your seasons and your arts the same,
    Your pleasures and your pains.

### V.

Like thee, in lowly, sylvan scenes,
On river banks and flowery greens
   My Muse delighted plays ;
Nor through the desert of the air,
Though swans or eagles triumph there,
   With fond ambition strays.

### VI.

Nor where the boding raven chaunts,
Nor near the owl's unhallow'd haunts
   Will she her cares employ ;
But flies from ruins and from tombs,
From Superstition's horrid glooms,
   To day-light and to joy.

### VII.

Nor will she tempt the barren waste ;
Nor deigns the lurking strength to taste
   Of any noxious thing ;
But leaves with scorn to Envy's use
The insipid nightshade's baneful juice,
   The nettle's sordid sting.

### VIII.

From all which Nature fairest knows,
The vernal blooms, the summer rose,
   She draws her blameless wealth ;
And, when the generous task is done,
She consecrates a double boon,
   To Pleasure and to Health.

## ODE II.

### ON THE WINTER-SOLSTICE.   1740.

### I.

THE radiant ruler of the year
   At length his wintry goal attains ;
Soon to reverse the long career,

And northward bend his steady reins.
Now, piercing half Potosi's height,
Prone rush the fiery floods of light
Ripening the mountain's silver stores :
While, in some cavern's horrid shade,
The panting Indian hides his head,
And oft the approach of eve implores.

II.

But lo, on this deserted coast
How pale the sun ! how thick the air !
Mustering his storms, a sordid host,
Lo, Winter desolates the year.
The fields resign their latest bloom ;
No more the breezes waft perfume,
No more the streams in music roll :
But snows fall dark, or rains resound ;
And, while great Nature mourns around,
Her griefs infect the human soul.

III.

Hence the loud city's busy throngs
Urge the warm bowl and splendid fire :
Harmonious dances, festive songs,
Against the spiteful heaven conspire.
Meantime perhaps with tender fears
Some village dame the curfew hears,
While round the hearth her children play :
At morn their father went abroad ;
The moon is sunk and deep the road ;
She sighs, and wonders at his stay.

IV.

But thou, my lyre, awake, arise,
And hail the sun's returning force :
Even now he climbs the northern skies,
And health and hope attend his course.
Then louder howl the aërial waste,
Be earth with keener cold embrac'd,
Yet gentle hours advance their wing ;
And Fancy, mocking Winter's might,

With flowers and dews and streaming light
Already decks the new-born spring.

### V.

O fountain of the golden day,
Could mortal vows promote thy speed,
How soon before thy vernal ray
Should each unkindly damp recede!
How soon each hovering tempest fly,
Whose stores for mischief arm the sky,
Prompt on our heads to burst amain,
To rend the forest from the steep,
Or, thundering o'er the Baltic deep,
To whelm the merchant's hopes of gain!

### VI.

But let not man's unequal views
Presume o'er Nature and her laws:
'Tis his with grateful joy to use
The indulgence of the Sovereign Cause;
Secure that health and beauty springs
Through this majestic frame of things,
Beyond what he can reach to know;
And that Heaven's all-subduing will,
With good, the progeny of ill,
Attempereth every state below.

### VII.

How pleasing wears the wintry night,
Spent with the old illustrious dead!
While, by the taper's trembling light,
I seem those awful scenes to tread
Where chiefs or legislators lie,
Whose triumphs move before my eye
In arms and antique pomp array'd;
While now I taste the Ionian song,
Now bend to Plato's godlike tongue
Resounding through the olive shade.

### VIII.

But should some cheerful, equal friend
Bid leave the studious page awhile,

Let mirth on wisdom then attend,
And social ease on learned toil.
Then while, at love's uncareful shrine,
Each dictates to the god of wine
Her name whom all his hopes obey,
What flattering dreams each bosom warm,
While absence, heightening every charm,
Invokes the slow-returning May!

### IX.

May, thou delight of heaven and earth,
When will thy genial star arise?
The auspicious morn, which gives thee birth,
Shall bring Eudora to my eyes.
Within her sylvan haunt behold,
As in the happy garden old,
She moves like that primeval fair:
Thither, ye silver-sounding lyres,
Ye tender smiles, ye chaste desires,
Fond hope and mutual faith, repair.

### X.

And if believing love can read
His better omens in her eye,
Then shall my fears, O charming maid,
And every pain of absence die:
Then shall my jocund harp, attun'd
To thy true ear, with sweeter sound
Pursue the free Horatian song:
Old Tyne shall listen to my tale,
And Echo, down the bordering vale,
The liquid melody prolong.

### FOR THE WINTER SOLSTICE, DECEMBER 11, 1740.

#### AS ORIGINALLY WRITTEN.

NOW to the utmost southern goal
The sun has trac'd his annual way,
And backward now prepares to roll,

And bless the north with earlier day.
Prone on Potosi's lofty brow
Floods of sublimer splendour flow,
Ripening the latent seeds of gold,
Whilst, panting in the lonely shade,
Th' afflicted Indian hides his head,
Nor dares the blaze of noon behold.

But lo! on this deserted coast
How faint the light, how chill the air!
Lo! arm'd with whirlwind, hail, and frost,
Fierce Winter desolates the year.
The fields resign their cheerful bloom,
No more the breezes breathe perfume,
No more the warbling waters roll;
Deserts of snow fatigue the eye,
Successive tempests bloat the sky,
And gloomy damps oppress the soul.

But let my drooping genius rise,
And hail the sun's remotest ray:
Now, now he climbs the northern skies
To-morrow nearer than to-day.
Then louder howl the stormy waste,
Be land and ocean worse defac'd,
Yet brighter hours are on the wing,
And Fancy, through the wintry gloom,
Radiant with dews and flowers in bloom,
Already hails th' emerging spring.

O fountain of the golden day!
Could mortal vows but urge thy speed,
How soon before thy vernal ray
Should each unkindly damp recede!
How soon each tempest hovering fly,
That now fermenting loads the sky,
Prompt on our heads to burst amain,
To rend the forest from the steep,
And thundering o'er the Baltic deep,
To whelm the merchant's hopes of gain!

But let not man's imperfect views
Presume to tax wise Nature's laws;
'Tis his with silent joy to use
Th' indulgence of the Sovereign Cause;
Secure that from the whole of things
Beauty and good consummate springs,
Beyond what he can reach to know,
And that the providence of Heaven
Has some peculiar blessing given
To each allotted state below.

Even now how sweet the wintry night
Spent with the old illustrious dead!
While by the taper's trembling light,
I seem those awful courts to tread,
Where chiefs and legislators lie,
Whose triumphs move before my eye,
With every laurel fresh display'd;
While charm'd I rove in classic song,
Or bend to freedom's fearless tongue,
Or walk the academic shade.

## ODE III.

### TO A FRIEND, UNSUCCESSFUL IN LOVE.

#### I.

INDEED, my Phædria, if to find
That wealth can female wishes gain,
Had e'er disturb'd your thoughtful mind,
Or caused one serious moment's pain,
I should have said that all the rules,
You learn'd of moralists and schools,
Were very useless, very vain.

#### II.

Yet I perhaps mistake the case—
Say, though with this heroic air,

P

Like one that holds a nobler chase,
You try the tender loss to bear,
Does not your heart renounce your tongue?
Seems not my censure strangely wrong
To count it such a slight affair?

### III.

When Hesper gilds the shaded sky,
Oft as you seek the well-known grove,
Methinks I see you cast your eye
Back to the morning scenes of love:
Each pleasing word you heard her say,
Her gentle look, her graceful way,
Again your struggling fancy move.

### IV.

Then tell me, is your soul entire?
Does Wisdom calmly hold her throne?
Then can you question each desire,
Bid this remain, and that be gone?
No tear half-starting from your eye?
No kindling blush you know not why?
No stealing sigh, nor stifled groan?

### V.

Away with this unmanly mood!
See where the hoary churl appears,
Whose hand hath seiz'd the favourite good
Which you reserv'd for happier years:
While, side by side, the blushing maid
Shrinks from his visage, half afraid,
Spite of the sickly joy she wears.

### VI.

Ye guardian powers of love and fame,
This chaste, harmonious pair behold;
And thus reward the generous flame
Of all who barter vows for gold.
O bloom of youth, O tender charms
Well-buried in a dotard's arms!
O equal price of beauty sold!

#### VII.

Cease then to gaze with looks of love :
Bid her adieu, the venal fair :
Unworthy she your bliss to prove ;
Then wherefore should she prove your care ?
No : lay your myrtle garland down ;
And let awhile the willow's crown
With luckier omens bind your hair.

#### VIII.

O just escap'd the faithless main,
Though driven unwilling on the land ;
To guide your favour'd steps again,
Behold your better Genius stand :
Where Truth revolves her page divine,
Where Virtue leads to Honour's shrine,
Behold, he lifts his awful hand.

#### IX.

Fix but on these your ruling aim,
And Time, the sire of manly care,
Will fancy's dazzling colours tame ;
A soberer dress will beauty wear :
Then shall esteem by knowledge led
Inthrone within your heart and head
Some happier love, some truer fair.


## ODE IV.

#### AFFECTED INDIFFERENCE.    TO THE SAME.

#### I.

YES : you contemn the perjur'd maid
        Who all your favourite hopes betray'd :
Nor, though her heart should home return,
Her tuneful tongue its falsehood mourn,
Her winning eyes your faith implore,
Would you her hand receive again,

Or once dissemble your disdain,
Or listen to the syren's theme,
Or stoop to love : since now esteem
And confidence, and friendship, is no more.

## II.

Yet tell me, Phædria, tell me why,
When summoning your pride you try
To meet her looks with cool neglect,
Or cross her walk with slight respect,
(For so is falsehood best repaid)
Whence do your cheeks indignant glow?
Why is your struggling tongue so slow?
What means that darkness on your brow?
As if with all her broken vow
You meant the fair apostate to upbraid?

## ODE V.

### AGAINST SUSPICION.

#### I.

OH fly! 'tis dire Suspicion's mien;
And, meditating plagues unseen,
The sorceress hither bends :
Behold her touch in gall imbrued :
Behold—her garment drops with blood
Of lovers and of friends.

#### II.

Fly far! Already in your eyes
I see a pale suffusion rise;
And soon through every vein,
Soon will her secret venom spread,
And all your heart and all your head
Imbibe the potent stain.

#### III.

Then many a demon will she raise
To vex your sleep, to haunt your ways;

While gleams of lost delight
Raise the dark tempest of the brain,
As lightning shines across the main
  Through whirlwinds and through night.

### IV.

No more can faith or candour move ;
But each ingenuous deed of love,
  Which reason would applaud,
Now, smiling o'er her dark distress,
Fancy malignant strives to dress
  Like injury and fraud.

### V.

Farewell to virtue's peaceful times :
Soon will you stoop to act the crimes
  Which thus you stoop to fear :
Guilt follows guilt ; and where the train
Begins with wrongs of such a stain,
  What horrors form the rear !

### VI.

'Tis thus to work her baleful power,
Suspicion waits the sullen hour
  Of fretfulness and strife,
When care the infirmer bosom wrings,
Or Eurus waves his murky wings
  To damp the seats of life.

### VII.

But come, forsake the scene unbless'd
Which first beheld your faithful breast
  To groundless fears a prey :
Come, where with my prevailing lyre
The skies, the streams, the groves conspire
  To charm your doubts away.

### VIII.

Thron'd in the sun's descending car,
What power unseen diffuseth far
  This tenderness of mind?
What Genius smiles on yonder flood ?

What God, in whispers from the wood,
     Bids every thought be kind ?

### IX.

O, thou, whate'er thy awful name,
Whose wisdom our untoward frame
     With social love restrains ;
Thou, who by fair affection's ties
Giv'st us to double all our joys
     And half disarm our pains ;

### X.

[1] If far from Dyson and from me
Suspicion took, by thy decree,
     Her everlasting flight ;
If firm on virtue's ample base
Thy parent hand has deign'd to raise
     Our friendship's honour'd height ;

### XI.

Let universal candour still,
Clear as yon heaven-reflecting rill,
     Preserve my open mind ;
Nor this nor that man's crooked ways
One sordid doubt within me raise
     To injure human kind.


# ODE VI.

## HYMN TO CHEERFULNESS.

HOW thick the shades of evening close !
     How pale the sky with weight of snows !
Haste, light the tapers, urge the fire,
And bid the joyless day retire.
—— Alas, in vain I try within
     To brighten the dejected scene,

----

[1] This stanza was found in a copy presented by Akenside.
                                        AMERICAN EDITOR.

While rous'd by grief these fiery pains
Tear the frail texture of my veins ;
While Winter's voice, that storms around,
And yon deep death-bell's groaning sound
Renew my mind's oppressive gloom,
Till starting Horror shakes the room.
    Is there in nature no kind power
To soothe affliction's lonely hour ?
To blunt the edge of dire disease,
And teach these wintry shades to please?
Come, Cheerfulness, triumphant fair,
Shine through the hovering cloud of care :
O sweet of language, mild of mien,
O Virtue's friend and Pleasure's queen,
Assuage the flames that burn my breast,
Compose my jarring thoughts to rest ;
And while thy gracious gifts I feel,
My song shall all thy praise reveal.
    As once ('twas in Astræa's reign)
The vernal powers renew'd their train,
It happen'd that immortal Love
Was ranging through the spheres above,
And downward hither cast his eye
The year's returning pomp to spy.
He saw the radiant god of day
Waft in his car the rosy May ;
The fragrant Airs and genial Hours
Were shedding round him dews and flowers ;
Before his wheels Aurora pass'd,
And Hesper's golden lamp was last.
But, fairest of the blooming throng,
When Health majestic mov'd along,
Delighted to survey below
The joys which from her presence flow,
While earth enliven'd hears her voice,
And swains, and flocks, and fields rejoice ;
Then mighty Love her charms confess'd,
And soon his vows inclin'd her breast,
And, known from that auspicious morn,

The pleasing Cheerfulness was born.
   Thou, Cheerfulness, by heaven design'd
To sway the movements of the mind,
Whatever fretful passion springs,
Whatever wayward fortune brings
To disarrange the power within,
And strain the musical machine;
Thou Goddess, thy attempering hand
Doth each discordant string command,
Refines the soft, and swells the strong;
And, joining Nature's general song,
Through many a varying tone unfolds
The harmony of human souls.
   Fair guardian of domestic life,
Kind banisher of homebred strife,
Nor sullen lip, nor taunting eye
Deforms the scene where thou art by:
No sickening husband damns the hour
Which bound his joys to female power;
No pining mother weeps the cares
Which parents waste on thankless heirs:
The officious daughters pleas'd attend;
The brother adds the name of friend:
By thee with flowers their board is crown'd,
With songs from thee their walks resound;
And morn with welcome lustre shines,
And evening unperceiv'd declines.
   Is there a youth, whose anxious heart
Labours with love's unpitied smart?
Though now he stray by rills and bowers,
And weeping waste the lonely hours,
Or if the nymph her audience deign,
Debase the story of his pain
With slavish looks, discolour'd eyes,
And accents faltering into sighs;
Yet thou, auspicious power, with ease
Canst yield him happier arts to please,
Inform his mien with manlier charms,
Instruct his tongue with nobler arms,

With more commanding passion move,
And teach the dignity of love.
    Friend to the Muse and all her train,
For thee I court the Muse again :
The Muse for thee may well exert
Her pomp, her charms, her fondest art,
Who owes to thee that pleasing sway
Which earth and peopled heaven obey.
Let Melancholy's plaintive tongue
Repeat what later bards have sung ;
But thine was Homer's ancient might,
And thine victorious Pindar's flight :
Thy hand each Lesbian wreath attir'd :
Thy lip Sicilian reeds inspir'd :
Thy spirit lent the glad perfume
Whence yet the flowers of Teos bloom ;
Whence yet from Tibur's Sabine vale
Delicious blows the enlivening gale,
While Horace calls thy sportive choir,
Heroes and nymphs, around his lyre.
    But see where yonder pensive sage
(A prey perhaps to fortune's rage,
Perhaps by tender griefs oppress'd,
Or glooms congenial to his breast)
Retires in desert scenes to dwell,
And bids the joyless world farewell.
Alone he treads the autumnal shade,
Alone beneath the mountain laid
He sees the nightly damps ascend,
And gathering storms aloft impend ;
He hears the neighbouring surges roll,
And raging thunders shake the pole :
Then, struck by every object round,
And stunn'd by every horrid sound,
He asks a clue for Nature's ways ;
But evil haunts him through the maze :
He sees ten thousand demons rise
To wield the empire of the skies,
And Chance and Fate assume the rod,

And Malice blot the throne of God.
—O thou, whose pleasing power I sing,
Thy lenient influence hither bring;
Compose the storm, dispel the gloom,
Till Nature wear her wonted bloom,
Till fields and shades their sweets exhale,
And music swell each opening gale:
Then o'er his breast thy softness pour,
And let him learn the timely hour
To trace the world's benignant laws,
And judge of that presiding cause
Who founds on discord beauty's reign,
Converts to pleasure every pain,
Subdues each hostile form to rest,
And bids the universe be bless'd.

O thou, whose pleasing power I sing,
If right I touch the votive string,
If equal praise I yield thy name,
Still govern thou thy poet's flame;
Still with the Muse my bosom share,
And soothe to peace intruding care.
But most exert thy pleasing power
On friendship's consecrated hour;
And while my Sophron points the road
To godlike wisdom's calm abode,
Or warm in freedom's ancient cause
Traceth the source of Albion's laws,
Add thou o'er all the generous toil
The light of thy unclouded smile.
But, if by fortune's stubborn sway
From him and friendship torn away,
I court the Muse's healing spell
For griefs that still with absence dwell,
Do thou conduct my fancy's dreams
To such indulgent placid themes,
As just the struggling breast may cheer,
And just suspend the starting tear,
Yet leave that sacred sense of woe
Which none but friends and lovers know.

## ODE VII.

### ON THE USE OF POETRY.

#### I.

NOT for themselves did human kind
   Contrive the parts by heaven assign'd
      On life's wide scene to play:
Not Scipio's force nor Cæsar's skill
Can conquer Glory's arduous hill,
      If Fortune close the way.

#### II.

Yet still the self-depending soul,
Though last and least in Fortune's roll,
      His proper sphere commands;
And knows what Nature's seal bestow'd,
And sees, before the throne of God,
      The rank in which he stands.

#### III.

Who train'd by laws the future age,
Who rescu'd nations from the rage
      Of partial, factious power,
My heart with distant homage views;
Content if thou, celestial Muse,
      Didst rule my natal hour.

#### IV.

Not far beneath the hero's feet,
Nor from the legislator's seat
      Stands far remote the bard.
Though not with public terrors crown'd,
Yet wider shall his rule be found,
      More lasting his award.

#### V.

Lycurgus fashion'd Sparta's fame,
And Pompey to the Roman name

Gave universal sway :
Where are they ?—Homer's reverend page
Holds empire to the thirtieth age,
And tongues and climes obey.

### VI.

And thus when William's acts divine
No longer shall from Bourbon's line
Draw one vindictive vow ;
When Sidney shall with Cato rest,
And Russel move the patriot's breast
No more than Brutus now ;

### VII.

Yet then shall Shakespeare's powerful art
O'er every passion, every heart,
Confirm his awful throne :
Tyrants shall bow before his laws ;
And Freedom's, Glory's, Virtue's cause,
Their dread assertor own.

## ODE VIII.

### ON LEAVING HOLLAND.

### I.  1.

FAREWELL to Leyden's lonely bound,
The Belgian Muse's sober seat ;
Where dealing frugal gifts around
To all the favourites at her feet,
She trains the body's bulky frame
For passive, persevering toils ;
And lest, from any prouder aim,
The daring mind should scorn her homely spoils,
She breathes maternal fogs to damp its restless flame.

### I.  2.

Farewell the grave, pacific air,
Where never mountain zephyr blew :

The marshy levels lank and bare,
Which Pan, which Ceres never knew:
The Naiads, with obscene attire,
Urging in vain their urns to flow;
While round them chaunt the croaking choir,
And haply soothe some lover's prudent woe,
Or prompt some restive bard and modulate his lyre.

### I. 3.

Farewell, ye nymphs, whom sober care of gain
Snatch'd in your cradles from the god of Love:
She render'd all his boasted arrows vain;
And all his gifts did he in spite remove.
Ye too, the slow-ey'd fathers of the land,
With whom dominion steals from hand to hand,
Unown'd, undignified by public choice,
I go where Liberty to all is known,
And tells a monarch on his throne,
He reigns not but by her preserving voice.

### II. 1.

O my lov'd England, when with thee
Shall I sit down, to part no more?
Far from this pale, discolour'd sea,
That sleeps upon the reedy shore:
When shall I plough thy azure tide?
When on thy hills the flocks admire,
Like mountain snows; till down their side
I trace the village and the sacred spire,   [vide?
While bowers and copses green the golden slope di-

### II. 2.

Ye nymphs who guard the pathless grove,
Ye blue-ey'd sisters of the streams,
With whom I wont at morn to rove,
With whom at noon I talk'd in dreams;
O! take me to your haunts again,
The rocky spring, the greenwood glade;
To guide my lonely footsteps deign,
To prompt my slumbers in the murmuring shade,
And soothe my vacant ear with many an airy strain.

II.   3.

And thou, my faithful harp, no longer mourn
Thy drooping master's inauspicious hand:
Now brighter skies and fresher gales return,
Now fairer maids thy melody demand.
Daughters of Albion, listen to my lyre!
O Phœbus, guardian of the Aonian choir,
Why sounds not mine harmonious as thy own,
When all the virgin deities above
   With Venus and with Juno move
In concert round the Olympian father's throne?

III.   1.

Thee too, protectress of my lays,
Elate with whose majestic call
Above degenerate Latium's praise,
Above the slavish boast of Gaul,
I dare from impious thrones reclaim,
And wanton sloth's ignoble charms,
   The honours of a poet's name
To Somers' counsels, or to Hampden's arms,
Thee, Freedom, I rejoin, and bless thy genuine flame,

III.   2.

Great citizen of Albion.   Thee
Heroic Valour still attends,
And useful Science pleas'd to see
How Art her studious toil extends:
While Truth, diffusing from on high
A lustre unconfin'd as day,
   Fills and commands the public eye;
Till, pierc'd and sinking by her powerful ray,
Tame Faith and monkish Awe, like nightly demons,
   fly.

III.   3.

Hence the whole land the patriot's ardour
   shares:
Hence dread Religion dwells with social Joy;
And holy passions and unsullied cares,
In youth, in age, domestic life employ.

O fair Britannia, hail!—With partial love
The tribes of men their native seats approve,
Unjust and hostile to each foreign fame:
But when for generous minds and manly laws
    A nation holds her prime applause,
There public zeal shall all reproof disclaim.


## ODE IX.

### TO CURIO. 1744.

#### I.

THRICE hath the spring beheld thy faded
    fame
Since I exulting grasp'd the tuneful shell:
Eager through endless years to sound thy name,
Proud that my memory with thine should dwell.
How hast thou stain'd the splendour of my choice!
Those godlike forms which hover'd round thy
    voice,
Laws, freedom, glory, whither are they flown?
What can I now of thee to Time report,
Save thy fond country made thy impious sport,
Her fortune and her hope the victims of thy own?

#### II.

There are with eyes unmov'd and reckless heart
Who saw thee from thy summit fall thus low,
Who deem'd thy arm extended but to dart
The public vengeance on thy private foe.
But, spite of every gloss of envious minds,
The owl-ey'd race whom virtue's lustre blinds,
Who sagely prove that each man hath his price,
I still believ'd thy aim from blemish free,
    I yet, even yet, believe it, spite of thee
And all thy painted pleas to greatness and to vice.

### III.

" Thou didst not dream of liberty decay'd,
Nor wish to make her guardian laws more strong:
But the rash many, first by thee misled,
Bore thee at length unwillingly along."
Rise from your sad abodes, ye curst of old
For faith deserted or for cities sold,
Own here one untried, unexampled, deed;
One mystery of shame from Curio learn,
To beg the infamy he did not earn,          [meed.
And scape in Guilt's disguise from Virtue's offer'd

### IV.

For saw we not that dangerous power avow'd
Whom Freedom oft hath found her mortal bane,
Whom public Wisdom ever strove to exclude,
And but with blushes suffereth in her train?
Corruption vaunted her bewitching spoils,
O'er court, o'er senate, spread in pomp her toils,
And call'd herself the state's directing soul:
Till Curio, like a good magician, tried
With Eloquence and Reason at his side,          [trol.
By strength of holier spells the inchantress to con-

### V.

Soon with thy country's hope thy fame extends:
The rescued merchant oft thy words resounds:
Thee and thy cause the rural hearth defends:
His bowl to thee the grateful sailor crowns:
The learn'd recluse, with awful zeal who read
Of Grecian heroes, Roman patriots dead,
Now with like awe doth living merit scan:
While he, whom virtue in his blest retreat
Bade social ease and public passions meet,
Ascends the civil scene, and knows to be a man.

### VI.

At length in view the glorious end appear'd:
We saw thy spirit through the senate reign;
And Freedom's friends thy instant omen heard
Of laws for which their fathers bled in vain.

Wak'd in the strife the public Genius rose
More keen, more ardent from his long repose:
Deep through her bounds the city felt his call:
Each crowded haunt was stirr'd beneath his power,
And murmuring challeng'd the deciding hour
Of that too vast event, the hope and dread of all.

### VII.

O ye good powers who look on human kind,
Instruct the mighty moments as they roll;
And watch the fleeting shapes in Curio's mind,
And steer his passions steady to the goal.
O Alfred, father of the English name,
O valiant Edward, first in civil fame,
O William, height of public virtue pure,
Bend from your radiant seats a joyful eye,
Behold the sum of all your labours nigh,
Your plans of law complete, your ends of rule secure.

### VIII.

'Twas then—O shame! O soul from faith
          estrang'd!
O Albion oft to flattering vows a prey!
'Twas then—Thy thought what sudden frenzy
          chang'd?
What rushing palsy took thy strength away?
Is this the man in Freedom's cause approv'd?
The man so great, so honour'd, so belov'd?
Whom the dead envied and the living bless'd?
This patient slave by tinsel bonds allur'd?
This wretched suitor for a boon abjur'd?
Whom those that fear'd him, scorn; that trusted
          him, detest?

### IX.

O lost alike to action and repose!
With all that habit of familiar fame,
Sold to the mockery of relentless foes,
And doom'd to exhaust the dregs of life in shame,
To act with burning brow and throbbing heart
A poor deserter's dull exploded part,

Q

To slight the favour thou canst hope no more,
Renounce the giddy crowd, the vulgar wind,
Charge thy own lightness on thy country's mind,
And from her voice appeal to each tame foreign
    shore.

### X.

But England's sons, to purchase thence applause,
Shall ne'er the loyalty of slaves pretend,
By courtly passions try the public cause;
Nor to the forms of rule betray the end.
O race erect! by manliest passions mov'd,
The labours which to Virtue stand approv'd,
Prompt with a lover's fondness to survey;
Yet, where Injustice works her wilful claim,
Fierce as the flight of Jove's destroying flame,
Impatient to confront, and dreadful to repay.

### XI.

These thy heart owns no longer. In their room
See the grave queen of pageants, Honour, dwell
Couch'd in thy bosom's deep tempestuous gloom
Like some grim idol in a sorcerer's cell.
Before her rites thy sickening reason flew,
Divine Persuasion from thy tongue withdrew,
While Laughter mock'd, or Pity stole a sigh:
Can Wit her tender movements rightly frame
Where the prime function of the soul is lame?
Can Fancy's feeble springs the force of Truth
    supply?

### XII.

But come: 'tis time: strong Destiny impends
To shut thee from the joys thou hast betray'd:
With princes fill'd, the solemn fane ascends,
By Infamy, the mindful demon sway'd.
There vengeful vows for guardian laws effac'd,
From nations fetter'd, and from towns laid waste,
For ever through the spacious courts resound:
There long posterity's united groan
And the sad charge of horrors not their own,
Assail the giant chiefs, and press them to the ground.

### XIII.

In sight old Time, imperious judge, awaits:
Above revenge, or fear, or pity, just,
He urgeth onward to those guilty gates
The Great, the Sage, the Happy, and August.
And still he asks them of the hidden plan
Whence every treaty, every war began,
Evolves their secrets and their guilt proclaims:
And still his hands despoil them on the road
Of each vain wreath by lying bards bestow'd,
And crush their trophies huge, and raze their
    sculptur'd names.

### XIV.

Ye mighty shades, arise, give place, attend:
Here his eternal mansion Curio seeks:
—Low doth proud Wentworth to the stranger
    bend,
And his dire welcome hardy Clifford speaks:
" He comes, whom fate with surer arts prepar'd
To accomplish all which we but vainly dar'd;
Whom o'er the stubborn herd she taught to reign:
Who sooth'd with gaudy dreams their raging
    power
Even to its last irrevocable hour;
Then baffled their rude strength, and broke them to
    the chain."

### XV.

But ye, whom yet wise Liberty inspires,
Whom for her champions o'er the world she claims,
(That household godhead whom of old your sires
Sought in the woods of Elbe and bore to Thames)
Drive ye this hostile omen far away;
Their own fell efforts on her foes repay;
Your wealth, your arts, your fame, be hers alone:
Still gird your swords to combat on her side;
Still frame your laws her generous test to abide;
And win to her defence the altar and the throne.

### XVI.

Protect her from yourselves, ere yet the flood
Of golden Luxury, which Commerce pours,
Hath spread that selfish fierceness through your
    blood,
Which not her lightest discipline endures :
Snatch from fantastic demagogues her cause :
Dream not of Numa's manners, Plato's laws :
A wiser founder, and a nobler plan,
O sons of Alfred, were for you assign'd :
Bring to that birthright but an equal mind,
And no sublimer lot will fate reserve for man.

## ODE X.

### TO THE MUSE.

#### I.

QUEEN of my songs, harmonious maid,
    Ah why hast thou withdrawn thy aid?
Ah why forsaken thus my breast
With inauspicious damps oppress'd ?
Where is the dread prophetic heat,
With which my bosom wont to beat ?
Where all the bright mysterious dreams
Of haunted groves and tuneful streams,
That woo'd my genius to divinest themes ?

#### II.

Say, goddess, can the festal board,
Or young Olympia's form ador'd;
Say, can the pomp of promis'd fame
Relume thy faint, thy dying flame ?
Or have melodious airs the power
To give one free, poetic hour?
Or, from amid the Elysian train,
The soul of Milton shall I gain,
To win thee back with some celestial strain ?

### III.

O powerful strain! O sacred soul!
His numbers every sense control:
And now again my bosom burns;
The Muse, the Muse herself returns.
Such on the banks of Tyne, confess'd,
I hail'd the fair immortal guest,
When first she seal'd me for her own,
Made all her blissful treasures known,
And bade me swear to follow Her alone.

## ODE XI.

### ON LOVE, TO A FRIEND.

### I.

NO, foolish youth—to virtuous fame
     If now thy early hopes be vow'd,
If true ambition's nobler flame
Command thy footsteps from the crowd,
Lean not to Love's enchanting snare;
His songs, his words, his looks beware,
Nor join his votaries, the young and fair.

### II.

By thought, by dangers, and by toils,
The wreath of just renown is worn;
Nor will ambition's awful spoils
The flowery pomp of ease adorn:
But Love unbends the force of thought;
By Love unmanly fears are taught;
And Love's reward with gaudy sloth is bought.

### III.

Yet thou hast read in tuneful lays,
And heard from many a zealous breast,
The pleasing tale of beauty's praise
In wisdom's lofty language dress'd;

Of beauty powerful to impart
Each finer sense, each comelier art,
And soothe and polish man's ungentle heart.

### IV.

If then, from Love's deceit secure,
Thus far alone thy wishes tend,
Go ; see the white-wing'd evening hour
On Delia's vernal walk descend :
Go, while the golden light serene,
The grove, the lawn, the soften'd scene
Becomes the presence of the rural queen.

### V.

Attend, while that harmonious tongue
Each bosom, each desire commands :
Apollo's lute by Hermes strung,
And touch'd by chaste Minerva's hands,
Attend.   I feel a force divine,
O Delia, win my thoughts to thine ;
That half the colour of thy life is mine.

### VI.

Yet conscious of the dangerous charm,
Soon would I turn my steps away ;
Nor oft provoke the lovely harm,
Nor lull my reason's watchful sway.
But thou, my friend—I hear thy sighs :
Alas, I read thy downcast eyes ;
And thy tongue falters ; and thy colour flies.

### VII.

So soon again to meet the fair ?
So pensive all this absent hour ?
—O yet, unlucky youth, beware,
While yet to think is in thy power.
In vain with friendship's flattering name
Thy passion veils its inward shame ;
Friendship, the treacherous fuel of thy flame !

### VIII.

Once, I remember, new to Love,
And dreading his tyrannic chain,

I sought a gentle maid to prove
What peaceful joys in friendship reign:
Whence we forsooth might safely stand,
And pitying view the lovesick band,
And mock the winged boy's malicious hand.

### IX.

Thus frequent pass'd the cloudless day,
To smiles and sweet discourse resign'd;
While I exulted to survey
One generous woman's real mind:
Till friendship soon my languid breast
Each night with unknown cares possess'd,
Dash'd my coy slumbers, or my dreams distress'd.

### X.

Fool that I was—And now, even now
While thus I preach the Stoic strain,
Unless I shun Olympia's view,
An hour unsays it all again.
O friend!—when Love directs her eyes
To pierce where every passion lies,
Where is the firm, the cautious, or the wise?

## ODE XII.

### TO SIR FRANCIS HENRY DRAKE, BARONET.

### I.

BEHOLD; the Balance in the sky
Swift on the wintry scale inclines:
To earthy caves the Dryads fly,
And the bare pastures Pan resigns.
Late did the farmer's fork o'erspread
With recent soil the twice-mown mead,
Tainting the bloom which Autumn knows:
He whets the rusty coulter now,
He binds his oxen to the plough,
And wide his future harvest throws.

### II.

Now, London's busy confines round,
By Kensington's imperial towers,
From Highgate's rough descent profound,
Essexian heaths, or Kentish bowers,
Where'er I pass, I see approach
Some rural statesman's eager coach
Hurried by senatorial cares :
While rural nymphs (alike, within,
Aspiring courtly praise to win)
Debate their dress, reform their airs.

### III.

Say, what can now the country boast,
O Drake, thy footsteps to detain,
When peevish winds and gloomy frost
The sunshine of the temper stain?
Say, are the priests of Devon grown
Friends to this tolerating throne,
Champions for George's legal right?
Have general freedom, equal law,
Won to the glory of Nassau
Each bold Wessexian squire and knight?

### IV.

I doubt it much ; and guess at least
That when the day, which made us free,
Shall next return, that sacred feast
Thou better may'st observe with me.
With me the sulphurous treason old
A far inferior part shall hold
In that glad day's triumphal strain ;
And generous William be rever'd,
Nor one untimely accent heard
Of James or his ignoble reign.

### V.

Then, while the Gascon's fragrant wine
With modest cups our joy supplies,
We'll truly thank the power divine
Who bade the chief, the patriot rise ;
Rise from heroic ease (the spoil

Due, for his youth's Herculean toil,
From Belgium to her saviour son)
Rise with the same unconquer'd zeal
For our Britannia's injured weal,
Her laws defac'd, her shrines o'erthrown.

### VI.

He came. The tyrant from our shore,
Like a forbidden demon, fled;
And to eternal exile bore
Pontific rage and vassal dread.
There sunk the mouldering Gothic reign:
New years came forth, a liberal train,
Call'd by the people's great decree.
That day, my friend, let blessings crown:
—Fill, to the demigod's renown
From whom thou hast that thou art free.

### VII.

Then, Drake, (for wherefore should we part
The public and the private weal?)
In vows to her who sways thy heart,
Fair health, glad fortune, will we deal.
Whether Aglaia's blooming cheek,
Or the soft ornaments that speak
So eloquent in Daphne's smile,
Whether the piercing lights that fly
From the dark heaven of Myrto's eye,
Haply thy fancy then beguile.

### VIII.

For so it is:—thy stubborn breast,
Though touched by many a slighter wound,
Hath no full conquest yet confess'd,
Nor the one fatal charmer found.
While I, a true and loyal swain,
My fair Olympia's gentle reign
Through all the varying seasons own.
Her genius still my bosom warms:
No other maid for me hath charms,
Or I have eyes for her alone.

## ODE XIII.

### ON LYRIC POETRY.

#### I. 1.

ONCE more I join the Thespian choir,
    And taste the inspiring fount again :
O parent of the Grecian lyre,
Admit me to thy powerful strain —
And lo, with ease my step invades
The pathless vale and opening shades,
Till now I spy her verdant seat;
And now at large I drink the sound,
While these her offspring, listening round,
By turns her melody repeat.

#### I. 2.

I see Anacreon smile and sing,
His silver tresses breathe perfume ;
His cheek displays a second spring
Of roses taught by wine to bloom.
Away, deceitful cares, away,
And let me listen to his lay;
Let me the wanton pomp enjoy,
While in smooth dance the light-wing'd Hours
Lead round his lyre its patron powers,
Kind Laughter and Convivial Joy.

#### I. 3.

Broke from the fetters of his native land,
Devoting shame and vengeance to her lords,
With louder impulse and a threatening hand
The Lesbian patriot[1] smites the sounding chords:
    Ye wretches, ye perfidious train,
    Ye cursèd of gods and free born men,
      Ye murderers of the laws,

[1] Alcæus.

Though now ye glory in your lust,
Though now ye tread the feeble neck in dust,
Yet Time and righteous Jove will judge your dread-
  ful cause.

## II.  1.

But lo, to Sappho's melting airs
Descends the radiant queen of love:
She smiles, and asks what fonder cares
Her suppliant's plaintive measures move:
Why is my faithful maid distress'd?
Who, Sappho, wounds thy tender breast?
Say, flies he?—Soon he shall pursue:
Shuns he thy gifts?—He soon shall give:
Slights he thy sorrows?—He shall grieve,
And soon to all thy wishes bow.

## II.  2.

But, O Melpomene, for whom
Awakes thy golden shell again?
What mortal breath shall e'er presume
To echo that unbounded strain?
Majestic in the frown of years,
Behold, the man of Thebes[2] appears:
For some there are, whose mighty frame
The hand of Jove at birth endow'd
With hopes that mock the gazing crowd;
As eagles drink the noontide flame,

## II.  3.

While the dim raven beats her weary wings,
And clamours far below.—Propitious Muse,
While I so late unlock thy purer springs,
And breathe whate'er thy ancient airs infuse,
 Wilt thou for Albion's sons around
 (Ne'er hadst thou audience more renown'd)
  Thy charming arts employ,
As when the winds from shore to shore
Thro' Greece thy lyre's persuasive language bore,
Till towns and isles and seas return'd the vocal joy?

   [2] Pindar.

### III. 1.

Yet then did Pleasure's lawless throng,
Oft rushing forth in loose attire,
Thy virgin dance, thy graceful song
Pollute with impious revels dire.
O fair, O chaste, thy echoing shade
May no foul discord here invade :
Nor let thy strings one accent move,
Except what earth's untroubled ear
'Mid all her social tribes may hear,
And heaven's unerring throne approve.

### III. 2.

Queen of the lyre, in thy retreat
The fairest flowers of Pindus glow ;
The vine aspires to crown thy seat,
And myrtles round thy laurel grow.
Thy strings adapt their varied strain
To every pleasure, every pain,
Which mortal tribes were born to prove ;
And straight our passions rise or fall,
As at the wind's imperious call
The ocean swells, the billows move.

### III. 3.

When midnight listens o'er the slumbering earth,
Let me, O Muse, thy solemn whispers hear :
When morning sends her fragrant breezes forth,
With airy murmurs touch my opening ear.
And ever watchful at thy side,
Let Wisdom's awful suffrage guide
The tenor of thy lay :
To her of old by Jove was given
To judge the various deeds of earth and heaven ;
'Twas thine by gentle arts to win us to her sway.

### IV. 1.

Oft as, to well-earn'd ease resign'd,
I quit the maze where Science toils,
Do thou refresh my yielding mind
With all thy gay, delusive spoils.

But, O indulgent, come not nigh
The busy steps, the jealous eye
Of wealthy care or gainful age;
Whose barren souls thy joys disdain,
And hold as foes to reason's reign
Whome'er thy lovely works engage.

### IV. 2.

When friendship and when letter'd mirth
Haply partake my simple board,
Then let thy blameless hand call forth
The music of the Teian chord.
Or if invok'd at softer hours,
O! seek with me the happy bowers
That hear Olympia's gentle tongue;
To beauty link'd with virtue's train,
To love devoid of jealous pain,
There let the Sapphic lute be strung.

### IV. 3.

But when from envy and from death to claim
A hero bleeding for his native land;
When to throw incense on the vestal flame
Of Liberty my genius gives command,
Nor Theban voice nor Lesbian lyre
From thee, O Muse, do I require;
While my presaging mind,
Conscious of powers she never knew,
Astonish'd grasps at things beyond her view,
Nor by another's fate submits to be confin'd.

## ODE XIV.

### TO THE HONOURABLE CHARLES TOWNSHEND;
### FROM THE COUNTRY.

SAY, Townshend, what can London boast
To pay thee for the pleasures lost,
The health to-day resign'd,

When Spring from this her favourite seat
Bade Winter hasten his retreat,
   And met the western wind.

### II.

O knew'st thou how the balmy air,
The sun, the azure heavens prepare
   To heal thy languid frame,
No more would noisy courts engage;
In vain would lying Faction's rage
   Thy sacred leisure claim.

### III.

Oft I look'd forth, and oft admir'd;
Till with the studious volume tir'd
   I sought the open day;
And sure, I cried, the rural gods
Expect me in their green abodes,
   And chide my tardy lay.

### IV.

But ah, in vain my restless feet
Trac'd every silent shady seat
   Which knew their forms of old:
Nor Naiad by her fountain laid,
Nor Wood-nymph tripping through her glade,
   Did now their rites unfold:

### V.

Whether to nurse some infant oak
They turn the slowly tinkling-brook
   And catch the pearly showers,
Or brush the mildew from the woods,
Or paint with noontide beams the buds,
   Or breathe on opening flowers.

### VI.

Such rites, which they with Spring renew,
The eyes of care can never view;
   And care hath long been mine:
And hence offended with their guest,
Since grief of love my soul oppress'd,
   They hide their toils divine.

## VII.

But soon shall thy enlivening tongue
This heart, by dear affliction wrung,
  With noble hope inspire:
Then will the sylvan powers again
Receive me in their genial train,
  And listen to my lyre.

## VIII.

Beneath yon Dryad's lonely shade
A rustic altar shall be paid,
  Of turf with laurel fram'd:
And thou the inscription wilt approve;
" This for the peace which, lost by love,
  By friendship was reclaim'd."

# ODE XV.

## TO THE EVENING STAR.

### I.

TO-NIGHT retir'd the queen of heaven
    With young Endymion stays:
And now to Hesper it is given
Awhile to rule the vacant sky,
Till she shall to her lamp supply
    A stream of brighter rays.

### II.

O Hesper, while the starry throng
    With awe thy path surrounds,
Oh, listen to my suppliant song,
If haply now the vocal sphere
Can suffer thy delighted ear
    To stoop to mortal sounds.

### III.

So may the bridegroom's genial strain
    Thee still invoke to shine:

So may the bride's unmarried train
To Hymen chaunt their flattering vow,
Still that his lucky torch may glow
    With lustre pure as thine.

### IV.

Far other vows must I prefer
    To thy indulgent power.
Alas, but now I paid my tear
On fair Olympia's virgin tomb:
And lo, from thence, in quest I roam
    Of Philomela's bower.

### V.

Propitious send thy golden ray,
    Thou purest light above:
Let no false flame seduce to stray
Where gulf or steep lie hid for harm:
But lead where music's healing charm
    May soothe afflicted love.

### VI.

To them, by many a grateful song
    In happier seasons vow'd,
These lawns, Olympia's haunt, belong:
Oft by yon silver stream we walk'd,
Or fix'd, while Philomela talk'd,
    Beneath yon copses stood.

### VII.

Nor seldom, where the beechen boughs
    That roofless tower invade,
We came while her enchanting Muse
The radiant moon above us held:
Till by a clamorous owl compell'd
    She fled the solemn shade.

### VIII.

But hark; I hear her liquid tone.
    Now, Hesper, guide my feet
Down the red marl with moss o'ergrown,
Through yon wild thicket next the plain,

Whose hawthorns choke the winding lane,
  Which leads to her retreat.

### IX.

See the green space : on either hand
  Enlarg'd it spreads around :
See, in the midst she takes her stand,
Where one old oak his awful shade
Extends o'er half the level mead
  Inclos'd in woods profound.

### X.

Hark, how through many a melting note
  She now prolongs her lays :
How sweetly down the void they float !
The breeze their magic path attends :
The stars shine out : the forest bends :
  The wakeful heifers gaze.

### XI.

Whoe'er thou art whom chance may bring
  To this sequester'd spot,
If then the plaintive Syren sing,
Oh softly tread beneath her bower,
And think of heaven's disposing power,
  Of man's uncertain lot.

### XII.

Oh think, o'er all this mortal stage,
  What mournful scenes arise :
What ruin waits on kingly rage :
How often virtue dwells with woe :
How many griefs from knowledge flow
  How swiftly pleasure flies.

### XIII.

O sacred bird, let me at eve,
  Thus wandering all alone,
Thy tender counsel oft receive,
Bear witness to thy pensive airs,
And pity Nature's common cares
  Till I forget my own.

R

## ODE XVI.

### TO CALEB HARDINGE, M. D.

#### I.

WITH sordid floods the wintry Urn [1]
Hath stain'd fair Richmond's level green:
Her naked hill the Dryads mourn,
No longer a poetic scene.
No longer there thy raptur'd eye
The beauteous forms of earth or sky
Surveys as in their Author's mind:
And London shelters from the year
Those whom thy social hours to share
The Attic Muse design'd.

#### II.

From Hampstead's airy summit me
Her guest the city shall behold,
What day the people's stern decree
To unbelieving kings is told,
When common men (the dread of fame)
Adjudg'd as one of evil name,
Before the sun, the anointed head.
Then seek thou too the pious town,
With no unworthy cares to crown
That evening's awful shade.

#### III.

Deem not I call thee to deplore
The sacred martyr of the day,
By fast and penitential lore
To purge our ancient guilt away.
For this, on humble faith I rest
That still our advocate, the priest,
From heavenly wrath will save the land:
Nor ask what rites our pardon gain,
Nor how his potent sounds restrain
The thunderer's lifted hand.

[1] Aquarius.

### IV.

No, Hardinge : peace to church and state !
That evening, let the Muse give law :
While I anew the theme relate
Which my first youth enamour'd saw.
Then will I oft explore thy thought,
What to reject which Locke hath taught,
What to pursue in Virgil's lay :
Till hope ascends to loftiest things,
Nor envies demagogues or kings
 Their frail and vulgar sway.

### V.

O vers'd in all the human frame,
Lead thou where'er my labour lies,
And English fancy's eager flame
To Grecian purity chastise :
While hand in hand, at Wisdom's shrine,
Beauty with truth I strive to join,
And grave assent with glad applause ;
To paint the story of the soul,
And Plato's visions to control
 By Verulamian [1] laws.

## ODE XVII.

### ON A SERMON AGAINST GLORY. 1747.

### I.

COME then, tell me, sage divine,
 Is it an offence to own
That our bosoms e'er incline
Toward immortal Glory's throne ?
For with me nor pomp, nor pleasure,
Bourbon's might, Braganza's treasure,

---

[1] Verulam gave one of his titles to Francis Bacon, author
of the Novum Organum.

So can Fancy's dream rejoice,
So conciliate Reason's choice,
As one approving word of her impartial voice.

### II.
If to spurn at noble praise
Be the passport to thy heaven,
Follow thou those gloomy ways;
No such law to me was given,
Nor, I trust, shall I deplore me,
Faring like my friends before me;
Nor an holier place desire
Than Timoleon's arms acquire,
And Tully's curule chair, and Milton's golden lyre.

## ODE XVIII.

### TO THE RIGHT HONOURABLE FRANCIS EARL
### OF HUNTINGDON. 1747.

#### I. 1.
THE wise and great of every clime,
    Through all the spacious walks of Time,
Where'er the Muse her power display'd,
With joy have listen'd and obey'd.
For, taught of heaven, the sacred Nine
Persuasive numbers, forms divine,
    To mortal sense impart:
They best the soul with glory fire;
They noblest counsels, boldest deeds inspire;
And high o'er Fortune's rage enthrone the fixed
    heart.

#### I. 2.
Nor less prevailing is their charm
The vengeful bosom to disarm;
To melt the proud with human woe,
And prompt unwilling tears to flow.

Can wealth a power like this afford ?
Can Cromwell's arts, or Marlborough's sword,
    An equal empire claim ?
No, Hastings.  Thou my words wilt own :
Thy breast the gifts of every Muse hath known ;
Nor shall the giver's love disgrace thy noble name.

### I. 3.

The Muse s awful art,
And the blest function of the poet's tongue,
Ne'er shalt thou blush to honour ; to assert
From all that scorned vice or slavish fear hath sung.
Nor shall the blandishment of Tuscan strings
Warbling at will in Pleasure's myrtle bower ;
Nor shall the servile notes to Celtic kings
By flattering minstrels paid in evil hour,
Move thee to spurn the heavenly Muse's reign.
    A different strain,
    And other themes
From her prophetic shades and hallow'd streams
(Thou well canst witness) meet the purged ear :
Such, as when Greece to her immortal shell
Rejoicing listen'd, godlike sounds to hear ;
    To hear the sweet instructress tell
    (While men and heroes throng'd around)
    How life its noblest use may find,
    How well for freedom be resign'd ;
And how, by glory, virtue shall be crown'd.

### II. 1.

Such was the Chian father's strain
To many a kind domestic train,
Whose pious hearth and genial bowl
Had cheer'd the reverend pilgrim's soul :
    When, every hospitable rite
    With equal bounty to requite,
        He struck his magic strings ;
    And pour'd spontaneous numbers forth,
And seiz'd their ears with tales of ancient worth,
And fill'd their musing hearts with vast heroic things.

### II. 2.

Now oft, where happy spirits dwell,
Where yet he tunes his charming shell,
Oft near him, with applauding hands,
The Genius of his country stands.
To listening gods he makes him known,
That man divine, by whom were sown
    The seeds of Grecian fame:
Who first the race with freedom fir'd;
From whom Lycurgus Sparta's sons inspir'd;
From whom Platæan palms and Cyprian trophies
    came.

### II. 3.

    O noblest, happiest age!
When Aristides rul'd, and Cimon fought;
When all the generous fruits of Homer's page
Exulting Pindar saw to full perfection brought.
O Pindar, oft shalt thou be hail'd of me:
Not that Apollo fed thee from his shrine;
Not that thy lips drank sweetness from the bee;
Nor yet that, studious of thy notes divine,
Pan danc'd their measure with the sylvan throng:
    But that thy song
    Was proud to unfold
What thy base rulers trembled to behold;
Amid corrupted Thebes was proud to tell
The deeds of Athens and the Persian shame:
Hence on thy head their impious vengeance fell.
    But thou, O faithful to thy fame,
    The Muse's law didst rightly know;
    That who would animate his lays,
    And other minds to virtue raise,
Must feel his own with all her spirit glow.

### III. 1.

Are there, approv'd of later times,
Whose verse adorn'd a tyrant's [1] crimes?
Who saw majestic Rome betray'd,

---

[1] Octavianus Cæsar.

And lent the imperial ruffian aid ?
Alas ! not one polluted bard,
No, not the strains that Mincius heard,
   Or Tibur's hills replied, ,
  Dare to the Muse's ear aspire ;
Save that, instructed by the Grecian lyre,
With Freedom's ancient notes their shameful task
   they hide.

### III.  2.

Mark, how the dread Pantheon stands,
Amid the domes of modern hands :
Amid the toys of idle state,
How simply, how severely great !
Then turn, and, while each western clime
Presents her tuneful sons to Time,
   So mark thou Milton's name ;
And add, " Thus differs from the throng
The spirit which inform'd thy awful song,
Which bade thy potent voice protect thy country's
   fame."

### III.  3.

   Yet hence barbaric zeal
-His memory with unholy rage pursues ;
  While from these arduous cares of public weal
She bids each bard begone, and rest him with his
   Muse.
O fool ! to think the man, whose ample mind
Must grasp at all that yonder stars survey ;
Must join the noblest forms of every kind,
The world's most perfect image to display,
Can e'er his country's majesty behold,
   Unmov'd or cold !
   O fool ! to deem
That he, whose thought must visit every theme,
Whose heart must every strong emotion know
Inspir'd by Nature, or by Fortune taught ;
That he, if haply some presumptuous foe,
  With false ignoble science fraught,

Shall spurn at Freedom's faithful band;
That he their dear defence will shun,
Or hide their glories from the sun,
Or deal their vengeance with a woman's hand!

### IV.  1.

I care not that in Arno's plain,
Or on the sportive banks of Seine,
From public themes the Muse's quire
Content with polish'd ease retire.
Where priests the studious head command,
Where tyrants bow the warlike hand
    To vile ambition's aim,
Say, what can public themes afford,
Save venal honours to a hateful lord,    [fame?
Reserv'd for angry heaven and scorn'd of honest

### IV.  2.

But here, where Freedom's equal throne
To all her valiant sons is known ;
Where all are conscious of her cares,
And each the power, that rules him, shares;
Here let the bard, whose dastard tongue
Leaves public arguments unsung,
    Bid public praise farewell:
Let him to fitter climes remove,
Far from the hero's and the patriot's love,
And lull mysterious monks to slumber in their cell.

### IV.  3.

O Hastings, not to all
Can ruling Heaven the same endowments lend :
Yet still doth Nature to her offspring call,
That to one general weal their different powers they
    bend,
Unenvious.   Thus alone, though strains divine
Inform the bosom of the Muse's son ;
Though with new honours the patrician's line
Advance from age to age ; yet thus alone
They win the suffrage of impartial fame.
    The poet's name

He best shall prove,
Whose lays the soul with noblest passions move.
But thee, O progeny of heroes old,
Thee to severer toils thy fate requires :
The fate which form'd thee in a chosen mould,
  The grateful country of thy sires,
  Thee to sublimer paths demand ;
  Sublimer than thy sires could trace,
  Or thy own Edward teach his race,
Tho' Gaul's proud genius sank beneath his hand.

### v. 1.

From rich domains, and subject farms,
  They led the rustic youth to arms ;
  And kings their stern achievements fear'd ;
  While private strife their banners rear'd.
But loftier scenes to thee are shown,
Where empire's wide establish'd throne
  No private master fills :
Where, long foretold, the People reigns :
Where each a vassal's humble heart disdains ;
And judgeth what he sees ; and, as he judgeth, wills.

### v. 2.

Here be it thine to calm and guide
  The swelling democratic tide ;
  To watch the state's uncertain frame,
  And baffle Faction's partial aim :
But chiefly, with determin'd zeal,
To quell that servile band, who kneel
  To Freedom's banish'd foes ;
That monster, which is daily found
Expert and bold thy country's peace to wound ;
Yet dreads to handle arms, nor manly counsel knows.

### v. 3.

'Tis highest Heaven's command,
That guilty aims should sordid paths pursue ;
That what ensnares the heart should maim the
    hand,
And Virtue's worthless foes be false to glory too.

But look on Freedom :—see, thro' every age,
What labours, perils, griefs, hath she disdain'd!
What arms, what regal pride, what priestly rage,
Have her dread offspring conquer'd or sustain'd!
For Albion well have conquer'd. Let the strains
   Of happy swains,
   Which now resound
Where Scarsdale's cliffs the swelling pastures
  bound,
Bear witness :—there, oft let the farmer hail
The sacred orchard which embowers his gate,
And show to strangers passing down the vale,
  Where Candish, Booth, and Osborne sate;
  When bursting from their country's chain,
  Even in the midst of deadly harms,
  Of papal snares and lawless arms,
They plann'd for Freedom this her noblest reign.

### VI. 1.

This reign, these laws, this public care,
Which Nassau gave us all to share,
Had ne'er adorn'd the English name,
Could Fear have silenc'd Freedom's claim.
But Fear in vain attempts to bind
Those lofty efforts of the mind
  Which social good inspires ;
Where men, for this, assault a throne,
Each adds the common welfare to his own;
And each unconquer'd heart the strength of all
  acquires.

### VI. 2.

Say, was it thus, when late we view'd
Our fields in civil blood imbru'd ?
When fortune crown'd the barbarous host,
And half the astonish'd isle was lost ?
Did one of all that vaunting train,
Who dare affront a peaceful reign,
  Durst one in arms appear ?
Durst one in counsels pledge his life ?

Stake his luxurious fortunes in the strife ?
Or lend his boasted name his vagrant friends to
    cheer ?

VI. 3.

    Yet, Hastings, these are they
Who challenge to themselves thy country's love;
The true ; the constant : who alone can weigh,
What glory should demand, or liberty approve!
But let their works declare them. Thy free powers,
The generous powers of thy prevailing mind,
Not for the tasks of their confederate hours,
Lewd brawls and lurking slander, were design'd.
Be thou thy own approver. Honest praise
        Oft nobly sways
        Ingenuous youth :
But, sought from cowards and the lying mouth,
Praise is reproach. Eternal God alone
For mortals fixeth that sublime award.
He, from the faithful records of his throne,
    Bids the historian and the bard
Dispose of honour and of scorn ;
Discern the patriot from the slave;
And write the good, the wise, the brave,
For lessons to the multitude unborn.

# BOOK II.

## ODE I.

### THE REMONSTRANCE OF SHAKESPEARE:

SUPPOSED TO HAVE BEEN SPOKEN AT THE THEATRE ROYAL,
WHILE THE FRENCH COMEDIANS WERE ACTING
BY SUBSCRIPTION. 1749.

IF, yet regardful of your native land,
  Old Shakespeare's tongue you deign to under-
    stand,

Lo, from the blissful bowers where heaven rewards
Instructive sages and unblemish'd bards,
I come, the ancient founder of the stage,
Intent to learn, in this discerning age,
What form of wit your fancies have embrac'd,
And whither tends your elegance of taste,
That thus at length our homely toils you spurn,
That thus to foreign scenes you proudly turn,
That from my brow the laurel wreath you claim
To crown the rivals of your country's fame.
　　What, though the footsteps of my devious Muse
The measur'd walks of Grecian art refuse?
Or though the frankness of my hardy style
Mock the nice touches of the critic's file?
Yet, what my age and climate held to view,
Impartial I survey'd and fearless drew.
And say, ye skilful in the human heart,
Who know to prize a poet's noblest part,
What age, what clime, could e'er an ampler field
For lofty thought, for daring fancy, yield?
I saw this England break the shameful bands
Forg'd for the souls of men by sacred hands :
I saw each groaning realm her aid implore ;
Her sons the heroes of each warlike shore :
Her naval standard (the dire Spaniard's bane)
Obey'd through all the circuit of the main.
Then too great Commerce, for a late-found world,
Around your coast her eager sails unfurl'd :
New hopes, new passions, thence the bosom fir'd ;
New plans, new arts, the genius thence inspir'd ;
Thence every scene, which private fortune knows,
In stronger life, with bolder spirit, rose.
　　Disgrac'd I this full prospect which I drew?
My colours languid, or my strokes untrue?
Have not your sages, warriors, swains, and kings,
Confess'd the living draught of men and things?
What other bard in any clime appears
Alike the master of your smiles and tears?
Yet have I deign'd your audience to entice

With wretched bribes to luxury and vice?
Or have my various scenes a purpose known
Which freedom, virtue, glory, might not own?
   Such from the first was my dramatic plan;
It should be yours to crown what I began:
And now that England spurns her Gothic chain,
And equal laws and social science reign,
I thought, Now surely shall my zealous eyes
View nobler bards and juster critics rise,
Intent with learned labour to refine
The copious ore of Albion's native mine,
Our stately Muse more graceful airs to teach,
And form her tongue to more attractive speech,
Till rival nations listen at her feet,
And own her polish'd as they own her great.
   But do you thus my favourite hopes fulfil?
Is France at last the standard of your skill?
Alas for you! that so betray a mind
Of art unconscious and to beauty blind.
Say; does her language your ambition raise,
Her barren, trivial, unharmonious phrase,
Which fetters eloquence to scantiest bounds,
And maims the cadence of poetic sounds?
Say; does your humble admiration choose
The gentle prattle of her Comic Muse,
While wits, plain-dealers, fops, and fools appear,
Charg'd to say nought but what the king may hear?
Or rather melt your sympathising hearts
Won by her tragic scene's romantic arts,
Where old and young declaim on soft desire,
And heroes never, but for love, expire?
   No. Though the charms of novelty, awhile,
Perhaps too fondly win your thoughtless smile,
Yet not for you design'd indulgent fate
The modes or manners of the Bourbon state.
And ill your minds my partial judgment reads,
And many an augury my hope misleads,
If the fair maids of yonder blooming train
To their light courtship would an audience deign,

Or those chaste matrons a Parisian wife
Choose for the model of domestic life ;
Or if one youth of all that generous band,
The strength and splendour of their native land,
Would yield his portion of his country's fame,
And quit old freedom's patrimonial claim,
With lying smiles oppression's pomp to see,
And judge of glory by a king's decree.
　　O blest at home with justly-envied laws,
O long the chiefs of Europe's general cause,
Whom heaven hath chosen at each dangerous hour
To check the inroads of barbaric power,
The rights of trampled nations to reclaim,
And guard the social world from bonds and shame ;
O let not luxury's fantastic charms
Thus give the lie to your heroic arms :
Nor for the ornaments of life embrace
Dishonest lessons from that vaunting race,
Whom fate's dread laws (for, in eternal fate
Despotic rule was heir to freedom's hate)
Whom in each warlike, each commercial part,
In civil council, and in pleasing art,
The judge of earth predestin'd for your foes,
And made it fame and virtue to oppose.

## ODE II.

### TO SLEEP.

#### I.

THOU silent power, whose welcome sway
　　Charms every anxious thought away;
In whose divine oblivion drown'd,
Sore pain and weary toil grow mild,
Love is with kinder looks beguil'd,
And grief forgets her fondly cherish'd wound ;
Oh whither hast thou flown, indulgent god ?

God of kind shadows and of healing dews,
Whom dost thou touch with thy Lethæan rod?
Around whose temples now thy opiate airs diffuse?

### II.

Lo, Midnight from her starry reign
Looks awful down on earth and main.
The tuneful birds lie hush'd in sleep,
With all that crop the verdant food,
With all that skim the crystal flood,
Or haunt the caverns of the rocky steep.
No rushing winds disturb the tufted bowers;
No wakeful sound the moonlight valley knows,
Save where the brook its liquid murmur pours,
And lulls the waving scene to more profound repose.

### III.

Oh let not me alone complain,
Alone invoke thy power in vain!
Descend, propitious, on my eyes;
Not from the couch that bears a crown,
Not from the courtly statesman's down,
Nor where the miser and his treasure lies:
Bring not the shapes that break the murderer's
rest,
Nor those the hireling soldier loves to see,
Nor those which haunt the bigot's gloomy breast:
Far be their guilty nights, and far their dreams
from me!

### IV.

Nor yet those awful forms present,
For chiefs and heroes only meant:
The figur'd brass, the choral song,
The rescued people's glad applause,
The listening senate, and the laws
Fix'd by the counsels of Timoleon's [1] tongue,

[1] After Timoleon had delivered Syracuse from the tyranny of Dionysius, the people on every important deliberation sent for him into the public assembly, asked his advice, and voted according to it. PLUTARCH.

Are scenes too grand for fortune's private ways :
And though they shine in youth's ingenuous view,
The sober gainful arts of modern days
To such romantic thoughts have bid a long adieu.

### v.

I ask not, god of dreams, thy care
To banish Love's presentments fair :
Nor rosy cheek nor radiant eye
Can arm him with such strong command
That the young sorcerer's fatal hand
Should round my soul his pleasing fetters tie.
Nor yet the courtier's hope, the giving smile
(A lighter phantom, and a baser chain)
Did e'er in slumber my proud lyre beguile
To lend the pomp of thrones her ill-according strain.

### VI.

But, Morpheus, on thy balmy wing
Such honourable visions bring,
As sooth'd great Milton's injur'd age,
When in prophetic dreams he saw
The race unborn with pious awe
Imbibe each virtue from his heavenly page :
Or such as Mead's benignant fancy knows
When health's deep treasures, by his art explor'd,
Have sav'd the infant from an orphan's woes,
Or to the trembling sire his age's hope restor'd.

## ODE III.

### TO THE CUCKOO.

### I.

O RUSTIC herald of the spring,
  At length in yonder woody vale
Fast by the brook I hear thee sing :
And, studious of thy homely tale,

Amid the vespers of the grove,
Amid the chaunting choir of love,
    Thy sage responses hail.

### II.

The time has been when I have frown'd
To hear thy voice the woods invade;
And while thy solemn accent drown'd
Some sweeter poet of the shade,
Thus, thought I, thus the sons of care
Some constant youth or generous fair
    With dull advice upbraid.

### III.

I said, " While Philomela's song
Proclaims the passion of the grove,
It ill beseems a cuckoo's tongue
Her charming language to reprove"—
Alas, how much a lover's ear
Hates all the sober truth to hear,
    The sober truth of love!

### IV.

When hearts are in each other bless'd,
When nought but lofty faith can rule
The nymph's and swain's consenting breast,
How cuckoo-like in Cupid's school,
With store of grave prudential saws
On fortune's power and custom's laws,
    Appears each friendly fool!

### V.

Yet think betimes, ye gentle train
Whom love and hope and fancy sway,
Who every harsher care disdain,
Who by the morning judge the day,
Think that, in April's fairest hours,
To warbling shades and painted flowers
    The cuckoo joins his lay.

S

## ODE IV.

### TO THE HONOURABLE CHARLES TOWNSHEND
### IN THE COUNTRY. 1750.

#### I. 1.

HOW oft shall I survey
 This humble roof, the lawn, the greenwood
  shade,
  The vale with sheaves o'erspread,
The glassy brook, the flocks which round thee stray?
  When will thy cheerful mind
Of these have utter'd all her dear esteem?
  Or, tell me, dost thou deem
No more to join in glory's toilsome race,
  But here content embrace
That happy leisure which thou hadst resign'd?

#### I. 2.

  Alas, ye happy hours,
When books and youthful sport the soul could share,
  Ere one ambitious care
Of civil life had aw'd her simpler powers;
  Oft as your winged train
Revisit here my friend in white array,
  O fail not to display
Each fairer scene where I perchance had part,
  That so his generous heart
The abode of even friendship may remain.

#### I. 3.

For not imprudent of my loss to come,
I saw from Contemplation's quiet cell
His feet ascending to another home
Where public praise and envied greatness dwell.
  But shall we therefore, O my lyre,
  Reprove ambition's best desire?

Extinguish glory's flame ?
Far other was the task injoin'd
When to my hand thy strings were first assign'd :
Far other faith belongs to friendship's honour'd
    name.

### II.  1.

Thee, Townshend, not the arms
Of slumbering Ease, nor Pleasure's rosy chain,
    Were destin'd to detain :
No, nor bright Science, nor the Muse's charms.
    For them high heaven prepares
Their proper votaries, an humbler band :
    And ne'er would Spenser's hand
Have deign'd to strike the warbling Tuscan shell,
    Nor Harrington to tell
What habit an immortal city wears,

### II.  2.

Had this been born to shield
The cause which Cromwell's impious hand betray'd,
    Or that, like Vere, display'd
His redcross banner o'er the Belgian field.
    Yet where the will divine
Hath shut those loftiest paths, it next remains,
    With reason clad in strains
Of harmony, selected minds to inspire,
    And virtue's living fire
To feed and eternize in hearts like thine.

### II.  3.

For never shall the herd, whom envy sways,
So quell my purpose or my tongue control,
That I should fear illustrious worth to praise,
Because its master's friendship mov'd my soul.
    Yet, if this undissembling strain
Should now perhaps thine ear detain
    With any pleasing sound,
Remember thou that righteous Fame
From hoary age a strict account will claim
Of each auspicious palm with which thy youth was
    crown'd.

### III. 1.

Nor obvious is the way
Where heaven expects thee, nor the traveller leads,
 Through flowers or fragrant meads,
Or groves that hark to Philomela's lay.
 The impartial laws of fate
To nobler virtues wed severer cares.
 Is there a man who shares
The summit next where heavenly natures dwell?
 Ask him (for he can tell)
What storms beat round that rough laborious height.

### III. 2.

Ye heroes, who of old
Did generous England Freedom's throne ordain;
 From Alfred's parent reign
To Nassau, great deliverer, wise and bold;
 I know your perils hard,
Your wounds, your painful marches, wintry seas,
 The night estrang'd from ease,
The day by cowardice and falsehood vex'd,
 The head with doubt perplex'd,
The indignant heart disdaining the reward

### III. 3.

Which envy hardly grants. But, O renown,
O praise from judging heaven and virtuous men,
If thus they purchas'd thy divinest crown,
Say, who shall hesitate? or who complain?
 And now they sit on thrones above:
 And when among the gods they move
  Before the Sovereign Mind,
 "Lo, these," he saith, "lo, these are they
 Who to the laws of mine eternal sway
From violence and fear asserted human kind."

### IV. 1.

Thus honour'd while the train
Of legislators in his presence dwell;
 If I may aught foretell,
The statesman shall the second palm obtain.

For dreadful deeds of arms
Let vulgar bards, with undiscerning praise,
    More glittering trophies raise :
But wisest Heaven what deeds may chiefly move
    To favour and to love ?
What, save wide blessings, or averted harms ?

### IV.   2.

Nor to the embattled field
Shall these achievements of the peaceful gown
    The green immortal crown
Of valour, or the songs of conquest, yield.
    Not Fairfax wildly bold,
While bare of crest he hew'd his fatal way,
    Through Naseby's firm array,
To heavier dangers did his breast oppose
    Than Pym's free virtue chose,
When the proud force of Strafford he control'd.

### IV.   3.

But what is man at enmity with truth ?
What were the fruits of Wentworth's copious mind
When (blighted all the promise of his youth)
The patriot in a tyrant's league had join'd ?
        Let Ireland's loud-lamenting plains,
        Let Tyne's and Humber's trampled swains,
            Let menac'd London tell
        How impious guile made wisdom base ;
        How generous zeal to cruel rage gave place ;
And how unbless'd he lived and how dishonour'd
    fell.

### V.   1.

Thence never hath the Muse
Around his tomb Pierian roses flung :
    Nor shall one poet's tongue
His name for music's pleasing labour choose.
    And sure, when Nature kind
Hath deck'd some favour'd breast above the throng,
    That man with grievous wrong
Affronts and wounds his genius, if he bends

To guilt's ignoble ends
The functions of his ill-submitting mind.

### V. 2.

For worthy of the wise
Nothing can seem but virtue; nor earth yield
Their fame an equal field,
Save where impartial Freedom gives the prize.
There Somers fixed his name,
Inroll'd the next to William. There shall Time
To every wondering clime
Point out that Somers, who from faction's crowd,
The slanderous and the loud,
Could fair assent and modest reverence claim.

### V. 3.

Nor aught did laws or social arts acquire,
Nor this majestic weal of Albion's land
Did aught accomplish, or to aught aspire,
Without his guidance, his superior hand.
And rightly shall the Muse's care
Wreaths like her own for him prepare,
Whose mind's enamour'd aim
Could forms of civil beauty draw
Sublime as ever sage or poet saw,
Yet still to life's rude scene the proud ideas tame.

### VI. 1.

Let none profane be near!
The Muse was never foreign to his breast:
On power's grave seat confess'd,
Still to her voice he bent a lover's ear.
And if the blessed know
Their ancient cares, even now the unfading groves,
Where haply Milton roves
With Spenser, hear the enchanted echoes round
Through farthest heaven resound
Wise Somers, guardian of their fame below.

### VI. 2.

He knew, the patriot knew,
That letters and the Muse's powerful art

Exalt the ingenuous heart,
And brighten every form of just and true.
    They lend a nobler sway
To civil wisdom, than corruption's lure
    Could ever yet procure :
They too from envy's pale malignant light
    Conduct her forth to sight
Cloth'd in the fairest colours of the day.

### VI.   3.

O Townshend, thus may Time, the judge severe,
Instruct my happy tongue of thee to tell :
And when I speak of one to Freedom dear
For planning wisely and for acting well,
    Of one whom Glory loves to own,
    Who still by liberal means alone
      Hath liberal ends pursu'd ;
    Then, for the guerdon of my lay,
" This man with faithful friendship," will I say,
" From youth to honour'd age my arts and me hath
    view'd."


## ODE V.

### ON LOVE OF PRAISE.

#### I.

OF all the springs within the mind
   Which prompt her steps in fortune's maze,
From none more pleasing aid we find
   Than from the genuine love of praise.

#### II.

Nor any partial, private end
   Such reverence to the public bears ;
Nor any passion, virtue's friend,
   So like to virtue's self appears.

### III.

For who in glory can delight
  Without delight in glorious deeds ?
What man a charming voice can slight,
  Who courts the echo that succeeds ?

### IV.

But not the echo on the voice
  More, than on virtue praise, depends;
To which, of course, its real price
  The judgment of the praiser lends.

### V.

If praise then with religious awe
  From the sole perfect judge be sought,
A nobler aim, a purer law,
  Nor priest, nor bard, nor sage hath taught.

### VI.

With which in character the same
  Though in an humbler sphere it lies,
I count that soul of human fame,
  The suffrage of the good and wise.

## ODE VI.

### TO WILLIAM HALL, ESQUIRE: WITH THE WORKS OF CHAULIEU.

### I.

ATTEND to Chaulieu's wanton lyre;
  While, fluent as the sky-lark sings
When first the morn allures its wings,
The epicure his theme pursues:
And tell me if, among the choir
Whose music charms the banks of Seine,
So full, so free, so rich a strain
E'er dictated the warbling Muse.

### II.

Yet, Hall, while thy judicious ear
Admires the well-dissembled art
That can such harmony impart
To the lame pace of Gallic rhymes;
While wit from affectation clear,
Bright images, and passions true,
Recall to thy assenting view
The envied bards of nobler times;

### III.

Say, is not oft his doctrine wrong?
This priest of Pleasure, who aspires
To lead us to her sacred fires,
Knows he the ritual of her shrine?
Say (her sweet influence to thy song
So may the goddess still afford)
Doth she consent to be ador'd
With shameless love and frantic wine?

### IV.

Nor Cato, nor Chrysippus here
Need we in high indignant phrase
From their Elysian quiet raise;
But Pleasure's oracle alone
Consult; attentive, not severe.
O Pleasure, we blaspheme not thee;
Nor emulate the rigid knee
Which bends but at the Stoic throne.

### V.

We own had fate to man assign'd
Nor sense, nor wish but what obey
Or Venus soft or Bacchus gay,
Then might our bard's voluptuous creed
Most haply govern human kind:
Unless perchance what he hath sung
Of tortur'd joints and nerves unstrung,
Some wrangling heretic should plead.

VI.

But now with all these proud desires
For dauntless truth and honest fame;
With that strong master of our frame,
The inexorable judge within,
What can be done?  Alas, ye fires
Of love;  alas, ye rosy smiles,
Ye nectar'd cups from happier soils,
—Ye have no bribe his grace to win.


## ODE VII.

### TO THE RIGHT REVEREND BENJAMIN LORD
### BISHOP OF WINCHESTER.   1754.

I. 1.

FOR toils which patriots have endur'd,
    For treason quell'd and laws secur'd,
In every nation Time displays
The palm of honourable praise.
Envy may rail; and Faction fierce
    May strive: but what, alas, can those
    (Though bold, yet blind and sordid foes)
    To Gratitude and Love oppose,
To faithful story and persuasive verse?

I. 2.

O nurse of freedom, Albion, say,
Thou tamer of despotic sway,
What man, among thy sons around,
Thus heir to glory hast thou found?
What page, in all thy annals bright,
Hast thou with purer joy survey'd
Than that where truth, by Hoadly's aid,
Shines through imposture's solemn shade,
Through kingly and through sacerdotal night?

### I. 3.

To him the Teacher bless'd,
Who sent religion, from the palmy field
By Jordan, like the morn to cheer the west,
And lifted up the veil which heaven from earth
    conceal'd,
To Hoadly thus his mandate he address'd:
"Go thou, and rescue my dishonour'd law
From hands rapacious and from tongues impure:
Let not my peaceful name be made a lure
Fell persecution's mortal snares to aid:
Let not my words be impious chains to draw
The freeborn soul in more than brutal awe,
To faith without assent, allegiance unrepaid."

### II. 1.

No cold or unperforming hand
Was arm'd by Heaven with this command.
The world soon felt it: and, on high,
To William's ear with welcome joy
Did Locke among the blest unfold
The rising hope of Hoadly's name;
Godolphin then confirm'd the fame;
And Somers, when from earth he came,
And generous Stanhope the fair sequel told.

### II. 2.

Then drew the lawgivers around,
(Sires of the Grecian name renown'd)
And listening ask'd, and wondering knew,
What private force could thus subdue
The vulgar and the great combin'd;
Could war with sacred folly wage;
Could a whole nation disengage
From the dread bonds of many an age,
And to new habits mould the public mind.

### II. 3.

For not a conqueror's sword,
Nor the strong powers to civil founders known,
Were his: but truth by faithful search explor'd,

And social sense, like seed, in genial plenty sown.
  Wherever it took root, the soul (restor'd
  To freedom) freedom too for others sought.
  Not monkish craft the tyrant's claim divine,
  Not regal zeal the bigot's cruel shrine
  Could longer guard from reason's warfare sage;
  Not the wild rabble to sedition wrought,
  Nor synods by the papal Genius taught,
Nor St. John's spirit loose, nor Atterbury's rage.

### III. 1.

  But where shall recompense be found?
  Or how such arduous merit crown'd?
  For look on life's laborious scene:
  What rugged spaces lie between
  Adventurous Virtue's early toils
  And her triumphal throne! The shade
  Of death, mean time, does oft invade
  Her progress; nor, to us display'd,
Wears the bright heroine her expected spoils.

### III. 2.

  Yet born to conquer is her power:
  —O Hoadly, if that favourite hour
  On earth arrive, with thankful awe
  We own just Heaven's indulgent law,
  And proudly thy success behold;
  We attend thy reverend length of days
  With benediction and with praise,
  And hail thee in our public ways
Like some great spirit fam'd in ages old.

### III. 3.

  While thus our vows prolong
  Thy steps on earth, and when by us resign'd
  Thou join'st thy seniors, that heroic throng
Who rescu'd or preserv'd the rights of human kind,
  O! not unworthy may thy Albion's tongue
  Thee still, her friend and benefactor, name:
  O! never, Hoadly, in thy country's eyes,
  May impious gold, or pleasure's gaudy prize,

Make public virtue, public freedom, vile;
Nor our own manners tempt us to disclaim
That heritage, our noblest wealth and fame,
Which thou hast kept entire from force and fac-
    tious guile.

## ODE VIII.

### I.

IF rightly tuneful bards decide,
    If it be fix'd in Love's decrees,
That Beauty ought not to be tried
    But by its native power to please,
Then tell me, youths and lovers, tell,
What fair can Amoret excel?

### II.

Behold that bright unsullied smile,
    And wisdom speaking in her mien:
Yet (she so artless all the while,
    So little studious to be seen)
We nought but instant gladness know,
Nor think to whom the gift we owe.

### III.

But neither music, nor the powers
    Of youth and mirth and frolic cheer,
Add half that sunshine to the hours,
    Or make life's prospect half so clear,
As memory brings it to the eye
From scenes where Amoret was by.

### IV.

Yet not a satirist could there
    Or fault or indiscretion find;
Nor any prouder sage declare
    One virtue, pictur'd in his mind,
Whose form with lovelier colours glows
Than Amoret's demeanor shows.

### v.

This sure is Beauty's happiest part:
  This gives the most unbounded sway:
This shall enchant the subject heart
  When rose and lily fade away;
And she be still, in spite of time,
Sweet Amoret in all her prime.

## ODE IX.

#### AT STUDY.

### I.

WHITHER did my fancy stray?
  By what magic drawn away
Have I left my studious theme?
From this philosophic page,
From the problems of the sage,
  Wandering through a pleasing dream?

### II.

'Tis in vain, alas! I find,
Much in vain, my zealous mind
  Would to learned Wisdom's throne
Dedicate each thoughtful hour:
Nature bids a softer power
  Claim some minutes for his own.

### III.

Let the busy or the wise
View him with contemptuous eyes;
  Love is native to the heart:
Guide its wishes as you will;
Without Love you'll find it still
  Void in one essential part.

### IV.

Me though no peculiar fair
Touches with a lover's care;

Though the pride of my desire
Asks immortal friendship's name,
Asks the palm of honest fame,
  And the old heroic lyre ;

### v.

Though the day have smoothly gone,
Or to letter'd leisure known,
  Or in social duty spent ;
Yet at eve my lonely breast
Seeks in vain for perfect rest ;
  Languishes for true content.

## ODE X.

TO THOMAS EDWARDS, ESQ.: ON THE LATE
EDITION OF MR. POPE'S WORKS. 1751.

### I.

BELIEVE me, Edwards, to restrain
  The license of a railer's tongue
Is what but seldom men obtain
By sense or wit, by prose or song :
A task for more Herculean powers,
Nor suited to the sacred hours
Of leisure in the Muse's bowers.

### II.

In bowers where laurel weds with palm,
The Muse, the blameless queen, resides :
Fair Fame attends, and Wisdom calm
Her eloquence harmonious guides :
While, shut for ever from her gate,
Oft trying, still repining, wait
Fierce Envy and calumnious Hate.

### III.

Who then from her delightful bounds
Would step one moment forth to heed

What impotent and savage sounds
From their unhappy mouths proceed?
No: rather Spenser's lyre again
Prepare, and let thy pious strain
For Pope's dishonour'd shade complain.

IV.

Tell how displeas'd was every bard,
When lately in the Elysian grove
They of his Muse's guardian heard,
His delegate to fame above;
And what with one accord they said
Of wit in drooping age misled,
And Warburton's officious aid:

V.

How Virgil mourn'd the sordid fate
To that melodious lyre assign'd
Beneath a tutor who so late
With Midas and his rout combin'd
By spiteful clamour to confound
That very lyre's enchanting sound,
Tho' listening realms admir'd around:

VI.

How Horace own'd he thought the fire
Of his friend Pope's satiric line
Did farther fuel scarce require
From such a militant divine:
How Milton scorn'd the sophist vain
Who durst approach his hallow'd strain
With unwash'd hands and lips profane.

VII.

Then Shakespeare debonair and mild
Brought that strange comment forth to view;
Conceits more deep, he said and smil'd,
Than his own fools or madmen knew:
But thank'd a generous friend above,
Who did with free adventurous love
Such pageants from his tomb remove.

VIII.

And if to Pope, in equal need,
The same kind office thou wouldst pay,
Then, Edwards, all the band decreed
That future bards with frequent lay
Should call on thy auspicious name,
From each absurd intruder's claim
To keep inviolate their fame.

## ODE XI.

### TO THE COUNTRY GENTLEMEN OF ENGLAND. 1758.

I.

WHITHER is Europe's ancient spirit fled?
 Where are those valiant tenants of her
  shore,
Who from the warrior bow the strong dart sped,
Or with firm hand the rapid pole-axe bore?
Freeman and Soldier was their common name.
Who late with reapers to the furrow came,
Now in the front of battle charg'd the foe:
Who taught the steer the wintry plough to endure,
Now in full councils check'd encroaching power,
And gave the guardian Laws their majesty to know.

II.

But who are ye? from Ebro's loitering sons
To Tiber's pageants, to the sports of Seine;
From Rhine's frail palaces to Danube's thrones
And cities looking on the Cimbric main,
Ye lost, ye self-deserted? whose proud lords
Have baffled your tame hands, and given your
  swords
To slavish ruffians, hir'd for their command:
These, at some greedy monk's or harlot's nod:
See rifled nations crouch beneath their rod:
These are the Public Will, the Reason of the land.

T

### III.

Thou, heedless Albion, what, alas, the while
Dost thou presume ?   O inexpert in arms,
Yet vain of Freedom, how dost thou beguile,
With dreams of hope, these near and loud alarms ?
Thy splendid home, thy plan of laws renown'd,
The praise and envy of the nations round,
What care hast thou to guard from Fortune's sway ?
Amid the storms of war, how soon may all
The lofty pile from its foundations fall,
Of ages the proud toil, the ruin of a day !

### IV.

No : thou art rich, thy streams and fertile vales
Add Industry's wise gifts to Nature's store :
And every port is crowded with thy sails,
And every wave throws treasure on thy shore.
What boots it ?   If luxurious Plenty charm
Thy selfish heart from Glory, if thy arm
Shrink at the frowns of Danger and of Pain,
Those gifts, that treasure is no longer thine.
Oh rather far be poor !   Thy gold will shine
Tempting the eye of Force, and deck thee to thy bane.

### V.

But what hath Force or War to do with thee ?
Girt by the azure tide and thron'd sublime
Amid thy floating bulwarks, thou canst see,
With scorn, the fury of each hostile clime
Dash'd ere it reach thee.   Sacred from the foe
Are thy fair fields : athwart thy guardian prow
No bold invader's foot shall tempt the strand—
Yet say, my country, will the waves and wind
Obey thee ?   Hast thou all thy hopes resign,d
To the sky's fickle faith ?   the pilot's wavering hand ?

### VI.

For oh may neither Fear nor stronger Love
(Love, by thy virtuous princes nobly won)
Thee, last of many wretched nations, move,
With mighty armies station'd round the throne

To trust thy safety.   Then, farewell the claims
Of Freedom! Her proud records to the flames
Then bear, an offering at Ambition's shrine;
Whate'er thy ancient patriots dar'd demand
From furious John's, or faithless Charles's hand,
Or what great William seal'd for his adopted line.

### VII.

But if thy sons be worthy of their name,
If liberal laws with liberal arts they prize,
Let them from conquest, and from servile shame
In War's glad school their own protectors rise.
Ye chiefly, heirs of Albion's cultur'd plains,
Ye leaders of her bold and faithful swains,
Now not unequal to your birth be found :
The public voice bids arm your rural state,
Paternal hamlets for your ensigns wait,
And grange and fold prepare to pour their youth
        around.

### VIII.

Why are ye tardy? what inglorious care
Detains you from their head, your native post?
Who most their country's fame and fortune share,
'Tis theirs to share her toils, her perils most.
Each man his task in social life sustains.
With partial labours, with domestic gains
Let others dwell : to you indulgent Heaven
By counsel and by arms the public cause
To serve for public love and love's applause,
The first employment far, the noblest hire, hath
        given.

### IX.

Have ye not heard of Lacedæmon's fame?
Of Attic chiefs in Freedom's war divine?
Of Rome's dread generals? the Valerian name?
The Fabian sons? the Scipios, matchless line?
Your lot was theirs : the farmer and the swain
Met his lov'd patron's summons from the plain;
The legions gather'd; the bright eagles flew:

Barbarian monarchs in the triumph mourn'd;
The conquerors to their household gods return'd,
And fed Calabrian flocks, and steer'd the Sabine
    plough.

### X.

Shall then this glory of the antique age,
This pride of men, be lost among mankind?
Shall war's heroic arts no more engage
The unbought hand, the unsubjected mind?
Doth valour to the race no more belong?
No more with scorn of violence and wrong
Doth forming Nature now her sons inspire,
That, like some mystery to few reveal'd,
The skill of arms abash'd and aw'd they yield,
And from their own defence with hopeless hearts
    retire?

### XI.

O shame to human life, to human laws!
The loose adventurer, hireling of a day,
Who his fell sword without affection draws,
Whose God, whose country, is a tyrant's pay,
This man the lessons of the field can learn;
Can every palm, which decks a warrior, earn,
And every pledge of conquest: while in vain,
To guard your altars, your paternal lands,
Are social arms held out to your free hands:
Too arduous is the lore; too irksome were the pain.

### XII.

Meantime by Pleasure's lying tales allur'd,
From the bright sun and living breeze ye stray;
And deep in London's gloomy haunts immur'd,
Brood o'er your fortune's, freedom's, health's
    decay.
O blind of choice and to yourselves untrue!
The young grove shoots, their bloom the fields
    renew,
The mansion asks its lord, the swains their friend;
While he doth riot's orgies haply share,

Or tempt the gamester's dark, destroying snare,
Or at some courtly shrine with slavish incense bend.

### XIII.

And yet full oft your anxious tongues complain
That lawless tumult prompts the rustic throng;
That the rude village-inmates now disdain
Those homely ties which rul'd their fathers long.
Alas, your fathers did by other arts
Draw those kind ties around their simple hearts,
And led in other paths their ductile will;
By succour, faithful counsel, courteous cheer,
Won them the ancient manners to revere,
To prize their country's peace and heaven's due
    rites fulfil.

### XIV.

But mark the judgment of experienc'd Time,
Tutor of nations.   Doth light discord tear
A state? and impotent sedition's crime?
The powers of warlike prudence dwell not there;
The powers who to command and to obey,
Instruct the valiant.   There would civil sway
The rising race to manly concord tame?
Oft let the marshal'd field their steps unite,
And in glad splendour bring before their sight
One common cause and one hereditary fame.

### XV.

Nor yet be aw'd, nor yet your task disown,
Though war's proud votaries look on severe;
Though secrets, taught erewhile to them alone,
They deem profan'd by your intruding ear.
Let them in vain, your martial hope to quell,
Of new refinements, fiercer weapons tell,
And mock the old simplicity, in vain:
To the time's warfare, simple or refin'd,
The time itself adapts the warrior's mind;
And equal prowess still shall equal palms obtain.

### XVI.

Say then; if England's youth, in earlier days,

On glory's field with well-train'd armies vied,
Why shall they now renounce that generous
    praise ?
Why dread the foreign mercenary's pride ?
Tho' Valois brav'd young Edward's gentle hand,
And Albert rush'd on Henry's way-worn band,
With Europe's chosen sons in arms renown'd,
Yet not on Vere's bold archers long they look'd,
Nor Audley's squires nor Mowbray's yeomen
    brook'd :
They saw their standard fall, and left their monarch
    bound.

### XVII.

Such were the laurels which your fathers won ;
Such glory's dictates in their dauntless breast :
—Is there no voice that speaks to every son ?
No nobler, holier call to You address'd ?
O ! by majestic Freedom, righteous Laws,
By heavenly Truth's, by manly Reason's cause,
Awake ; attend ; be indolent no more :
By friendship, social peace, domestic love,
Rise ; arm ; your country's living safety prove ;
And train her valiant youth, and watch around her
    shore.

## ODE XII.

#### ON RECOVERING FROM A FIT OF SICKNESS,

#### IN THE COUNTRY. 1758.

### I.

THY verdant scenes, O Goulder's Hill,
    Once more I seek, a languid guest :
With throbbing temples and with burden'd breast
Once more I climb thy steep aerial way.
O faithful cure of oft-returning ill,

Now call thy sprightly breezes round,
Dissolve this rigid cough profound,      [play.
And bid the springs of life with gentler movement

### II.

How gladly 'mid the dews of dawn
By weary lungs thy healing gale,
The balmy west or the fresh north inhale !
How gladly, while my musing footsteps rove
Round the cool orchard or the sunny lawn,
Awak'd I stop, and look to find
What shrub perfumes the pleasant wind,
Or what wild songster charms the Dryads of the
grove.

### III.

Now, ere the morning walk is done,
The distant voice of Health I hear
Welcome as beauty's to the lover's ear.
" Droop not, nor doubt of my return," she cries;
" Here will I, 'mid the radiant calm of noon,
Meet thee beneath yon chestnut bower,
And lenient on thy bosom pour      [skies."
That indolence divine which lulls the earth and

### IV.

The goddess promis'd not in vain.
I found her at my favourite time.
Nor wish'd to breathe in any softer clime,
While (half-reclin'd, half-slumbering as I lay)
She hover'd o'er me.   Then, among her train
Of Nymphs and Zephyrs, to my view
Thy gracious form appear'd anew,      [day.
Then first, O heavenly Muse, unseen for many a

### V.

In that soft pomp the tuneful maid
Shone like the golden star of love.
I saw her hand in careless measures move ;
I heard sweet preludes dancing on her lyre,
While my whole frame the sacred sound obey'd.
New sunshine o'er my fancy springs,

New colours clothe external things,
And the last glooms of pain and sickly plaint retire.

### VI.

O Goulder's Hill, by thee restor'd
Once more to this enliven'd hand,
My harp, whice late resounded o'er the land
The voice of glory, solemn and severe,
My Dorian harp shall now with mild accord
    To thee her joyful tribute pay,
    And send a less-ambitious lay
Of friendship and of love to greet thy master's ear.

### VII.

For when within thy shady seat
First from the sultry town he chose,
And the tir'd senate's cares, his wish'd repose,
Then wast thou mine; to me a happier home
For social leisure : where my welcome feet,
    Estrang'd from all the entangling ways
    In which the restless vulgar strays,
Through Nature's simple paths with ancient Faith
    might roam.

### VIII.

And while around his sylvan scene
My Dyson led the white-wing'd hours,
Oft from the Athenian Academic bowers
Their sages came : oft heard our lingering walk
The Mantuan music warbling o'er the green :
    And oft did Tully's reverend shade,
    Though much for liberty afraid,
With us of letter'd ease or virtuous glory talk.

### IX.

But other guests were on their way,
    And reach'd ere long this favour'd grove;
Even the celestial progeny of Jove,
Bright Venus, with her all-subduing son,
Whose golden shaft most willingly obey
    The best and wisest.  As they came,

Glad Hymen wav'd his genial flame,
And sang their happy gifts, and prais'd their spot-
　　less throne.

### X.

I saw when through yon festive gate
He led along his chosen maid,
And to my friend with smiles presenting said;
" Receive that fairest wealth which Heaven as-
　　sign'd
To human fortune.　Did thy lonely state
　One wish, one utmost hope confess?
　Behold, she comes, to adorn and bless:
Comes, worthy of thy heart, and equal to thy mind."

## ODE XIII.

### TO THE AUTHOR OF MEMOIRS OF THE HOUSE
### OF BRANDENBURGH.　1751.

### I.

THE men renown'd as chiefs of human race,
　And born to lead in counsels or in arms,
Have seldom turn'd their feet from glory's chace
To dwell with books or court the Muse's charms.
Yet, to our eyes if haply time hath brought
Some genuine transcript of their calmer thought,
There still we own the wise, the great, or good;
And Cæsar there and Xenophon are seen,
　As clear in spirit and sublime of mien,
As on Pharsalian plains, or by the Assyrian flood.

### II.

Say thou too, Frederic, was not this thy aim?
Thy vigils could the student's lamp engage,
Except for this? except that future Fame
Might read thy genius in the faithful page?
That if hereafter Envy shall presume

With words irreverent to inscribe thy tomb,
And baser weeds upon thy palms to fling,
That hence posterity may try thy reign,
Assert thy treaties, and thy wars explain,
And view in native lights the hero and the king.

### III.

O evil foresight and pernicious care!
Wilt thou indeed abide by this appeal?
Shall we the lessons of thy pen compare
With private honour or with public zeal?
Whence then at things divine those darts of
    scorn?                                    [borne
Why are the woes, which virtuous men have
For sacred truth, a prey to laughter given?
What fiend, what foe of Nature urg'd thy arm
The Almighty of his sceptre to disarm?
To push this earth adrift and leave it loose from
    Heaven?

### IV.

Ye godlike shades of legislators old,
Ye who made Rome victorious, Athens wise,
Ye first of mortals with the bless'd enroll'd,
Say did not horror in your bosoms rise,
When thus by impious vanity impell'd
A magistrate, a monarch, ye beheld
Affronting civil order's holiest bands?
Those bands which ye so labour'd to improve?
Those hopes and fears of justice from above,
Which tam'd the savage world to your divine
    commands?

## ODE XIV.

### THE COMPLAINT.

### I.

AWAY! away!
    Tempt me no more, insidious love:

Thy soothing sway
Long did my youthful bosom prove :
At length thy treason is discern'd,
At length some dear-bought caution earn'd :
Away ! nor hope my riper age to move.

## II.

I know, I see
Her merit.   Needs it now be shown,
Alas, to me ?
How often, to myself unknown,
The graceful, gentle, virtuous maid
Have I admir'd ! How often said,
What joy to call a heart like hers one's own !

## III.

But, flattering god,
O squanderer of content and ease,
In thy abode
Will care's rude lesson learn to please ?
O say, deceiver, hast thou won
Proud Fortune to attend thy throne,
Or plac'd thy friends above her stern decrees ?

## ODE XV.

### ON DOMESTIC MANNERS.

#### (UNFINISHED.)

## I.

MEEK Honour, female shame,
O ! whither, sweetest offspring of the sky,
From Albion dost thou fly ;
Of Albion's daughters once the favourite fame ?
O beauty's only friend,
Who giv'st her pleasing reverence to inspire ;
Who selfish, bold desire

Dost to esteem and dear affection turn ;
 Alas, of thee forlorn
What joy, what praise, what hope can life pretend ?

### II.

 Behold ; our youths in vain
Concerning nuptial happiness inquire :
 Our maids no more aspire
The arts of bashful Hymen to attain ;
 But with triumphant eyes
And cheeks impassive, as they move along,
 Ask homage of the throng.
The lover swears that in a harlot's arms
 Are found the self-same charms,
And worthless and deserted lives and dies.

### III.

 Behold ; unbless'd at home,
The father of the cheerless household mourns :
 The night in vain returns,
For Love and glad Content at distance roam ;
 While she, in whom his mind
Seeks refuge from the day's dull task of cares,
 To meet him she prepares,
Thro' noise and spleen and all the gamester's art,
 A listless, harass'd heart,
Where not one tender thought can welcome find.

### IV.

 'Twas thus, along the shore
Of Thames, Britannia's guardian Genius heard,
 From many a tongue preferr'd,
Of strife and grief the fond invective lore :
 At which the queen divine
Indignant, with her adamantine spear
 Like thunder sounding near,
Smote the red cross upon her silver shield,
 And thus her wrath reveal'd.
(I watch'd her awful words and made them mine.)

  *   *   *   *

## NOTES ON THE TWO BOOKS OF ODES.

### B. i. Ode xviii. Stanza ii. 2.

LYCURGUS the Lacedæmonian lawgiver brought into Greece from Asia Minor the first complete copy of Homer's works. At Platæa was fought the decisive battle between the Persian army and the united militia of Greece under Pausanias and Aristides.—Cimon the Athenian erected a trophy in Cyprus for two great victories gained on the same day over the Persians by sea and land. Diodorus Siculus has preserved the inscription which the Athenians affixed to the consecrated spoils, after this great success; in which it is very remarkable that the greatness of the occasion has raised the manner of expression above the usual simplicity and modesty of all other ancient inscriptions. It is this:

ΕΞ. ΟΥ. Γ'. ΕΥΡΩΠΗΝ. ΑΣΙΑΣ. ΔΙΧΑ. ΠΟΝΤΟΣ.
   ΕΝΕΙΜΕ.
ΚΑΙ. ΠΟΛΕΑΣ. ΘΝΗΤΩΝ. ΘΟΥΡΟΣ. ΑΡΗΣ. ΕΠΕΧΕΙ.
ΟΥΔΕΝ. ΠΩ. ΤΟΙΟΥΤΟΝ. ΕΠΙΧΘΟΝΙΩΝ. ΓΕΝΕΤ'.
   ΑΝΔΡΩΝ.
ΕΡΓΟΝ. ΕΝ. ΗΠΕΙΡΩΙ. ΚΑΙ. ΚΑΤΑ. ΠΟΝΤΟΝ. ΑΜΑ.
ΟΙΔΕ. ΓΑΡ. ΕΝ. ΚΥΠΡΩΙ. ΜΗΔΟΥΣ. ΠΟΛΛΟΥΣ. ΟΛΕ-
   ΣΑΝΤΕΣ.
ΦΟΙΝΙΚΩΝ. ΕΚΑΤΟΝ. ΝΑΥΣ. ΕΛΟΝ. ΕΝ. ΠΕΛΑΓΕΙ.
ΑΝΔΡΩΝ. ΠΛΗΘΟΥΣΑΣ. ΜΕΓΑ. Δ'. ΕΣΤΕΝΕΝ. ΑΣΙΣ.
   ΥΠ'. ΑΥΤΩΝ.
ΠΛΗΓΕΙΣ'. ΑΜΦΟΤΕΡΑΙΣ. ΧΕΡΣΙ. ΚΡΑΤΕΙ. ΠΟ-
   ΛΕΜΟΥ.

The following translation is almost literal:

> Since first the sea from Asia's hostile coast
> Divided Europe, and the god of war
> Assail'd imperious cities; never yet,
> At once among the waves and on the shore,
> Hath such a labour been achieved by men
> Who earth inhabit. They, whose arms the Medes
> In Cyprus felt pernicious, they, the same,
> Have won from skilful Tyre an hundred ships
> Crowded with warriors. Asia groans, in both
> Her hands sore smitten, by the might of war.

Stanza ii. 3.] Pindar was cotemporary with Aristides and Cimon, in whom the glory of ancient Greece was at its height. When Xerxes invaded Greece, Pindar was true to the common interest of his country ; though his fellow citizens, the Thebans, had sold themselves to the Persian king. In one of his odes he expresses the great distress and anxiety of his mind, occasioned by the vast preparations of Xerxes against Greece. *(Isthm.* 8.) In another he celebrates the victories of Salamis, Platæa, and Himera. *(Pyth.* 1.) It will be necessary to add two or three other particulars of his life, real or fabulous, in order to explain what follows in the text concerning him. First then, he was thought to be so great a favourite of Apollo, that the priests of that deity allotted him a constant share of their offerings. It was said of him, as of some other illustrious men, that at his birth a swarm of bees lighted on his lips, and fed him with their honey. It was also a tradition concerning him, that Pan was heard to recite his poetry, and seen dancing to one of his hymns on the mountains near Thebes. But a real historical fact in his life is, that the Thebans imposed a large fine upon him on account of the veneration which he expressed in his poems for that heroic spirit, shown by the people of Athens in defence of the common liberty, which his own fellow citizens had shamefully betrayed. And, as the argument of this ode implies, that great poetical talents, and high sentiments of liberty, do reciprocally produce and assist each other, so Pindar is perhaps the most exemplary proof of this connection, which occurs in history. The Thebans were remarkable, in general, for a slavish disposition through all the fortunes of their common-wealth ; at the time of its ruin by Philip ; and even in its best state, under the administration of Pelopidas and Epaminondas : and every one knows, they were no less remarkable for great dulness, and want of all genius. That Pindar should have equally distinguished himself from the rest of his fellow citizens in both these respects, seems somewhat extraordinary, and is scarce to be accounted for but by the preceding observation.

Stanza iii. 3.] Alluding to his Defence of the people of England against Salmasius. See particularly the manner in which he himself speaks of that undertaking, in the introduction to his reply to Morus.

Stanza iv. 3.] Edward the Third; from whom descended Henry Hastings, third Earl of Huntingdon, by the daughter of the Duke of Clarence, brother to Edward the Fourth.

Stanza v. 3.] At Whittington, a village on the edge of

Scarsdale in Derbyshire, the Earls of Devonshire and Danby, with the Lord Delamere, privately concerted the plan of the Revolution. The house in which they met is at present a farm-house, and the country people distinguish the room where they sat, by the name of the plotting parlour.

B. ii. Ode vii. Stanza ii. 1.] Mr. Locke died in 1704, when Mr. Hoadly was beginning to distinguish himself in the cause of civil and religious liberty: Lord Godolphin in 1712, when the doctrines of the Jacobite faction were chiefly favoured by those in power: Lord Somers in 1716, amid the practices of the nonjuring clergy against the protestant establishment; and Lord Stanhope in 1721, during the controversy with the lower house of convocation.

B. ii. Ode x. Stanza v.] During Mr. Pope's war with Theobald, Concanen, and the rest of their tribe, Mr. Warburton, the present Lord Bishop of Gloucester, did with great zeal cultivate their friendship; having been introduced, forsooth, at the meetings of that respectable confederacy; a favour which he afterwards spoke of in very high terms of complacency and thankfulness. At the same time in his intercourse with them he treated Mr. Pope in a most contemptuous manner, and as a writer without genius. Of the truth of these assertions his lordship can have no doubt, if he recollects his own correspondence with Concanen; a part of which is still in being, and will probably be remembered as long as any of this prelate's writings.

B. ii. Ode xiii.] In the year 1751 appeared a very splendid edition, in quarto, of "Memoires pour servir à l'Histoire de la Maison de Brandebourg, à Berlin et à la Haye;" with a privilege signed Frederic; the same being engraved in imitation of hand-writing. In this edition, among other extraordinary passages, are the two following, to which the third stanza of this ode more particularly refers:

Page 163.] "Il se fit une migration (the author is speaking of what happened of the revocation of the edict of Nantes) dont on n'avoit guere vu d'exemples dans l'histoire: un peuple entier sortit du royaume par l'esprit de parti en haine du pape, et pour recevoir sous un autre ciel la communion sous les deux especes: quatre cens mille ames s'expatrierent ainsi et abandonnerent tous leur biens pour detonner dans d'autres temples les vieux pseaumes de Clement Marot."

Page 242.] "La crainte donna le jour à la credulité, et l'amour propre interessa bientot le ciel au destin des hommes."

# HYMN TO THE NAIADS. 1746.

### ARGUMENT.

THE Nymphs, who preside over springs and rivulets, are
addressed at day-break, in honour of their several
functions, and of the relations which they bear to the natural and to the moral world. Their origin is deduced from
the first allegorical deities, or powers of nature; according
to the doctrine of the old mythological poets, concerning the
generation of the gods and the rise of things. They are
then successively considered, as giving motion to the air and
exciting summer-breezes; as nourishing and beautifying the
vegetable creation; as contributing to the fulness of navi-
gable rivers, and consequently to the maintenance of commerce; and by that means to the maritime part of military
power. Next is represented their favourable influence
upon health, when assisted by rural exercise : which intro-
duces their connection with the art of physic, and the happy
effects of mineral medicinal springs. Lastly, they are celebrated for the friendship which the Muses bear them, and
for the true inspiration which temperance only can receive ;
in opposition to the enthusiasm of the more licentious poets.

O'ER yonder eastern hill the twilight pale
Walks forth from darkness; and the God of day,
With bright Astræa seated by his side,
Waits yet to leave the ocean. Tarry, Nymphs,
Ye Nymphs, ye blue-ey'd progeny of Thames,
Who now the mazes of this rugged heath
Trace with your fleeting steps : who all night long
Repeat, amid the cool and tranquil air,
Your lonely murmurs, tarry : and receive
My offer'd lay. To pay you homage due,      10
I leave the gates of sleep ; nor shall my lyre
Too far into the splendid hours of morn
Engage your audience : my observant hand

Shall close the strain ere any sultry beam
Approach you.  To your subterranean haunts
Ye then may timely steal; to pace with care
The humid sands ; to loosen from the soil
The bubbling sources ; to direct the rills
To meet in wider channels; or beneath
Some grotto's dripping arch, at height of noon  20
To slumber, shelter'd from the burning heaven.
    Where shall my song begin, ye Nymphs ? or end ?
Wide is your praise and copious—first of things,
First of the lonely powers, ere Time arose,
Were Love and Chaos.  Love, the sire of Fate ;
Elder than Chaos.  Born of Fate was Time,
Who many sons and many comely births
Devour'd, relentless father; till the child
Of Rhea drove him from the upper sky,
And quell'd his deadly might.  Then social reign'd
The kindred powers, Tethys, and reverend Ops,
And spotless Vesta; while supreme of sway
Remain'd the Cloud-Compeller.  From the couch
Of Tethys sprang the sedgy-crowned race,
Who from a thousand urns, o'er every clime,
Send tribute to their parent ; and from them
Are ye, O Naiads : Arethusa fair,
And tuneful Aganippe; that sweet name,
Bandusia; that soft family which dwelt
With Syrian Daphne ; and the honour'd tribes  40
Belov'd of Pæon.  Listen to my strain,
Daughters of Tethys : listen to your praise.
    You, Nymphs, the winged offspring, which of old
Aurora to divine Astræus bore,
Owns ; and your aid beseecheth.  When the might
Of Hyperíon, from his noontide throne,
Unbends their languid pinions, aid from you
They ask ; Favonius and the mild South-west
From you relief implore.  Your sallying streams
Fresh vigour to their weary wings impart.  50
Again they fly, disporting ; from the mead
Half ripen'd and the tender blades of corn,

To sweep the noxious mildew; or dispel
Contagious steams, which oft the parched earth
Breathes on her fainting sons.  From noon to eve,
Along the river and the paved brook,
Ascend the cheerful breezes : hail'd of bards
Who, fast by learned Cam, the Æolian lyre
Solicit; nor unwelcome to the youth
Who on the heights of Tibur, all inclin'd        60
O'er rushing Anio, with a pious hand
The reverend scene delineates, broken fanes,
Or tombs, or pillar'd aqueducts, the pomp
Of ancient Time ; and haply, while he scans
The ruins, with a silent tear revolves
The fame and fortune of imperious Rome.
    You too, O Nymphs, and your unenvious aid
The rural powers confess ; and still prepare
For you their choicest treasures.  Pan commands,
Oft as the Delian king with Sirius holds         70
The central heavens, the father of the grove
Commands his Dryads over your abodes
To spread their deepest umbrage.  Well the god
Remembereth how indulgent ye supplied
Your genial dews to nurse them in their prime.
    Pales, the pasture's queen, where'er ye stray,
Pursues your steps, delighted; and the path
With living verdure clothes.  Around your haunts
The laughing Chloris, with profusest hand,
Throws wide her blooms, her odours.  Still with you
Pomona seeks to dwell : and o'er the lawns,
And o'er the vale of Richmond, where with Thames
Ye love to wander, Amalthea pours
Well-pleas'd the wealth of that Ammonian horn,
Her dower ; unmindful of the fragrant isles
Nysæan or Atlantic.  Nor canst thou,
(Albeit oft, ungrateful, thou dost mock
The beverage of the sober Naiad's urn,
O Bromius, O Lenæan) nor canst thou
Disown the powers whose bounty, ill repaid,        90
With nectar feeds thy tendrils.  Yet from me,

Yet, blameless Nymphs, from my delighted lyre,
Accept the rites your bounty well may claim;
Nor heed the scoffings of the Edonian band.
　For better praise awaits you.　Thames, your sire,
As down the verdant slope your duteous rills
Descend, the tribute stately Thames receives,
Delighted; and your piety applauds;
And bids his copious tide roll on secure,
For faithful are his daughters; and with words   100
Auspicious gratulates the bark which, now
His banks forsaking, her adventurous wings
Yields to the breeze, with Albion's happy gifts
Extremest isles to bless.　And oft at morn,
When Hermes, from Olympus bent o'er earth
To bear the words of Jove, on yonder hill
Stoops lightly-sailing; oft intent your springs
He views: and waving o'er some new-born stream
His blest pacific wand, "And yet," he cries,
" Yet," cries the son of Maia, " though recluse
And silent be your stores, from you, fair Nymphs,
Flows wealth and kind society to men.
By you my function and my honour'd name
Do I possess; while o'er the Bœtic vale,
Or through the towers of Memphis, or the palms
By sacred Ganges water'd, I conduct
The English merchant: with the buxom fleece
Of fertile Ariconium while I clothe
Sarmatian kings; or to the household gods
Of Syria, from the bleak Cornubian shore,        120
Dispense the mineral treasure which of old
Sidonian pilots sought, when this fair land
Was yet unconscious of those generous arts
Which wise Phœnicia from their native clime
Transplanted to a more indulgent heaven."
　Such are the words of Hermes: such the praise,
O Naiads, which from tongues celestial waits
Your bounteous deeds.　From bounty issueth power:
And those who, sedulous in prudent works,
Relieve the wants of nature, Jove repays        130

With noble wealth, and his own seat on earth,
Fit judgments to pronounce, and curb the might
Of wicked men.   Your kind unfailing urns
Not vainly to the hospitable arts
Of Hermes yield their store.   For, O ye Nymphs,
Hath he not won the unconquerable queen
Of arms to court your friendship? You she owns
The fair associates who extend her sway
Wide o'er the mighty deep ; and grateful things
Of you she uttereth, oft as from the shore      140
Of Thames, or Medway's vale, or the green banks
Of Vecta, she her thundering navy leads
To Calpe's foaming channel, or the rough
Cantabrian surge ; her auspices divine
Imparting to the senate and the prince
Of Albion, to dismay barbaric kings,
The Iberian, or the Celt.   The pride of kings
Was ever scorn'd by Pallas : and of old
Rejoic'd the virgin, from the brazen prow
Of Athens o'er Ægina's gloomy surge,      150
To drive her clouds and storms ; o'erwhelming all
The Persian's promis'd glory, when the realms
Of Indus and the soft Ionian clime,
When Libya's torrid champaign and the rocks
Of cold Imaüs join'd their servile bands,
To sweep the sons of Liberty from earth.
In vain : Minerva on the bounding brow
Of Athens stood, and with the thunder's voice
Denounc'd her terrors on their impious heads,
And shook her burning ægis.   Xerxes saw :      160
From Heracléum, on the mountain's height
Thron'd in his golden car, he knew the sign
Celestial ; felt unrighteous hope forsake
His faltering heart, and turn'd his face with shame.
    Hail, ye who share the stern Minerva's power ;
Who arm the hand of Liberty for war :
And give to the renown'd Britannic name
To awe contending monarchs : yet benign,
Yet mild of nature : to the works of peace

More prone, and lenient of the many ills          170
Which wait on human life.   Your gentle aid
Hygeia well can witness ; she who saves,
From poisonous cates and cups of pleasing bane,
The wretch devoted to the entangling snares
Of Bacchus and of Comus.   Him she leads
To Cynthia's lonely haunts.   To spread the toils,
To beat the coverts, with the jovial horn
At dawn of day to summon the loud hounds,
She calls the lingering sluggard from his dreams :
And where his breast may drink the mountain
          breeze,                                              180
And where the fervour of the sunny vale
May beat upon his brow, through devious paths
Beckons his rapid courser.   Nor when ease,
Cool ease and welcome slumbers have becalm'd
His eager bosom, does the queen of health
Her pleasing care withhold.   His decent board
She guards, presiding ;  and the frugal powers
With joy sedate leads in :  and while the brown
Ennæan dame with Pan presents her stores ;
While changing still, and comely in the change,
Vertumnus and the Hours before him spread     191
The garden's banquet :  you to crown his feast,
To crown his feast, O Naiads, you the fair
Hygeia calls :  and from your shelving seats,
And groves of poplar, plenteous cups ye bring,
To slake his veins :  till soon a purer tide
Flows down those loaded channels ;  washeth off
The dregs of luxury, the lurking seeds
Of crude disease ;  and through the abodes of life
Sends vigour, sends repose.   Hail, Naiads :  hail,
Who give, to labour, health ;  to stooping age,
The joys which youth had squander'd.   Oft your
          urns
Will I invoke ;  and frequent in your praise,
Abash the frantic Thyrsus with my song.
     For not estrang'd from your benignant arts
Is he, the god, to whose mysterious shrine

My youth was sacred, and my votive cares
Belong; the learned Pæon.  Oft when all
His cordial treasures he hath search'd in vain;
When herbs, and potent trees, and drops of balm
Rich with the genial influence of the sun,        211
(To rouse dark fancy from her plaintive dreams,
To brace the nerveless arm, with food to win
Sick appetite, or hush the unquiet breast
Which pines with silent passion) he in vain
Hath prov'd; to your deep mansions he descends.
Your gates of humid rock, your dim arcades,
He entereth; where impurpled veins of ore
Gleam on the roof; where through the rigid mine
Your trickling rills insinuate.  There the god  220
From your indulgent hands the streaming bowl
Wafts to his pale-ey'd suppliants; wafts the seeds
Metallic and the elemental salts            [soon
Wash'd from the pregnant glebe.  They drink: and
Flies pain; flies inauspicious care: and soon
The social haunt or unfrequented shade
Hears Io, Io Pæan; as of old,
When Python fell.  And, O propitious Nymphs,
Oft as for hapless mortals I implore
Your sultry springs, through every urn        230
Oh shed your healing treasures!  With the first
And finest breath, which from the genial strife
Of mineral fermentation springs, like light
O'er the fresh morning's vapours, lustrate then
The fountain, and inform the rising wave.

My lyre shall pay your bounty.  Scorn not ye
That humble tribute.  Though a mortal hand
Excite the strings to utterance, yet for themes
Not unregarded of celestial powers,
I frame their language; and the Muses deign  240
To guide the pious tenor of my lay.
The Muses (sacred by their gifts divine)
In early days did to my wondering sense
Their secrets oft reveal: oft my rais'd ear
In slumber felt their music: oft at noon

Or hour of sunset, by some lonely stream,
In field or shady grove, they taught me words
Of power from death and envy to preserve [mind,
The good man's name.   Whence yet with grateful
And offerings unprofan'd by ruder eye,         250
My vows I send, my homage, to the seats
Of rocky Cirrha, where with you they dwell :
Where you their chaste companions they admit :
Through all the hallow'd scene : where oft intent,
And leaning o'er Castalia's mossy verge,
They mark the cadence of your confluent urns,
How tuneful, yielding gratefullest repose
To their consorted measure : till again,
With emulation all the sounding choir,
And bright Apollo, leader of the song,         260
Their voices through the liquid air exalt,
And sweep their lofty strings : those powerful strings
That charm the mind of gods : that fill the courts
Of wide Olympus with oblivion sweet
Of evils, with immortàl rest from cares ;
Assuage the terrors of the throne of Jove ;
And quench the formidable thunderbolt
Of unrelenting fire.   With slacken'd wings,
While now the solemn concert breathes around,
Incumbent o'er the sceptre of his lord         270
Sleeps the stern eagle ; by the number'd notes,
Possess'd ; and satiate with the melting tone :
Sovereign of birds.   The furious god of war,
IIis darts forgetting, and the winged wheels
That bear him vengeful o'er the embattled plain,
Relents, and soothes his own fierce heart to ease,
Most welcome ease.   The sire of gods and men
In that great moment of divine delight,
Looks down on all that live ; and whatsoe'er
He loves not, o'er the peopled earth and o'er     280
The interminated ocean, he beholds
Curs'd with abhorrence by his doom severe,
And troubled at the sound.   Ye, Naiads, ye
With ravish'd ears the melody attend

Worthy of sacred silence.  But the slaves
Of Bacchus with tempestuous clamours strive
To drown the heavenly strains ; of highest Jove,
Irreverent ; and by mad presumption fir'd
Their own discordant raptures to advance
With hostile emulation.   Down they rush        290
From Nysa's vine-impurpled cliff, the dames
Of Thrace, the Satyrs, and the unruly Fauns,
With old Silenus, reeling through the crowd
Which gambols round him, in convulsions wild
Tossing their limbs, and brandishing in air
The ivy-mantled thyrsus, or the torch
Thro' black smoke flaming, to the Phrygian pipe's
Shrill voice ; and to the clashing cymbals, mix'd
With shrieks and frantic uproar.   May the gods
From every unpolluted ear avert            300
Their orgies !  If within the seats of men,
Within the walls, the gates, where Pallas holds
The guardian key, if haply there be found
Who loves to mingle with the revel-band
And hearken to their accents ; who aspires
From such instructors to inform his breast
With verse : let him, fit votarist, implore
Their inspiration.   He perchance the gifts
Of young Lyæus, and the dread exploits,
May sing in aptest numbers : he the fate        310
Of sober Pentheus, he the Paphian rites,
And naked Mars with Cytherea chain'd,
And strong Alcides in the spinster's robes,
May celebrate, applauded.   But with you,
O Naiads, far from that unhallow'd rout,
Must dwell the man whoe'er to praised themes
Invokes the immortal Muse.   The immortal Muse
To your calm habitations, to the cave
Corycian or the Delphic mount, will guide
His footsteps ; and with your unsullied streams  320
His lips will bathe : whether the eternal lore
Of Themis, or the majesty of Jove,
To mortals he reveal ;  or teach his lyre

The unenvied guerdon of the patriot's toils,
In those unfading islands of the bless'd,
Where sacred bards abide.  Hail, honour'd Nymphs;
Thrice hail.    For you the Cyrenaïc shell
Behold, I touch, revering.    To my songs
Be present ye with favourable feet,
And all profaner audience far remove.          330

## NOTES ON THE HYMN TO THE NAIADS.

Line 25. *Love* ——

*Elder than Chaos.*] Hesiod in his Theogony, gives a different account, and makes Chaos the eldest of beings; though he assigns to Love neither father nor superior: which circumstance is particularly mentioned by Phædrus, in Plato's Banquet, as being observable not only in Hesiod, but in all other writers both of verse and prose: and on the same occasion he cites a line from Parmenides, in which Love is expressly styled the eldest of all the gods. Yet Aristophanes, in "The Birds," affirms, that "Chaos, and Night, and Erebus, and Tartarus were first; and that Love was produced from an egg, which the sable-winged night deposited in the immense bosom of Erebus." But it must be observed, that the Love designed by this comic poet was always distinguished from the other, from that original and self-existent being the ΤΟ ΟΝ or ΑΓΑΘΟΝ of Plato, and meant only the ΔΗΜΙΟΥΡΓΟΣ or second person of the old Grecian trinity; to whom is inscribed a hymn among those which pass under the name of Orpheus, where he is called Protogonos, or the first-begotten, is said to have been born of an egg, and is represented as the principal or origin of all these external appearances of nature. In the fragments of Orpheus, collected by Henry Stephens, he is named Phanes, the discoverer or discloser; who unfolded the ideas of the supreme intelligence, and exposed them to the perception of inferior beings in this visible frame of the world; as Macrobius, and Proclus, and Athenagoras, all agree to interpret the several passages of Orpheus which they have preserved.

But the Love designed in our text, is the one self-existent and infinite mind, whom if the generality of ancient mythologists have not introduced or truly described in accounting for the production of the world and its appearances; yet, to a modern poet, it can be no objection that he hath ventured to differ from them in this particular; though, in other respects, he professeth to imitate their manner and conform to their opinions. For, in these great points of natural theology, they differ no less remarkably among themselves; and are perpetually confounding the philosophical relations of things with the traditionary circumstances of mythic history; upon which very account, Callimachus, in his hymn to Jupiter, declareth his dissent from them concerning even an article of the national creed; adding that the ancient bards were by no means to be depended on. And yet in the exordium of the old Argonautic poem, ascribed to Orpheus, it is said, that " Love, whom mortals in later times call Phanes, was the father of the eternally-begotten Night;" who is generally represented by these mythological poets, as being herself the parent of all things; and who, in the " Indigitamenta," or Orphic Hymns, is said to be the same with Cypris, or Love itself. Moreover, in the body of this Argonautic poem where the personated Orpheus introduceth himself singing to his lyre in reply to Chiron; he celebrateth " the obscure memory of Chaos, and the natures which it contained within itself in a state of perpetual vicissitude; how the heaven had its boundary determined, the generation of the earth, the depth of the ocean, and also the sapient Love, the most ancient, the self-sufficient; with all the beings which he produced when he separated one thing from another." Which noble passage is more directly to Aristotle's purpose in the first book of his metaphysics than any of those which he has there quoted, to show that the ancient poets and mythologists agreed with Empedocles, Anaxagoras, and the other more sober philosophers, in that natural anticipation and common notion of mankind concerning the necessity of mind and reason to account for the connection, motion, and good order of the world. For, though neither this poem, nor the hymns which pass under the same name, are, it should seem, the work of the real Orpheus: yet beyond all question, they are very ancient. The hymns, more particularly, are allowed to be older than the invasion of Greece by Xerxes; and were probably a set of public and solemn forms of devotion : as appears by a passage in one of them, which Demosthenes hath almost literally cited in his first oration against Aristogiton, as the saying of Orpheus, the founder of their most holy mysteries. On this account, they are of higher authority than any other mythological work now extant, the Theogony of Hesiod himself not excepted. The poetry of them is often extremely noble; and the mysterious air which prevails in them, together with its delightful impression upon the mind, cannot be better expressed than in that remarkable description with which they inspired the German editor Eschenbach, when he accidentally met with them at Leipsic: " Thesaurum me reperisse credidi," says he, " et profecto thesaurum reperi. Incredibile dictu quo me sacro horrore afflaverint indigitamenta ista deorum: nam et tempus ad illorum lectionem eligere cogebar, quod vel solum horrorem incutere animo potest, nocturnum ; cum enim totam diem consumserim in contemplando urbis splendore, et in adeundis, quibus scatet urbs illa, viris doctis ; sola nox restabat, quam Orpheo consecrare potui. In abyssum quendam mysteriorum venerandæ antiquitatis descendere videbar, quotiescunque silente mundo, solis vigilantibus astris et luna, μελανηφάτϛ istos hymnos ad manus sumsi."

Line 25. *Chaos.*] The unformed, undigested mass of Moses and Plato: which Milton calls,

" The womb of nature."

Line 25. *Love, the sire of Fate.*] Fate is the universal system of natural causes ; the work of the Omnipotent Mind, or of Love : so Minucius Felix : " Quid enim aliud est fatum, quam quod de unoquoque nostrum deus fatus est." So also Cicero, in the First Book on Divination : " Fatum autem id appello, quod Græci EIPMAPMENHN : id est, ordinem seriemque causarum, cum causa causæ nexa rem ex se gignat—ex quo intelligitur, ut fatum sit non id quod superstitiose, sed id quod physice dicitur causa æterna rerum." To the same purpose, is the doctrine of Hierocles, in that excellent fragment concerning Providence and Destiny. As to the three Fates, or Destinies of the poets, they represented that part of the general system of natural causes which relates to man, and to other mortal beings : for so we are told in the hymn addressed to them among the Orphic Indigitamenta, where they are called the daughters of Night (or Love), and, contrary to the vulgar notion, are distinguished by the epithets of gentle, and tender-hearted. According to Hesiod, Theog. ver. 904, they were the daughters of Jupiter and Themis : but in the Orphic Hymn to Venus, or Love, that goddess is directly styled the mother of Necessity, and is represented, immediately after, as governing the three Destinies, and conducting the whole system of natural causes.

Line 26. *Born of Fate was Time.*] Cronos, Saturn, or Time, was, according to Apollodorus, the son of Cælum and Tellus. But the author of the Hymns gives it quite undisguised by mythological language, and calls him plainly the offspring of the earth and the starry heaven ; that is, of Fate, as explained in the preceding note.

Line 27. *Who many sons devour'd.*] The known fable of Saturn devouring his children was certainly meant to imply the dissolution of natural bodies ; which are produced and destroyed by Time.

Line 28. *The Child of Rhea.*] Jupiter, so called by Pindar.

Line 29. *Drove him from the upper sky.*] That Jupiter dethroned his father Saturn, is recorded by all the mythologists. Phurnutus, or Cornutus, the author of a little Greek treatise on the nature of the gods, informs us that by Jupiter was meant the vegetable soul of the world, which restrained and prevented those uncertain alterations which Saturn, or Time, used formerly to cause in the mundane system.

Line 30. *Then social reign'd.*] Our mythology here supposeth, that before the establishment of the vital, vegetative, plastic nature (represented by Jupiter), the four elements were in a variable and unsettled condition; but afterwards, well-disposed and at peace among themselves. Tethys was the wife of the Ocean; Ops, or Rhea, the Earth; Vesta, the eldest daughter of Saturn, Fire; and the cloud compeller, or Ζεὺς νεφεληγερέτης, the Air: though he also represented the plastic principle of nature, as may be seen in the Orphic hymn inscribed to him.

Line 34. *The sedgy crowned race.*] The river-gods; who, according to Hesiod's Theogony, were the sons of Oceanus and Tethys.

Line 36. *From them are ye, O Naiads.*] The descent of the Naiads is less certain than most points of the Greek mythology. Homer, Odyss. xiii. κёραι Διός. Virgil, in The Eighth Book of the Æneid, speaks as if the Nymphs, or Naiads, were the parents of the rivers: but in this he contradicts the testimony of Hesiod, and evidently departs from the orthodox system, which representeth several nymphs as retaining to every single river. On the other hand, Callimachus, who was very learned in all the schooldivinity of those times, in his hymn to Delos, maketh Peneus, the great Thessalian river-god, the father of his nymphs: and Ovid, in the fourteenth book of his Metamorphoses, mentions the Naiads of Latium as the immediate daughters of the neighbouring river-gods. Accordingly, the Naiads of particular rivers are occasionally, both by Ovid and Statius, called by patronymic, from the name of the river to which they belong.

Line 40. *Syrian Daphne.*] The grove of Daphne in Syria, near Antioch, was famous for its delightful fountains.

Line 40. *The tribes belov'd by Pæon.*] Mineral and medicinal springs. Pæon was the physician of the gods.

Line 43. *The winged offspring.*] The Winds; who, according to Hesiod and Apollodorus, were the sons of Astræus and Aurora.

Line 46. *Hyperion.*] A son of Cælum and Tellus, and father of the Sun, who is thence called, by Pindar, Hyperionides. But Hyperion is put by Homer in the same manner as here, for the Sun himself.

Line 49. *Your sallying streams.*] The state of the atmosphere with respect to rest and motion is, in several ways, affected by rivers and running streams; and that more especially in hot seasons: first, they destroy its equilibrium, by cooling those parts of it with which they are in contact; and secondly, they communicate their own motion: and the air which is thus moved by them, being left heated, is of consequence more elastic than other parts of the atmosphere, and therefore fitter to preserve and to propagate that motion.

Line 70. *Delian king.*] One of the epithets of Apollo, or the Sun, in the Orphic hymn inscribed to him.

Line 79. *Chloris.*] The ancient Greek name for Flora.

Line 83. *Amalthea.*] The mother of the first Bacchus, whose birth and education was written, as Diodorus Siculus informs us, in the old Pelasgic character, by Thymœtes, grandson to Laomedon, and contemporary with Orpheus. Thymœtes had travelled over Libya to the country which borders on the western ocean; there he saw the island of Nysa, and learned from the inhabitants, that "Ammon, King of Libya, was married in former ages to Rhea, sister of Saturn and the Titans: that he afterwards fell in love with a beautiful virgin whose name was Amalthea; had by her a son, and gave her possession of a neighbouring tract of land, wonderfully fertile; which in shape nearly resembling the horn of an ox, was thence called the Hesperian horn, and afterwards the horn of Amalthea: that fearing the jealousy of Rhea, he concealed the young Bacchus, with his mother, in the island of Nysa;" the beauty of which, Diodorus describes with great dignity and pomp of style. This fable is one of the noblest in all the ancient mythology, and seems to have made a particular impression on the imagination of Milton; the only modern poet (unless perhaps it be necessary to except Spenser) who, in these mysterious traditions of the poetic story, had a heart to feel, and words to express, the simple and solitary genius of antiquity. To raise the idea of his Paradise, he prefers it even to,—

——" that Nysean isle
Girt by the river Triton, where old Cham,
(Whom Gentiles Ammon call, and Libyan Jove)
Hid Amalthea, and her florid son,
Young Bacchus, from his stepdame Rhea's eye."

Line 94. *Edonian band.*] The priestesses and other ministers of Bacchus: so called from Edonus, a mountain of Thrace, where his rites were celebrated.

Line 105. *When Hermes.*] Hermes, or Mercury, was

the patron of commerce; in which benevolent character he is addressed by the author of the Indigitamenta, in these beautiful lines:

Ἑρμηνεῦ πάντων, κερδέμπορε, λυσιμέριμνε,
Ὃς χείρεσθιν ἔχεις εἰρήνης ὅπλον ἀμέμφες.

Line 121. *Dispense the mineral treasure.*] The merchants of Sidon and Tyre made frequent voyages to the coast of Cornwall, from whence they carried home great quantities of tin.

Line 136. *Hath he not won.*] Mercury, the patron of commerce, being so greatly dependent on the good offices of the Naiads, in return obtains for them the friendship of Minerva, the goddess of war: for military power, at least the naval part of it, hath constantly followed the establishment of trade; which exemplifies the preceding observation, that " from bounty issueth power."

Line 143. *Calpe—Cantabrian surge.*] Gibraltar and the Bay of Biscay.

Line 150. *Ægina's gloomy surge.*] Near this island, the Athenians obtained the victory of Salamis, over the Persian navy.

Line 160. *Xerxes saw.*] This circumstance is recorded in that passage, perhaps the most splendid among all the remains of ancient history, where Plutarch, in his Life of Themistocles, describes the sea-fights of Artemisium and Salamis.

Line 204. *Thyrsus.*] A staff, or spear, wreathed round with ivy: of constant use in the bacchanalian mysteries.

Line 227. *Io, Pæan.*] An exclamation of victory and triumph, derived from Apollo's encounter with Python.

Line 252. *Cirrha.*] One of the summits of Parnassus, and sacred to Apollo. Near it were several fountains, said to be frequented by the Muses. Nysa, the other eminence of the same mountain, was dedicated to Bacchus.

Line 263. *Charm the mind of gods.*] This whole passage, concerning the effects of sacred music among the gods, is taken from Pindar's first Pythian ode.

Line 297. *Phrygian pipe's.*] The Phrygian music was fantastic and turbulent, and fit to excite disorderly passions.

Line 302. *The gates where Pallas holds*
        *The guardian key.*] It was the office of Minerva to be the guardian of walled cities; whence she was named ΠΟΛΙΑΣ and ΠΟΛΙΟΥΧΟΣ, and had her statues placed in their gates, being supposed to keep the keys; and on that account styled ΚΛΗΔΟΥΧΟΣ.

Line 310. *Fate of sober Pentheus.*] Pentheus was torn in

pieces by the bacchanalian priests and women, for despising their mysteries.

Line 318. *The cave Corycian.*] Of this cave Pausanias, in his Tenth Book, gives the following description: " Between Delphi and the eminences of Parnassus, is a road to the grotto of Corycium, which has its name from the nymph Corycia, and is by far the most remarkable which I have seen. One may walk a great way into it without a torch. 'Tis of a considerable height, and hath several springs within it; and yet a much greater quantity of water distills from the shell and roof, so as to be continually dropping on the ground. The people round Parnassus hold it sacred to the Corycian nymphs and to Pan."

Line 319. *Delphic mount.*] Delphi, the seat and oracle of Apollo, had a mountainous and rocky situation, on the skirts of Parnassus.

Line 327. *Cyrenäic shell.*] Cyrene was the native country of Callimachus, whose hymns are the most remarkable example of that mythological passion which is assumed in the preceding poem, and have always afforded particular pleasure to the author of it, by reason of the mysterious solemnity with which they affect the mind. On this account he was induced to attempt somewhat in the same manner; solely by way of exercise: the manner itself being now almost entirely abandoned in poetry. And as the mere genealogy, or the personal adventures of heathen gods, could have been but little interesting to a modern reader; it was therefore thought proper to select some convenient part of the history of nature, and to employ these ancient divinities as it is probable they were first employed; to wit, in personifying natural causes, and in representing the mutual agreement or opposition of the corporeal and moral powers of the world : which hath been accounted the very highest office of poetry.

# INSCRIPTIONS.

## I.

### FOR A GROTTO.

TO me, whom in their lays the shepherds call
    Actæa, daughter of the neighbouring stream,
This cave belongs.  The fig-tree and the vine,
Which o'er the rocky entrance downward shoot,
Were placed by Glycon.  He with cowslips pale,
Primrose, and purple lychnis, deck'd the green
Before my threshold, and my shelving walls
With honeysuckle cover'd.  Here at noon,
Lull'd by the murmur of my rising fount,
I slumber: here my clustering fruits I tend:
Or from the humid flowers at break of day,
Fresh garlands weave, and chace from all my bounds
Each thing impure or noxious.  Enter in,
O stranger, undismay'd.  Nor bat, nor toad
Here lurks: and if thy breast of blameless thoughts
Approve thee, not unwelcome shalt thou tread
My quiet mansion: chiefly, if thy name
Wise Pallas and the immortal Muses own.

## II.

### FOR A STATUE OF CHAUCER AT WOODSTOCK.

SUCH was old Chaucer; such the placid mien
    Of him who first with harmony inform'd
The language of our fathers.  Here he dwelt
For many a cheerful day.  These ancient walls
Have often heard him, while his legends blithe

X

He sang; of love, or knighthood, or the wiles
Of homely life: through each estate and age,
The fashions and the follies of the world
With cunning hand portraying.  Though perchance
From Blenheim's towers, O stranger, thou art come
Glowing with Churchill's trophies; yet in vain
Dost thou applaud them if thy breast be cold
To him, this other hero; who, in times
Dark and untaught, began with charming verse
To tame the rudeness of his native land.


## III.

WHOE'ER thou art whose path in summer
              lies
Thro' yonder village, turn thee where the grove
Of branching oaks a rural palace old
Imbosoms.   There dwells Albert, generous lord
Of all the harvest round.   And onward thence
A low plain chapel fronts the morning light
Fast by a silent rivulet.   Humbly walk,
O stranger, o'er the consecrated ground;
And on that verdant hillock, which thou seest
Beset with osiers, let thy pious hand
Sprinkle fresh water from the brook, and strew
Sweet-smelling flowers.   For there doth Edmund
The learned shepherd; for each rural art      [rest,
Fam'd, and for songs harmonious, and the woes
Of ill-requited love.   The faithless pride
Of fair Matilda sank him to the grave         [ven
In manhood's prime.   But soon did righteous Hea-
With tears, with sharp remorse, and pining care,
Avenge her falsehood.   Nor could all the gold
And nuptial pomp, which lur'd her plighted faith
From Edmund to a loftier husband's home,
Relieve her breaking heart, or turn aside

The strokes of death. Go, traveller; relate
The mournful story. Haply some fair maid
May hold it in remembrance, and be taught
That riches cannot pay for truth or love.


## IV.

O YOUTHS and virgins: O declining eld:
 O pale misfortune's slaves: O ye who dwell
Unknown with humble quiet; ye who wait
In courts, or fill the golden seat of kings:
O sons of sport and pleasure: O thou wretch
That weep'st for jealous love, or the sore wounds
Of conscious guilt, or death's rapacious hand
Which left thee void of hope: O ye who roam
In exile; ye who through the embattled field
Seek bright renown; or who for nobler palms
Contend, the leaders of a public cause;
Approach: behold this marble. Know ye not
The features? Hath not oft his faithful tongue
Told you the fashion of your own estate,
The secrets of your bosom? Here then, round
His monument with reverence while ye stand,
Say to each other: " This was Shakespeare's form;
Who walk'd in every path of human life,
Felt every passion; and to all mankind
Doth now, will ever, that experience yield
Which his own genius only could acquire."


## V.

GVLIELMVS III. FORTIS, PIVS, LIBERATOR, CVM
INEVNTE AETATE PATRIAE LABENTI ADFVISSET
SALVS IPSE VNICA; CVM MOX ITIDEM REIPVB-

LICAE BRITANNICAE VINDEX RENVNCIATVS ES-
SET ATQVE STATOR; TVM DENIQVE AD ID SE
NATVM RECOGNOVIT ET REGEM FACTVM, VT
CVRARET NE DOMINO IMPOTENTI CEDERENT
PAX, FIDES, FORTVNA, GENERIS HVMANI.
AVCTORI PVBLICAE FELICITATIS
P. G. A. M. A.


## VI.

### FOR A COLUMN AT RUNNYMEDE.

THOU, who the verdant plain dost traverse here,
    While Thames among his willows from thy view
Retires; O stranger, stay thee, and the scene
Around contemplate well. This is the place
Where England's ancient barons, clad in arms
And stern with conquest, from their tyrant king
(Then render'd tame) did challenge and secure
The charter of thy freedom. Pass not on
Till thou hast bless'd their memory, and paid
Those thanks which God appointed the reward
Of public virtue. And if chance thy home
Salute thee with a father's honour'd name,
Go, call thy sons: instruct them what a debt
They owe their ancestors; and make them swear
To pay it, by transmitting down entire
Those sacred rights to which themselves were born.


## VII.

### THE WOOD NYMPH.

APPROACH in silence. Tis no vulgar tale
    Which I, the Dryad of this hoary oak,
Pronounce to mortal ears. The second age
Now hasteneth to its period, since I rose

On this fair lawn.   The groves of yonder vale
Are, all, my offspring: and each Nymph, who guards
The copses and the furrow'd fields beyond,
Obeys me.   Many changes have I seen
In human things, and many awful deeds
Of justice, when the ruling hand of Jove
Against the tyrants of the land, against
The unhallow'd sons of luxury and guile,
Was arm'd for retribution.   Thus at length
Expert in laws divine, I know the paths
Of wisdom, and erroneous folly's end
Have oft presag'd : and now well-pleas'd I wait
Each evening till a noble youth, who loves
My shade, awhile releas'd from public cares,
Yon peaceful gate shall enter, and sit down
Beneath my branches.   Then his musing mind
I prompt, unseen; and place before his view
Sincerest forms of good ; and move his heart
With the dread bounties of the sire supreme
Of gods and men, with freedom's generous deeds,
The lofty voice of glory and the faith
Of sacred friendship.   Stranger, I have told
My function.   If within thy bosom dwell
Aught which may challenge praise, thou wilt not leave
Unhonour'd my abode, nor shall I hear
A sparing benediction from thy tongue.


## VIII.

YE powers unseen, to whom, the bards of Greece
     Erected altars ; ye who to the mind
More lofty views unfold, and prompt the heart
With more divine emotions ; if ere while
Not quite unpleasing have my votive rites
Of you been deem'd, when oft this lonely seat
To you I consecrated ; then vouchsafe
Here with your instant energy to crown

My happy solitude.  It is the hour
When most I love to invoke you, and have felt
Most frequent your glad ministry divine.
The air is calm: the sun's unveiled orb
Shines in the middle heaven.  The harvest round
Stands quiet, and among the golden sheaves
The reapers lie reclin'd.  The neighbouring groves
Are mute; nor even a linnet's random strain
Echoeth amid the silence.  Let me feel
Your influence, ye kind powers.  Aloft in heaven,
Abide ye? or on those transparent clouds
Pass ye from hill to hill? or on the shades
Which yonder elms cast o'er the lake below
Do you converse retir'd? From what lov'd haunt
Shall I expect you? Let me once more feel
Your influence, O ye kind inspiring powers:
And I will guard it well; nor shall a thought
Rise in my mind, nor shall a passion move
Across my bosom unobserv'd, unstor'd
By faithful memory.  And then at some
More active moment, will I call them forth
Anew; and join them in majestic forms,
And give them utterance in harmonious strains;
That all mankind shall wonder at your sway.


## IX.

ME though in life's sequester'd vale
The Almighty Sire ordain'd to dwell,
Remote from glory's toilsome ways,
And the great scenes of public praise;
Yet let me still with grateful pride
Remember how my infant frame
He temper'd with prophetic flame,
And early music to my tongue supplied.

'Twas then my future fate he weigh'd,
And, this be thy concern, he said,

At once with Passion's keen alarms,
And Beauty's pleasurable charms,
And sacred Truth's eternal light,
To move the various mind of Man ;
Till under one unblemish'd plan,
His Reason, Fancy, and his Heart unite.


## AN EPISTLE TO CURIO.[1]

THRICE has the spring beheld thy faded fame,
    And the fourth winter rises on thy shame,
Since I exulting grasp'd the votive shell,
In sounds of triumph all thy praise to tell;
Blest could my skill through ages make thee shine,
And proud to mix my memory with thine.
But now the cause that wak'd my song before,
With praise, with triumph, crowns the toil no more.
If to the glorious man whose faithful cares,
Nor quell'd by malice, nor relax'd by years,
Had aw'd Ambition's wild audacious hate,
And dragg'd at length Corruption to her fate ;
If every tongue its large applauses ow'd,
And well-earn'd laurels every Muse bestow'd;

[1] Curio was a young Roman senator of distinguished birth and parts, who upon his first entrance into the forum, had been committed to the care of Cicero. Being profuse and extravagant, he soon dissipated a large and splendid fortune; to supply the want of which, he was driven to the necessity of abetting the designs of Cæsar against the liberties of his country, although he had before been a professed enemy to him. Cicero exerted himself with great energy to prevent his ruin, but without effect, and he became one of the first victims in the civil war. This epistle was first published in the year 1744, when a celebrated patriot, after a long, and at last successful opposition to an unpopular minister, had deserted the cause of his country, and became the foremost in support and defence of the same measures he had so steadily and for such a length of time contended against.

If public Justice urg'd the high reward,
And Freedom smil'd on the devoted bard;
Say then, to him whose levity or lust
Laid all a people's generous hopes in dust;
Who taught Ambition firmer heights of power,
And sav'd Corruption at her hopeless hour;
Does not each tongue its execrations owe?
Shall not each Muse a wreath of shame bestow?
And public Justice sanctify th' award?
And Freedom's hand protect the impartial bard?
Yet long reluctant I forbore thy name,
Long watch'd thy virtue like a dying flame,
Hung o'er each glimmering spark with anxious eyes,
And wish'd and hop'd the light again would rise.
But since thy guilt still more entire appears,
Since no art hides, no supposition clears;
Since vengeful Slander now too sinks her blast,
And the first rage of Party-hate is past;
Calm as the judge of truth, at length I come
To weigh thy merits, and pronounce thy doom:
So may my trust from all reproach be free;
And Earth and Time confirm the fair decree.
There are who say they view'd without amaze
The sad reverse of all thy former praise:
That through the pageants of a patriot's name,
They pierced the foulness of thy secret aim;
Or deem'd thy arm exalted but to throw
The public thunder on a private foe.
But I, whose soul consented to thy cause,
Who felt thy genius stamp its own applause,
Who saw the spirits of each glorious age
Move in thy bosom, and direct thy rage;
I scorn'd the ungenerous gloss of slavish minds,
The owl-ey'd race, whom Virtue's lustre blinds.
Spite of the learned in the ways of vice,
And all who prove that each man has his price,
I still believ'd thy end was just and free;
And yet, even yet believe it—spite of thee.
Even tho' thy mouth impure has dar'd disclaim,

Urg'd by the wretched impotence of shame,
Whatever filial cares thy zeal had paid
To laws infirm, and liberty decay'd ;
Has begg'd Ambition to forgive the show ;
Has told Corruption thou wert ne'er her foe ;
Has boasted in thy country's awful ear,
Her gross delusion when she held thee dear ;
How tame she followed thy tempestuous call,
And heard thy pompous tales, and trusted all—
Rise from your sad abodes, ye curst of old
For laws subverted, and for cities sold !
Paint all the noblest trophies of your guilt,
The oaths you perjur'd, and the blood you spilt ;
Yet must you one untempted vileness own,
One dreadful palm reserv'd for him alone ;
With studied arts his country's praise to spurn,
To beg the infamy he did not earn,
To challenge hate when honour was his due,
And plead his crimes where all his virtue knew.
Do robes of state the guarded heart enclose
From each fair feeling human nature knows ?
Can pompous titles stun the enchanted ear
To all that reason, all that sense would hear ?
Else could thou e'er desert thy sacred post,
In such unthankful baseness to be lost ?
Else couldst thou wed the emptiness of vice,
And yield thy glories at an idiot's price ?
    When they who, loud for liberty and laws,
In doubtful times had fought their country's cause,
When now of conquest and dominion sure,
They sought alone to hold their fruits secure ;
When taught by these, Oppression hid the face,
To leave Corruption stronger in her place,
By silent spells to work the public fate,
And taint the vitals of the passive state,
Till healing Wisdom should avail no more,
And Freedom loath to tread the poison'd shore ;
Then, like some guardian god that flies to save,
The weary pilgrim from an instant grave,

Whom, sleeping and secure, the guileful snake
Steals near and nearer thro' the peaceful brake;
Then Curio rose to ward the public woe,
To wake the heedless, and incite the slow,
Against Corruption Liberty to arm,
And quell the enchantress by a mightier charm.
    Swift o'er the land the fair contagion flew,
And with thy country's hopes thy honours grew.
Thee, patriot, the patrician roof confess'd;
Thy powerful voice the rescued merchant bless'd;
Of thee with awe the rural hearth resounds;
The bowl to thee the grateful sailor crowns;
Touch'd in the sighing shade with manlier fires,
To trace thy steps the love-sick youth aspires;
The learn'd recluse, who oft amaz'd had read
Of Grecian heroes, Roman patriots dead,
With new amazement hears a living name
Pretend to share in such forgotten fame;
And he who scorning courts and courtly ways,
Left the tame track of these dejected days,
The life of nobler ages to renew
In virtues sacred from a monarch's view,
Rous'd by thy labours from the bless'd retreat,
Where social ease and public passions meet,
Again ascending treads the civil scene,
To act and be a man, as thou hadst been.
    Thus by degrees thy cause superior grew,
And the great end appear'd at last in view:
We heard the people in thy hopes rejoice,
We saw the senate bending to thy voice;
The friends of freedom hail'd the approaching reign
Of laws for which our fathers bled in vain;
While venal Faction, struck with new dismay,
Shrunk at their frown, and self-abandon'd lay.
Wak'd in the shock the public Genius rose,
Abash'd and keener from his long repose;
Sublime in ancient pride, he rais'd the spear
Which slaves and tyrants long were wont to fear:
The city felt his call: from man to man,

From street to street, the glorious horror ran ;
Each crowded haunt was stirr'd beneath his power,
And, murmuring, challeng'd the decided hour.
　Lo! the deciding hour at last appears ;
The hour of every freeman's hopes and fears !
Thou, Genius ! guardian of the Roman name,
O ever prompt tyrannic rage to tame !
Instruct the mighty moments as they roll,
And guide each movement steady to the goal.
Ye spirits by whose providential art
Succeeding motives turn the changeful heart,
Keep, keep the best in view to Curio's mind,
And watch his fancy, and his passions bind !
Ye shades immortal, who by Freedom led,
Or in the field or on the scaffold bled,
Bend from your radiant seats a joyful eye,
And view the crown of all your labours nigh.
See Freedom mounting her eternal throne !
The sword submitted, and the laws her own :
See ! public Power chastis'd beneath her stands,
With eyes intent, and uncorrupted hands !
See private Life by wisest arts reclaim'd !
See ardent youth to noblest manners fram'd !
See us acquire whate'er was sought by you,
If Curio, only Curio will be true.
　'Twas then—O shame ! O trust how ill repaid !
O Latium, oft by faithless sons betray'd !—
'Twas then—What frenzy on thy reason stole ?
What spells unsinew'd thy determin'd soul ?
—Is this the man in Freedom's cause approv'd ?
The man so great, so honour'd, so belov'd ?
This patient slave by tinsel chains allur'd ?
This wretched suitor for a boon abjur'd ?
This Curio, hated and despis'd by all ?
Who fell himself to work his country's fall ?
　O lost, alike to action and repose !
Unknown, unpitied in the worst of woes !
With all that conscious, undissembled pride,
Sold to the insults of a foe defied !

With all that habit of familiar fame,
Doom'd to exhaust the dregs of life in shame!
The sole sad refuge of thy baffled art
To act a statesman's dull, exploded part,
Renounce the praise no longer in thy power,
Display thy virtue, though without a dower,
Contemn the giddy crowd, the vulgar wind,
And shut thy eyes that others may be blind.
—Forgive me, Romans, that I bear to smile,
When shameless mouths your majesty defile,
Paint you a thoughtless, frantic, headlong crew,
And cast their own impieties on you.
For witness, Freedom, to whose sacred power,
My soul was vow'd from reason's earliest hour,
How have I stood exulting, to survey
My country's virtues, opening in thy ray!
How, with the sons of every foreign shore
The more I match'd them, honour'd hers the more!
O race erect! whose native strength of soul,
Which kings, nor priests, nor sordid laws control,
Bursts the tame round of animal affairs,
And seeks a noble centre for its cares;
Intent the laws of life to comprehend,
And fix dominion's limits by its end.
Who, bold and equal in their love or hate,
By conscious reason judging every state,
The man forget not, though in rags he lies,
And know the mortal through a crown's disguise:
Thence prompt alike with witty scorn to view
Fastidious Grandeur lift his solemn brow,
Or, all awake at pity's soft command,
Bend the mild ear, and stretch the gracious hand:
Thence large of heart, from envy far remov'd,
When public toils to virtue stand approv'd,
Not the young lover fonder to admire,
Not more indulgent the delighted sire;
Yet high and jealous of their free-born name,
Fierce as the flight of Jove's destroying flame,
Where'er Oppression works her wanton sway,

Proud to confront, and dreadful to repay.
But if to purchase Curio's sage applause,
My country must with him renounce her cause,
Quit with a slave the path a patriot trod,
Bow the meek knee, and kiss the regal rod ;
Then still, ye powers, instruct his tongue to rail,
Nor let his zeal, nor let his subject fail :
Else, ere he change the style, bear me away
To where the Gracchi,[1] where the Bruti stay !
　O long rever'd, and late resign'd to shame !
If this uncourtly page thy notice claim
When the loud cares of business are withdrawn,
Nor well-drest beggars round thy footsteps fawn ;
In that still, thoughtful, solitary hour,
When Truth exerts her unresisted power,
Breaks the false optics ting'd with fortune's glare,
Unlocks the breast, and lays the passions bare ;
Then turn thy eyes on that important scene,
And ask thyself—if all be well within.
Where is the heart-felt worth and weight of soul,
Which labour could not stop, nor fear control ?
Where the known dignity, the stamp of awe,
Which, half abash'd, the proud and venal saw ?
Where the calm triumphs of an honest cause ?
Where the delightful taste of just applause ?
Where the strong reason, the commanding tongue,
On which the senate fir'd or trembling hung !
All vanish'd, all are sold—and in their room,
Couch'd in thy bosom's deep, distracted gloom,
See the pale form of barbarous Grandeur dwell,
Like some grim idol in a sorcerer's cell !
To her in chains thy dignity was led ;
At her polluted shrine thy honour bled ;
With blasted weeds thy awful brow she crown'd,

[1] The two brothers, Tiberius and Caius Gracchus, lost
their lives in attempting to introduce the only regulation
that could give stability and good order to the Roman re-
public.  L. Junius Brutus founded the commonwealth, and
died in its defence.

Thy powerful tongue with poison'd philters bound,
That baffled Reason straight indignant flew,
And fair Persuasion from her seat withdrew :
For now no longer Truth supports thy cause ;
No longer Glory prompts thee to applause ;
No longer Virtue breathing in thy breast,
With all her conscious majesty confest,
Still bright and brighter wakes the almighty flame,
To rouse the feeble, and the wilful tame,
And where she sees the catching glimpses roll,
Spreads the strong blaze, and all involves the soul ;
But cold restraints thy conscious fancy chill,
And formal passions mock thy struggling will ;
Or, if thy Genius e'er forget his chain,
And reach impatient at a nobler strain,
Soon the sad bodings of contemptuous mirth
Shoot thro' thy breast, and stab the generous birth,
Till, blind with smart, from truth to frenzy tost,
And all the tenor of thy reason lost,
Perhaps thy anguish drains a real tear ;
While some with pity, some with laughter hear.
—Can art, alas ! or genius, guide the head,
Where truth and freedom from the heart are fled ?
Can lesser wheels repeat their native stroke,
When the prime function of the soul is broke ?
  But come, unhappy man ! thy fates impend :
Come, quit thy friends, if yet thou hast a friend ;
Turn from the poor rewards of guilt like thine,
Renounce thy titles, and thy robes resign ;
For see the hand of Destiny display'd
To shut thee from the joys thou hast betray'd !
See the dire fane of Infamy arise !
Dark as the grave, and spacious as the skies ;
Where, from the first of time, thy kindred train,
The chiefs and princes of the unjust remain.
Eternal barriers guard the pathless road
To warn the wanderer of the curst abode ;
But prone as whirlwinds scour the passive sky,
The heights surmounted, down the steep they fly.

There, black with frowns, relentless Time awaits,
And goads their footsteps to the guilty gates ;
And still he asks them of their unknown aims,
Evolves their secrets, and their guilt proclaims ;
And still his hands despoil them on the road
Of each vain wreath, by lying bards bestow'd,
Break their proud marbles, crush their festal cars,
And rend the lawless trophies of their wars.
At last the gates his potent voice obey ;
Fierce to their dark abode he drives his prey ;
Where, ever arm'd with adamantine chains,
The watchful demon o'er her vassals reigns,
O'er mighty names and giant-powers of lust,
The great, the sage, the happy, and august.[1]
No gleam of hope their baleful mansion cheers,
No sound of honour hails their unblest ears ;
But dire reproaches from the friend betray'd,
The childless sire and violated maid ;
But vengeful vows for guardian laws effac'd,
From towns enslaved, and continents laid waste ;
But long posterity's united groan,
And the sad charge of horrors not their own,
For ever through the trembling space resound,
And sink each impious forehead to the ground.
    Ye mighty foes of liberty and rest,
Give way, do homage to a mightier guest !
Ye daring spirits of the Roman race,
See Curio's toil your proudest claims efface !
—Aw'd at the name, fierce Appius [2] rising bends,
And hardy Cinna from his throne attends :
" He comes," they cry, " to whom the fates assign'd
With surer arts to work what we design'd,
From year to year the stubborn herd to sway,
Mouth all their wrongs, and all their rage obey ;

[1] Titles which have been generally ascribed to the most
pernicious of men.
[2] Appius Claudius the Decemvir, and L. Cornelius Cinna
both attempted to establish a tyrannical dominion in Rome,
and both perished by the treason.

Till own'd their guide, and trusted with their power,
He mock'd their hopes in one decisive hour;
Then, tir'd and yielding, led them to the chain,
And quench'd the spirit we provok'd in vain."
But thou, Supreme, by whose eternal hands
Fair Liberty's heroic empire stands;
Whose thunders the rebellious deep control,
And quell the triumphs of the traitor's soul,
O turn this dreadful omen far away!
On Freedom's foes their own attempts repay:
Relume her sacred fire so near suppress'd,
And fix her shrine in every Roman breast:
Though bold corruption boast around the land,
" Let virtue, if she can, my baits withstand?"
Though bolder now she urge the accursed claim,
Gay with her trophies rais'd on Curio's shame;
Yet some there are who scorn her impious mirth,
Who know what conscience and a heart are worth.
—O friend and father of the human mind,
Whose art for noblest ends our frame design'd!
If I, though fated to the studious shade
Which party-strife, nor anxious power invade,
If I aspire in public virtue's cause,
To guide the Muses by sublimer laws,
Do thou her own authority impart,
And give my numbers entrance to the heart.
Perhaps the verse might rouse her smother'd flame,
And snatch the fainting patriot back to fame:
Perhaps by worthy thoughts of human kind,
To worthy deeds exalt the conscious mind;
Or dash Corruption in her proud career,
And teach her slaves that Vice was born to fear.

# THE VIRTUOSO;

## IN IMITATION OF SPENSER'S STYLE AND STANZA.

—————————— Videmus
Nugari solitos.    PERSIUS.

WHILOM by silver Thames's gentle stream,
　　In London town there dwelt a subtile wight;
A wight of mickle wealth, and mickle fame,
　　Book-learn'd and quaint; a Virtuoso hight.
Uncommon things, and rare, were his delight;
　　From musings deep his brain ne'er gotten ease,
Nor ceasen he from study, day or night;
　　Until (advancing onward by degrees)
He knew whatever breeds on earth, or air, or seas.

He many a creature did anatomize,
　　Almost unpeopling water, air, and land;
Beasts, fishes, birds, snails, caterpillars, flies,
　　Were laid full low by his relentless hand,
That oft with gory crimson was distain'd:
　　He many a dog destroy'd, and many a cat;
Of fleas his bed, of frogs the marshes drain'd,
　　Could tellen if a mite were lean or fat,
And read a lecture o'er the entrails of a gnat.

He knew the various modes of ancient times,
　　Their arts and fashions of each different guise,
Their weddings, funerals, punishments for crimes,
　　Their strength, their learning eke, and rareties;
Of old habiliments, each sort and size,
　　Male, female, high and low, to him were known;
Each gladiator-dress, and stage disguise;
　　With learned, clerkly phrase he could have shown
How the Greek tunic differ'd from the Roman
　　　gown.

Y

A curious medalist, I wot, he was,
    And boasted many a course of ancient coin;
Well as his wife's he knewen every face,
    From Julius Cæsar down to Constantine:
For some rare sculptor he would oft ypine,
    (As green-sick damosels for husbands do;)
And when obtained, with enraptur'd eyne,
    He'd run it o'er and o'er with greedy view,
    And look, and look again, as he would look it
        thro'.

His rich museum, of dimensions fair,    [fraught:
    With goods that spoke the owner's mind was
Things ancient, curious, value-worth, and rare,
    From sea and land, from Greece and Rome
        were brought,
Which he with mighty sums of gold had bought:
    On these all tides with joyous eyes he por'd;
And, sooth to say, himself he greater thought,
    When he beheld his cabinets thus stor'd,
    Than if he'd been of Albion's wealthy cities lord.

Here in a corner stood a rich scrutoire,
    With many a curiosity replete;
In seemly order furnished every drawer,
    Products of art or nature as was meet:
Air-pumps and prisms were plac'd beneath his feet,
    A Memphian mummy-king hung o'er his head;
Here phials with live insects small and great,
    There stood a tripod of the Pythian maid;
    Above, a crocodile diffus'd a grateful shade.

Fast by the window did a table stand,
    Where hodiern and antique rarities,    [land,
From Egypt, Greece, and Rome, from sea and
    Were thick-besprent of every sort and size:
Here a Bahaman-spider's carcass lies,
    There a dire serpent's golden skin doth shine;
Here Indian feathers, fruits, and glittering flies;

There gums and amber found beneath the line,
The beak of Ibis here, and there an Antonine.

Close at his back, or whispering in his ear,
　There stood a spright ycleped Phantasy ;
Which, wheresoe'er he went, was always near :
　Her look was wild, and roving was her eye ;
Her hair was clad with flowers of every dye ;
　Her glistering robes were of more various hue,
Than the fair bow that paints the cloudy sky,
　Or all the spangled drops of morning dew ;
　Their colour changing still at every different view.

Yet in this shape all tides she did not stay,
　Various as the chameleon that she bore ;
Now a grand monarch with a crown of hay,
　Now mendicant in silks and golden ore :
A statesman, now equipp'd to chase the boar,
　Or cowled monk, lean, feeble, and unfed ;
A clown-like lord, or swain of courtly lore ;
　Now scribbling dunce in sacred laurel clad,
　Or papal father now, in homely weeds array'd.

The wight whose brain this phantom's power doth fill,
　On whom she doth with constant care attend,
Will for a dreadful giant take a mill,
　Or a grand palace in a hogsty find :
(From her dire influence me may heaven defend !)
　All things with vitiated sight he spies ;
Neglects his family, forgets his friend,
　Seeks painted trifles and fantastic toys,
　And eagerly pursues imaginary joys.

# AMBITION AND CONTENT;

## A FABLE.

Optat quietem. HOR.

WHILE yet the world was young, and men
  were few,
Nor lurking fraud, nor tyrant rapine knew,
In virtue rude, the gaudy arts they scorn'd,
Which, virtue lost, degenerate times adorn'd:
No sumptuous fabrics yet were seen to rise,
Nor gushing fountains taught to invade the skies;
With nature, art had not begun the strife,
Nor swelling marble rose to mimic life;
No pencil yet had learn'd to express the fair;
The bounteous earth was all their homely care.
 Then did Content exert her genial sway,
And taught the peaceful world her power to obey;
Content, a female of celestial race,
Bright and complete in each celestial grace.
Serenely fair she was, as rising day,
And brighter than the sun's meridian ray;
Joy of all hearts, delight of every eye,
Nor grief nor pain appear'd when she was by;
Her presence from the wretched banish'd care,
Dispers'd the swelling sigh and stopt the falling tear.
 Long did the nymph her regal state maintain,
As long mankind were blest beneath her reign;
Till dire Ambition, hellish fiend, arose,
To plague the world, and banish man's repose:
A monster sprung from that rebellious crew,
Which mighty Jove's Phlegræan thunder slew.
Resolv'd to dispossess the royal fair,
On all her friends he threaten'd open war:
Fond of the novelty, vain, fickle man,

In crowds to his infernal standard ran;
And the weak maid, defenceless left alone,
To avoid his rage, was forc'd to quit the throne.
   It chanc'd as wandering thro' the fields she stray'd,
Forsook of all, and destitute of aid,
Upon a rising mountain's flowery side,
A pleasant cottage roof'd with turf she spied:
Fast by a gloomy, venerable wood
Of shady planes, and ancient oaks it stood.
Around a various prospect charm'd the sight;
Here waving harvests clad the field with white;
Here a rough shaggy rock the clouds did pierce,
From which a torrent rush'd with rapid force;
Here mountain-woods diffus'd a dusky shade;
Here flocks and herds in flowery valleys play'd,
While o'er the matted grass the liquid crystal stray'd.
In this sweet place there dwelt a cheerful pair,
Tho' bent beneath the weight of many a year;
Who wisely flying public noise and strife,
In this obscure retreat had pass'd their life;
The husband Industry was call'd, Frugality the wife.
With tenderest friendship mutually blest,
No household jars had e'er disturb'd their rest.
A numerous offspring grac'd their homely board,
That still with nature's simple gifts was stor'd.
The father rural business only knew;
The sons the same delightful art pursue.
An only daughter, as a goddess fair,
Above the rest was the fond mother's care;
Plenty; the brightest nymph of all the plain,
Each heart's delight, ador'd by every swain.
Soon as Content this charming scene espied,
Joyful within herself the goddess cried;
" This happy sight my drooping heart doth raise;
The gods, I hope, will grant me gentler days.
When with prosperity my life was blest,
In yonder house I've been a welcome guest:
There now, perhaps, I may protection find;
For royalty is banish'd from my mind;

I'll thither haste : how happy should I be,
If such a refuge were reserv'd for me ! "    [way
   Thus spoke the fair ; and straight she bent her
To the tall mountain, where the cottage lay :
Arriv'd she makes her chang'd condition known ;
Tells how the rebels drove her from the throne ;
What painful, dreary wilds she'd wander'd o'er ;
And shelter from the tyrant doth implore.
   The faithful, aged pair at once were seiz'd
With joy and grief, at once were pain'd and pleas'd ;
Grief for their banish'd queen their hearts possest,
And joy succeeded for their future guest ;
" And if you'll deign, bright goddess, here to dwell,
And with your presence grace our humble cell,
Whate'er the gods have given with bounteous hand,
Our harvests, fields and flocks, our all command."
   Meantime, Ambition, on his rival's flight,
Sole lord of man, attain'd his wish's height ;
Of all dependance on his subjects eas'd,
He rag'd without a curb, and did whate'er he pleas'd ;
As some wild flame, driven on by furious winds,
Wide spreads destruction, nor resistance finds ;
So rush'd the fiend destructive o'er the plain,
Defac'd the labours of th' industrious swain ;
Polluted every stream with human gore,
And scatter'd plagues and death from shore to shore.
   Great Jove beheld it from the Olympian towers,
Where sate assembled all the heavenly powers ;
Then with a nod that shook the empyrean throne,
Thus the Saturnian thunderer begun :
" You see, immortal inmates of the skies,
How this vile wretch almighty power defies ;
His daring crimes, the blood which he has spilt,
Demand a torment equal to his guilt.
Then, Cyprian goddess, let thy mighty boy
Swift to the tyrant's guilty palace fly ;
There let him choose his sharpest, hottest dart,
And with his former rival wound his heart.
And thou, my son, (the god to Hermes said)

Snatch up thy wand, and plume thy heels and head;
Dart thro' the yielding air with all thy force,
And down to Pluto's realms direct thy course;
There rouse Oblivion from her sable cave,
Where dull she sits by Lethe's sluggish wave;
Command her to secure the sacred bound,
Where lives Content retir'd, and all around
Diffuse the deepest glooms of Stygian night,
And screen the virgin from the tyrant's sight;
That the vain purpose of his life may try
Still to explore, what still eludes his eye."
He spoke; loud praises shake the bright abode,
And all applaud the justice of the god.

## THE POET. A RHAPSODY.

OF all the various lots around the ball,
    Which fate to man distributes, absolute;
Avert, ye gods! that of the Muse's son,
Curs'd with dire poverty! poor hungry wretch!
What shall he do for life? he cannot work
With manual labour: shall those sacred hands,
That brought the counsels of the gods to light;
Shall that inspired tongue, which every Muse
Has touch'd divine, to charm the sons of men;
These hallow'd organs! these! be prostitute
To the vile service of some fool in power,
All his behests submissive to perform,
Howe'er to him ingrateful? Oh! he scorns
The ignoble thought; with generous disdain,
More eligible deeming it to starve,
Like his fam'd ancestors renown'd in verse,
Than poorly bend to be another's slave,—
Than feed and fatten in obscurity.
—These are his firm resolves, which fate, nor time,
Nor poverty can shake. Exalted high

In garret vile he lives ; with remnants hung
Of tapestry.   But oh ! precarious state
Of this vain transient world ! all powerful time,
What dost thou not subdue ?  See what a chasm
Gapes wide, tremendous !  see where Saul, enrag'd,
High on his throne, encompass'd by his guards,
With levell'd spear, and arm extended, sits,
Ready to pierce old Jesse's valiant son,
Spoil'd of his nose !—around in tottering ranks,
On shelves pulverulent, majestic stands
His library ; in ragged plight, and old ;
Replete with many a load of criticism,
Elaborate products of the midnight toil
Of Belgian brains ; snatch'd from the deadly hands
Of murderous grocer, or the careful wight,
Who vends the plant, that clads the happy shore
Of Indian Patomack ; which citizens
In balmy fumes exhale, when, o'er a pot
Of sage-inspiring coffee, they dispose
Of kings and crowns, and settle Europe's fate.
　　Elsewhere the dome is fill'd with various heaps
Of old domestic lumber : that huge chair
Has seen six monarchs fill the British throne :
Here a broad massy table stands, o'erspread
With ink and pens, and scrolls replete with rhyme :
Chests, stools, old razors, fractur'd jars, half full
Of muddy Zythum, sour and spiritless :
Fragments of verse, hose, sandals, utensils
Of various fashion, and of various use,
With friendly influence hide the sable floor.
　　This is the bard's museum, this the fane
To Phœbus sacred, and the Aonian maids :
But oh ! it stabs his heart, that niggard fate
To him in such small measure should dispense
Her better gifts : to him ! whose generous soul
Could relish, with as fine an elegance,
The golden joys of grandeur, and of wealth ;
He who could tyrannize o'er menial slaves,
Or swell beneath a coronet of state,

Or grace a gilded chariot with a mien,
Grand as the haughtiest Timon of them all.
   But 'tis in vain to rave at destiny,
Here he must rest and brook the best he can,
To live remote from grandeur, learning, wit;
Immur'd amongst th' ignoble, vulgar herd,
Of lowest intellect; whose stupid souls
But half inform their bodies; brains of lead
And tongues of thunder; whose insensate breasts
Ne'er felt the rapturous, soul-entrancing fire
Of the celestial Muse; whose savage ears
Ne'er heard the sacred rules, nor even the names
Of the Venusian bard, or critic sage
Full-fam'd of Stagyra: whose clamorous tongues
Stun the tormented ear with colloquy,
Vociferate, trivial, or impertinent;
Replete with boorish scandal; yet, alas!
This, this! he must endure, or muse alone,
Pensive and moping o'er the stubborn rhyme,
Or line imperfect—No! the door is free,
And calls him to evade their deafening clang,
By private ambulation;—'tis resolved:
Off from his waist he throws the tatter'd gown,
Beheld with indignation; and unloads
His pericranium of the weighty cap,
With sweat and grease discolour'd: then explores
The spacious chest, and from its hollow womb
Draws his best robe, yet not from tincture free
Of age's reverend russet, scant and bare;
Then down his meagre visage waving flows
The shadowy peruke; crown'd with gummy hat
Clean brush'd; a cane supports him. Thus equipp'd
He sallies forth; swift traverses the streets,
And seeks the lonely walk. "Hail sylvan scenes,
Ye groves, ye valleys, ye meand'ring brooks,
Admit me to your joys," in rapturous phrase,
Loud he exclaims; while with the inspiring Muse
His bosom labours; and all other thoughts,
Pleasure and wealth, and poverty itself,

Before her influence vanish. Rapt in thought,
Fancy presents before his ravished eyes
Distant posterity, upon his page          [sons
With transport dwelling; while bright learning's
That ages hence must tread this earthly ball,
Indignant, seem to curse the thankless age,
That starv'd such merit. Meantime swallow'd up
In meditation deep, he wanders on,
Unweeting of his way.—But ah! he starts!
With sudden fright! his glaring eye-balls roll,
Pale turn his cheeks, and shake his loosen'd joints;
His cogitations vanish into air,
Like painted bubbles, or a morning dream.
Behold the cause! see! thro' the opening glade,
With rosy visage, and abdomen grand,
A cit, a dun!—As in Apulia's wilds,
Or where the Thracian Hebrus rolls his wave,
A heedless kid, disportive, roves around,
Unheeding, till upon the hideous cave
Of the dire wolf she treads; half-dead she views
His bloodshot eye-balls, and his dreadful fangs,
And swift as Eurus from the monster flies.
So fares the trembling bard; amaz'd he turns,
Scarce by his legs upborne; yet fear supplies
The place of strength; straight home he bends his
Nor looks behind him till he safe regain    [course,
His faithful citadel; there spent, fatigu'd,
He lays him down to ease his heaving lungs,
Quaking, and of his safety scarce convinc'd.
Soon as the panic leaves his panting breast,
Down to the Muse's sacred rites he sits,
Volumes pil'd round him; see! upon his brow
Perplex'd anxiety, and struggling thought,
Painful as female throes: whether the bard
Display the deeds of heroes; or the fall
Of vice, in lay dramatic; or expand
The lyric wing; or in elegiac strains
Lament the fair; or lash the stubborn age,
With laughing satire; or in rural scenes

With shepherds sport; or rack his hard-bound brains
For the unexpected turn.   Arachne so,
In dusty kitchen corner, from her bowels
Spins the fine web; but spins with better fate,
Than the poor bard: she! caitiff! spreads her snares,
And with their aid enjoys luxurious life,
Bloated with fat of insects, flesh'd in blood:
He! hard, hard, lot! for all his toil and care,
And painful watchings, scarce protracts awhile
His meagre, hungry days! ungrateful world!
If with his drama he adorn the stage,
No worth-discerning concourse pays the charge,
Or of the orchestra, or the enlightening torch.
He who supports the luxury and pride
Of craving Lais; he! whose carnage fills
Dogs, eagles, lions; has not yet enough,
Wherewith to satisfy the greedier maw
Of that most ravenous, that devouring beast,
Yclep'd a poet.   What new Halifax,
What Somers, or what Dorset canst thou find,
Thou hungry mortal ? break, wretch, break thy quill,
Blot out the studied image; to the flames
Commit the Stagyrite; leave this thankless trade;
Erect some pedling stall, with trinkets stock'd,
There earn thy daily halfpence, nor again
Trust the false Muse; so shall the cleanly meal
Repel intruding hunger.—Oh! 'tis vain,
The friendly admonition's all in vain;
The scribbling itch has seized him, he is lost
To all advice, and starves for starving's sake.
     Thus sung the sportful Muse, in mirthful mood,
Indulging gay the frolic vein of youth;
But, oh! ye gods, avert th' impending stroke
This luckless omen threatens! Hark! methinks
I hear my better angel cry, " Retreat,
Rash youth! in time retreat! let those poor bards,
Who slighted all, all! for the flattering Muse,
Yet curs'd with pining want, as landmarks stand,
To warn thee from the service of the ingrate."

# A BRITISH PHILIPPIC:

## OCCASIONED BY THE INSULTS OF THE SPANIARDS, AND THE PRESENT PREPARATIONS FOR WAR. 1738.

WHENCE this unwonted transport in my
　　breast?
Why glow my thoughts, and whither would the
　　Muse
Aspire with rapid wing? Her country's cause
Demands her efforts: at that sacred call
She summons all her ardour, throws aside
The trembling lyre, and with the warrior's trump
She means to thunder in each British ear;
And if one spark of honour or of fame,
Disdain of insult, dread of infamy,
One thought of public virtue yet survive,
She means to wake it, rouse the generous flame,
With patriot zeal inspirit every breast,
And fire each British heart with British wrongs.
　　Alas the vain attempt! what influence now
Can the Muse boast! or what attention now
Is paid to fame or virtue? Where is now
The British spirit, generous, warm, and brave,
So frequent wont from tyranny and woe
To free the suppliant nations? Where, indeed!
If that protection, once to strangers given,
Be now withheld from sons? Each nobler thought,
That warm'd our sires, is lost and buried now
In luxury and avarice. Baneful vice!
How it unmans a nation! yet I'll try,
I'll aim to shake this vile degenerate sloth;
I'll dare to rouse Britannia's dreaming sons
To fame, to virtue, and impart around

A generous feeling of compatriot woes.
　　Come then the various powers of forceful speech,
All that can move, awaken, fire, transport!
Come the bold ardour of the Theban bard!
The arousing thunder of the patriot Greek!
The soft persuasion of the Roman sage!
Come all! and raise me to an equal height,
A rapture worthy of my glorious cause!
Lest my best efforts, failing, should debase
The sacred theme; for with no common wing
The Muse attempts to soar.　Yet what need these?
My country's fame, my free-born British heart,
Shall be my best inspirers, raise my flight
High as the Theban's pinion, and with more
Than Greek or Roman flame exalt my soul.
Oh! could I give the vast ideas birth
Expressive of the thoughts that flame within,
No more should lazy Luxury detain
Our ardent youth; no more should Britain's sons
Sit tamely passive by, and careless hear
The prayers, sighs, groans, (immortal infamy!)
Of fellow Britons, with oppression sunk,
In bitterness of soul demanding aid,
Calling on Britain, their dear native land,
The land of Liberty; so greatly fam'd
For just redress; the land so often dyed
With her best blood, for that arousing cause,
The freedom of her sons; those sons that now
Far from the manly blessings of her sway,
Drag the vile fetters of a Spanish lord.
And dare they, dare the vanquish'd sons of Spain
Enslave a Briton? Have they then forgot,
So soon forgot, the great, the immortal day,
When rescued Sicily with joy beheld
The swift-wing'd thunder of the British arm
Disperse their navies? when their coward bands
Fled, like the raven from the bird of Jove,
From swift impending vengeance fled in vain?
Are these our lords? And can Britannia see

Her foes oft vanquish'd, thus defy her power,
Insult her standard, and enslave her sons,
And not arise to justice? Did our sires,
Unaw'd by chains, by exile, or by death,
Preserve inviolate her guardian rights,
To Britons ever sacred! that their sons    [eyes,
Might give them up to Spaniards?—Turn your
Turn ye degenerate, who with haughty boast
Call yourselves Britons, to that dismal gloom,
That dungeon dark and deep, where never thought
Of joy or peace can enter; see the gates
Harsh-creaking open; what a hideous void,
Dark as the yawning grave! while still as death
A frightful silence reigns.  There on the ground
Behold your brethren chain'd like beasts of prey:
There mark your numerous glories, there behold
The look that speaks unutterable woe;
The mangled limb, the faint, the deathful eye,
With famine sunk, the deep heart-bursting groan
Suppress'd in silence; view the loathsome food,
Refus'd by dogs, and oh! the stinging thought!
View the dark Spaniard glorying in their wrongs,
The deadly priest triumphant in their woes,
And thundering worse damnation on their souls:
While that pale form, in all the pangs of death,
Too faint to speak, yet eloquent of all,
His native British spirit yet untam'd,
Raises his head; and with indignant frowns
Of great defiance, and superior scorn,
Looks up and dies.—Oh! I am all on fire!
But let me spare the theme, lest future times
Should blush to hear that either conquer'd Spain
Durst offer Britain such outrageous wrong,
Or Britain tamely bore it—
Descend, ye guardian heroes of the land!
Scourges of Spain, descend! Behold your sons;
See! how they run the same heroic race,
How prompt, how ardent in their country's cause,
How greatly proud to assert their British blood,

And in their deeds reflect their fathers' fame!
Ah! would to heaven ye did not rather see
How dead to virtue in the public cause,
How cold, how careless, how to glory deaf,
They shame your laurels, and belie their birth!
   Come, ye great spirits, Ca'ndish, Raleigh, Blake!
And ye of latter name, your country's pride,
Oh! come, disperse these lazy fumes of sloth,
Teach British hearts with British fires to glow!
In wakening whispers rouse our ardent youth,
Blazon the triumphs of your better days,
Paint all the glorious scenes of rightful war
In all its splendours; to their swelling souls
Say how ye bow'd th' insulting Spaniards' pride,
Say how ye thunder'd o'er their prostrate heads,
Say how ye broke their lines and fir'd their ports,
Say how not death, in all its frightful shapes,
Could damp your souls, or shake the great resolve
For right and Britain: then display the joys
The patriot's soul exalting, while he views
Transported millions hail with loud acclaim
The guardian of their civil, sacred rights.
How greatly welcome to the virtuous man
Is death for others' good! the radiant thoughts
That beam celestial on his passing soul,
Th' unfading crowns awaiting him above,
Th' exalting plaudit of the Great Supreme,
Who in his actions with complacence views
His own reflected splendour; then descend,
Though to a lower, yet a nobler scene;
Paint the just honours to his reliques paid,
Show grateful millions weeping o'er his grave;
While his fair fame in each progressive age
For ever brightens; and the wise and good
Of every land in universal choir
With richest incense of undying praise
His urn encircle, to the wondering world
His numerous triumphs blazon; while with awe,
With filial reverence, in his steps they tread,

And, copying every virtue, every fame,
Transplant his glories into second life,
And, with unsparing hand, make nations blest
By his example. Vast, immense rewards!
For all the turmoils which the virtuous mind
Encounters here. Yet, Britons, are ye cold?
Yet deaf to glory, virtue, and the call
Of your poor injured countrymen? Ah! no:
I see ye are not; every bosom glows
With native greatness, and in all its state
The British spirit rises: glorious change!
Fame, virtue, freedom, welcome! O forgive
The Muse, that, ardent in her sacred cause,
Your glory question'd; she beholds with joy,
She owns, she triumphs in her wish'd mistake.
See! from her sea-beat throne in awful march
Britannia towers: upon her laurel crest
The plumes majestic nod; behold she heaves
Her guardian shield, and terrible in arms
For battle shakes her adamantine spear:
Loud at her foot the British lion roars,
Frighting the nations; haughty Spain full soon
Shall hear and tremble. Go then, Britons, forth,
Your country's daring champions: tell your foes,
Tell them in thunders o'er their prostrate land,
You were not born for slaves: let all your deeds
Show that the sons of those immortal men,
The stars of shining story, are not slow
In virtue's path to emulate their sires,
T' assert their country's rights, avenge her sons,
And hurl the bolts of justice on her foes.

# HYMN TO SCIENCE.

" O Vitæ Philosophia Dux! O Virtutis indagatrix, ex-
pultrixque Vitiorum.—Tu Urbes peperisti; tu inventrix
Legum, tu magistra Morum et Disciplinæ fuisti: Ad te con-
fugimus, a te Opem petimus."　　　　*Cic. Tusc. Quæst.*

SCIENCE! thou fair effusive ray
　From the great source of mental day,
　　Free, generous, and refin'd!
Descend with all thy treasures fraught,
Illumine each bewilder'd thought,
　　And bless my labouring mind.

But first with thy resistless light,
Disperse those phantoms from my sight,
　　Those mimic shades of thee:
The scholiast's learning, sophist's cant,
The visionary bigot's rant,
　　The monk's philosophy.

O! let thy powerful charms impart
The patient head, the candid heart,
　　Devoted to thy sway;
Which no weak passions e'er mislead,
Which still with dauntless steps proceed
　　Where reason points the way.

Give me to learn each secret cause;
Let Number's, Figure's, Motion's laws
　　Reveal'd before me stand;
These to great Nature's scenes apply,
And round the globe, and through the sky,
　　Disclose her working hand.

Next, to thy nobler search resign'd,
The busy, restless, Human Mind
　　Through every maze pursue;

z

Detect Perception where it lies,
Catch the Ideas as they rise,
   And all their changes view.

Say from what simple springs began
The vast ambitious thoughts of man,
   Which range beyond control,
Which seek eternity to trace,
Dive through the infinity of space,
   And strain to grasp the whole.

Her secret stores let Memory tell,
Bid Fancy quit her fairy cell,
   In all her colours drest;
While prompt her sallies to control,
Reason, the judge, recalls the soul
   To Truth's severest test.

Then launch through Being's wide extent;
Let the fair scale, with just ascent
   And cautious steps be trod;
And from the dead, corporeal mass,
Through each progressive order pass
   To Instinct, Reason, God.

There, Science! veil thy daring eye;
Nor dive too deep, nor soar too high,
   In that divine abyss;
To Faith content thy beams to lend,
Her hopes t' assure, her steps befriend
   And light her way to bliss.

Then downwards take thy flight again,
Mix with the policies of men,
   And social Nature's ties;
The plan, the genius of each state,
Its interest and its powers relate,
   Its fortunes and its rise.

Through private life pursue thy course,
Trace every action to its source,
   And means and motives weigh:

Put tempers, passions, in the scale;
Mark what degrees in each prevail,
　And fix the doubtful sway.

That last best effort of thy skill,
To form the life, and rule the will,
　Propitious power! impart:
Teach me to cool my passion's fires,
Make me the judge of my desires,
　The master of my heart.

Raise me above the vulgar's breath,
Pursuit of fortune, fear of death,
　And all in life that's mean:
Still true to reason be my plan,
Still let my actions speak the man,
　Through every various scene.

Hail! queen of manners, light of truth;
Hail! charm of age, and guide of youth;
　Sweet refuge of distress:
In business, thou! exact, polite;
Thou giv'st retirement its delight,
　Prosperity its grace.

Of wealth, power, freedom, thou the cause;
Foundress of order, cities, laws,
　Of arts inventress thou!
Without thee, what were human-kind?
How vast their wants, their thoughts how blind!
　Their joys how mean, how few!

Sun of the soul! thy beams unveil:
Let others spread the daring sail,
　On Fortune's faithless sea:
While, undeluded, happier I
From the vain tumult timely fly,
　And sit in peace with thee.

# LOVE, AN ELEGY.

TOO much my heart of Beauty's power hath
    known,
Too long to Love hath reason left her throne;
Too long my genius mourn'd his myrtle chain,
And three rich years of youth consum'd in vain.
My wishes, lull'd with soft inglorious dreams,
Forgot the patriot's and the sage's themes:
Through each Elysian vale and fairy grove,
Through all the enchanted paradise of love,
Misled by sickly Hope's deceitful flame,
Averse to action, and renouncing fame.
    At last the visionary scenes decay,
My eyes, exulting, bless the new-born day,
Whose faithful beams detect the dangerous road
In which my heedless feet securely trod,
And strip the phantoms of their lying charms
That lur'd my soul from Wisdom's peaceful arms.
    For silver streams and banks bespread with
    flowers,
For mossy couches and harmonious bowers,
Lo! barren heaths appear, and pathless woods,
And rocks hung dreadful o'er unfathom'd floods:
For openness of heart, for tender smiles,
Looks fraught with love, and wrath-disarming wiles;
Lo! sullen Spite, and perjur'd Lust of Gain,
And cruel Pride, and crueller Disdain;
Lo! cordial Faith to idiot airs refin'd,
Now coolly civil, now transporting kind.
For graceful Ease, lo! Affectation walks;
And dull Half-sense, for Wit and Wisdom talks.
New to each hour what low delight succeeds,
What precious furniture of hearts and heads!
By nought their prudence, but by getting, known,
And all their courage in deceiving shown.

See next what plagues attend the lover's state,
What frightful forms of Terror, Scorn, and Hate!
See burning Fury heaven and earth defy!
See dumb Despair in icy fetters lie!
See black Suspicion bend his gloomy brow,
The hideous image of himself to view!
And fond Belief, with all a lover's flame,
Sink in those arms that point his head with shame!
There wan Dejection, faltering as he goes,
In shades and silence vainly seeks repose;
Musing through pathless wilds, consumes the day,
Then lost in darkness weeps the hours away.
Here the gay crowd of Luxury advance,
Some touch the lyre, and others urge the dance;
On every head the rosy garland glows,
In every hand the golden goblet flows.
The Syren views them with exulting eyes,
And laughs at bashful Virtue as she flies.
But see behind, where Scorn and Want appear,
The grave remonstrance and the witty sneer;
See fell Remorse in action, prompt to dart
Her snaky poison through the conscious heart;
And Sloth to cancel, with oblivious shame,
The fair memorial of recording Fame.
Are these delights that one would wish to gain?
Is this the Elysium of a sober brain?
To wait for happiness in female smiles,
Bear all her scorn, be caught with all her wiles,
With prayers, with bribes, with lies, her pity crave,
Bless her hard bonds, and boast to be her slave;
To feel, for trifles, a distracting train
Of hopes and terrors equally in vain;
This hour to tremble, and the next to glow,
Can Pride, can Sense, can Reason, stoop so low?
When Virtue, at an easier price, displays
The sacred wreaths of honourable praise;
When Wisdom utters her divine decree,
To laugh at pompous Folly, and be free.
I bid adieu, then, to these woful scenes;

I bid adieu to all the sex of queens;
Adieu to every suffering, simple soul,
That lets a woman's will his ease control.
There laugh, ye witty; and rebuke, ye grave!
For me, I scorn to boast that I'm a slave.
I bid the whining brotherhood be gone;
Joy to my heart! my wishes are my own!
Farewell the female heaven, the female hell;
To the great God of Love a glad farewell.
Is this the triumph of thy awful name;
Are these the splendid hopes that urg'd thy aim,
When first my bosom own'd thy haughty sway?
When thus Minerva heard thee boasting, say,
" Go, martial maid, elsewhere thy arts employ,
Nor hope to shelter that devoted boy.
Go teach the solemn sons of Care and Age,
The pensive statesman, and the midnight sage;
The young with me must other lessons prove,
Youth calls for Pleasure, Pleasure calls for Love.
Behold, his heart thy grave advice disdains;
Behold, I bind him in eternal chains."
Alas! great Love, how idle was the boast!
Thy chains are broken, and thy lessons lost;
Thy wilful rage has tir'd my suffering heart,
And passion, reason, forc'd thee to depart.
But wherefore dost thou linger on thy way?
Why vainly search for some pretence to stay,
When crowds of vassals court thy pleasing yoke,
And countless victims bow them to the stroke?
Lo! round thy shrine a thousand youths advance,
Warm with the gentle ardours of romance;
Each longs to assert thy cause with feats of arms,
And make the world confess Dulcinea's charms.
Ten thousand girls with flowery chaplets crown'd,
To groves and streams thy tender triumph sound:
Each bids the stream in murmurs speak her flame,
Each calls the grove to sigh her shepherd's name.
But, if thy pride such easy honour scorn,
If nobler trophies must thy toil adorn,

Behold yon flowery antiquated maid
Bright in the bloom of threescore years display'd;
Her shalt thou bind in thy delightful chains,
And thrill with gentle pangs her wither'd veins,
Her frosty cheek with crimson blushes dye,
With dreams of rapture melt her maudlin eye.
  Turn then thy labours to the servile crowd,
Entice the wary, and control the proud;
Make the sad miser his best gains forego,
The solemn statesman sigh to be a beau,
The bold coquette with fondest passion burn,
The Bacchanalian o'er his bottle mourn;
And that chief glory of thy power maintain,
" To poise ambition in a female brain."
Be these thy triumphs; but no more presume
That my rebellious heart will yield thee room:
I know thy puny force, thy simple wiles;
I break triumphant through thy flimsy toils;
I see thy dying lamp's last languid glow,
Thy arrows blunted and unbrac'd thy bow.
I feel diviner fires my breast inflame,
To active science, and ingenuous fame;
Resume the paths my earliest choice began,
And lose, with pride, the lover in the man.

## TO CORDELIA.

### JULY 1740.

FROM pompous life's dull masquerade,
  From Pride's pursuits, and Passion's war,
  Far, my Cordelia, very far,
To thee and me may Heaven assign
The silent pleasures of the shade,
The joys of peace, unenvied, though divine!

Safe in the calm embowering grove,
   As thy own lovely brow serene;
   Behold the world's fantastic scene!
What low pursuits employ the great,
What tinsel things their wishes move,
The forms of Fashion, and the toys of State.

In vain are all Contentment's charms,
   Her placid mien, her cheerful eye,
   For look, Cordelia, how they fly!
Allur'd by Power, Applause, or Gain,
They fly her kind protecting arms;
Ah, blind to pleasure, and in love with pain!

Turn and indulge a fairer view,
   Smile on the joys which here conspire;
   O joys harmonious as my lyre!
O prospect of enchanting things,
As ever slumbering poet knew,
When Love and Fancy wrapt him in their wings!

Here, no rude storm of Passion blows,
   But Sports, and Smiles, and Virtues play,
   Cheer'd by Affection's purest ray;
The air still breathes Contentment's balm,
And the clear stream of Pleasure flows
For ever active, yet for ever calm.

## SONG.

THE shape alone let others prize,
   The features of the fair;
I look for spirit in her eyes,
   And meaning in her air.

A damask cheek, an ivory arm,
   Shall ne'er my wishes win;

Give me an animated form,
    That speaks a mind within.

A face where awful honour shines,
    Where sense and sweetness move,
And angel innocence refines
    The tenderness of love.

These are the soul of beauty's frame;
    Without whose vital aid,
Unfinish'd all her features seem,
    And all her roses dead.

But ah! where both their charms unite,
    How perfect is the view,
With every image of delight,
    With graces ever new:

Of power to charm the greatest woe,
    The wildest rage control,
Diffusing mildness o'er the brow,
    And rapture through the soul.

Their power but faintly to express
    All language must despair;
But go, behold Arpasia's face,
    And read it perfect there.

THE END.

A A